Law Reform For All

Law Reform For All

Edited by

DAVID BEAN

BLACKSTONE
PRESS LIMITED

First published in Great Britain 1996 by Blackstone Press Limited, 9–15 Aldine Street, London W12 8AW. Telephone: 0181-740 1173

© Blackstone Press Limited, 1996
The contributors hold the copyright for their respective chapters jointly with the Society of Labour Lawyers.

ISBN: 1 85431 472 6

British Library Cataloguing in Publication Data
A CIP catalogue record for this book is available from the British Library.

Typeset by Montage Studios Limited, Tonbridge, Kent
Printed by Livesey Limited, Shrewsbury, Shropshire

Contents

Contents

Contributors

Foreword

Rt Hon Tony Blair, MP was called to the Bar by Lincoln's Inn in 1976. He practised as a barrister until he became MP for Sedgefield in 1983. In July 1994 he was elected Leader of the Labour Party.

The editor

David Bean is a practising barrister specialising in employment law and other common law and commercial work. He is secretary of the Employment Labour Bar Association and an elected member of the Bar Council, and sits as an Assistant Recorder in the county courts and Crown Court. In 1983 he was Labour candidate in Orpington. He is a Deputy Chair of the Society of Labour Lawyers, and was Chair of the Fabian Society in 1989–90.

The authors

Lord Archer of Sandwell PC QC (Peter Archer) was Solicitor General 1974–79, and subsequently for six years a member of the Shadow Cabinet. He was Chair of the Society of Labour Lawyers 1971–74 and 1980–93, and joint editor of *More Law Reform Now*. He is currently Chairman of the Council on Tribunals and President of the Fabian Society and an Honorary President of the Society of Labour Lawyers.

Geoffrey Bindman, solicitor, is senior partner of Bindman & Partners which he founded in 1974. He is a visiting professor in the Faculty of Laws at University College, London. He is a former Chair of the Legal Action Group and the Lawyers' Group of Amnesty International. He acted as legal adviser to the Race Relations Board and Commission for Racial Equality, 1966–83. He is the Chair of the Society of Labour Lawyers' media law sub-committee.

Contributors

Ross Cranston is Cassel Professor of Commercial Law at the London School of Economics and is in practice at the Bar. He is also deputy chair of the Trustees of Public Concern at Work (the whistleblowers' charity), and an assessor to Lord Woolf's inquiry into Access to Justice.

Martyn Day is the Joint Senior Partner at Leigh Day & Co. where he heads the Environmental Team specialising in acting for the individual rather than for corporations. He has been the main lawyer for the plaintiffs in the Sellafield leukaemia actions, actions related to the impact of electro-magnetic fields, traffic caused pollution and tobacco smoke. He is the co-author of the *Personal Injury Practice Handbook* (1994), *Pollution and Personal Injury: Toxic Torts 2* (1995) and the *Multi-Party Action Handbook* (1995).

Andrew Dismore is a solicitor with Russell Jones & Walker. He is Chair of Association of Personal Injury Lawyers Damages Special Interest Group; and an assessor for the Law Society Personal Injury Panel. He is a member of the Association of Trial Lawyers of America. He developed the new head of damages for loss of congenial employment and represented the plaintiffs in some of the first post-traumatic stress disorder cases. He was solicitor in the judicial review proceedings before the House of Lords which successfully challenged government cuts in the Criminal Injuries Compensation Scheme.

Colin Ettinger is a solicitor and partner with Irwin Mitchell. He has extensive experience in employment law and has been involved in several major cases in the field.

Maria Fernandes formerly a barrister, became a solicitor in 1991. She has served on the Law Society's committees on Immigration and Equal Opportunities and was Secretary to the International Bar Association's Migration Committee until 1994. She specialises in immigration law and writes and lectures widely. She has recently written a book on visitors. Founder of the London law firm Fernandes Vaz.

James Goudie QC is Chair of the Society of Labour Lawyers. He is also Chair both of the Administrative Law Bar Association and of the Law Reform Committee of the Bar Council. He was a Labour Councillor for 11 years, latterly as leader, and a Parliamentary candidate in 1974. He is co-editor of *Supperstone and Goudie on Judicial Review*.

John Hobson studied at the College of Law, Guildford, and St John's College Cambridge. He worked as a solicitor in private practice, local government and in law centres in Stepney and Southwark before being called to the Bar in 1980. He specialises in local government, planning and environmental law.

Stephen Hockman QC was called to the Bar in 1970 and appointed QC in 1990. He is a Recorder of the Crown Court. He has a general practice with particular emphasis on local government, planning and environmental law. He has been a member of the Labour Party since 1975.

Henry Hodge has since 1977 been senior partner of the firm of Hodge Jones & Allen. He is a Deputy Chair of the Society of Labour Lawyers. He has served on the Council of the Law Society since 1984 and was Deputy Vice President in 1994–95. He was an Islington Councillor from 1974 to 1978 and Labour candidate in Croydon South in February 1974. He was the Deputy Director of the Child Poverty Action Group from 1972 to 1977.

Benet Hytner QC was called to the Bar in February 1952 and appointed QC in 1970. He has practised on the Northern Circuit and was elected its Leader from 1984–88. He was appointed as a Crown Court Recorder in 1977 and Judge of Appeal, Isle of Man in 1980. He has served several terms on the Bar Council and the Council of the of Inns of Court. He has been a member of the Labour Party since 1943.

Lord Irvine of Lairg QC is an Honorary President of the Society of Labour Lawyers. As Shadow Lord Chancellor, he is the Opposition's senior Legal Affairs Spokesman in the House of Lords. He became a QC in 1978 and a peer in 1987. A practising QC, he specialises in Commercial and Administrative Law and is the Head of 11 King's Bench Walk Chambers.

Jenny Jeger was appointed in 1978 at the age of 26 as the youngest member of the Inner London Juvenile Panel (now the Youth Court). She was a member of the Lord Chancellor's Advisory Committee for the appointment of magistrates in Inner London from 1989 to December 1994.

Peter Jones is Professor of Professional Development at Nottingham Law School with responsibility for practice-based courses. A founding partner of Hodge Jones and Allen, he was later a community lawyer at Nottingham Citizens Advice Bureau and is now a consultant with Freeth Cartwright Hunt Dickins.

Wendy Mantle is a solicitor, a sole practitioner specialising in family law. She is a mediator with the Family Mediators Association. She has written for the general public a *Handbook of Separation and Divorce* which will be published shortly and is the author of *Child Support: The New System Explained* (1993) a book for practitioners.

Maggie Rae is a family solicitor and partner in the firm of Mishcon de Reya. She is Chair of the Fabian Society for 1996. She writes and teaches extensively on all aspects of Family Law.

Rabinder Singh is a practising barrister specialising in public law, employment law and human rights.

Roger Smith, solicitor, has been Director of the Legal Action Group since 1986. He has been a solicitor with the Child Poverty Action Group, director of West Hampstead Law Centre and a solicitor at Camden Law Centre. He is a writer and commentator on legal affairs, and an honorary Professor of law at the University of Kent.

Paul Stinchcombe took a double first in Law at Cambridge University before becoming a Fellow of Harvard Law School where he took his LLM. He practises as a barrister, specialising in planning law. He was a Camden Councillor 1990–94, and is the Labour Party's prospective Parliamentary candidate for Wellingborough.

Jack Straw MP was called to the Bar by the Inner Temple in 1972. He was an Islington Councillor from 1971–78 and during this period served as a special adviser to Barbara Castle and Peter Shore. He was elected MP for Blackburn in 1979. He has been a member of the Shadow Cabinet since 1987 and, after shadowing the Education and Environment Departments, is now Shadow Home Secretary.

Michael Supperstone QC is an Assistant Recorder of the Crown Court and vice-chairman of the Administrative Law Bar Association. He has written extensively on public law. Works include the Administrative Law title of *Halsbury's Laws of England, Judicial Review, Law of Public Order and National Security*, and *Immigration Law and Practice*. He is a member of the editorial committee of *Public Law*.

Keith Vaz, barrister, has been MP for Leicester East since 1987. He was a member, Select Committee Home Affairs 1987–92 and Shadow Local Government spokesman 1992–94. He is currently Shadow Minister for Planning and Regeneration.

John Wadham spent some years working for law centres in London before he qualified as a solicitor and moved to private practice. He is now Director of Liberty (the National Council for Civil Liberties) and is editor of 'Your Rights: The Liberty Guide', the civil liberties section of the *Penguin Guide to the Law* and the Case Reports of the *European Human Rights Law Review*. He has also contributed to many other publications and written a number of articles on human rights and civil liberties.

Fraser Whitehead is a partner in Russell Jones & Walker which specialises in work-related legal issues including health and safety, personal injury, individual and collective employment issues and regulatory law, with particular involvement in industrial disease and multiple tort claims. He is a former President of Holborn Law Society, a trustee and former Chair of Child Accident Prevention Trust. He is a member of the management committee of the Mary Ward Law Centre, a member of ATLA and APIL, the Fabian Society and many others. He is Secretary of the Society of Labour Lawyers.

Lord Williams of Mostyn QC (Gareth Williams) became a QC in 1978. He was appointed as a Recorder in 1978 and a Deputy High Court Judge in 1986. In 1992 he served as Chairman of the Bar Council and President of the Commonwealth and Ethnic Bar Association. In 1995 he became Pro-Chancellor of the University of Wales. He is a member of the Council of Justice and a trustee of the NSPCC.

Foreword

Rt Hon Tony Blair MP

Legally enforceable rights and duties underpin a democratic society, and access to justice is essential in order to make these rights and duties real. That is why I welcome debate on law reform — through official policy-making channels within the Labour Party and thought provoking works of this kind.

Over the last 16 years more and more ordinary people have effectively been excluded from the legal system. In 1979 79 per cent of the population were eligible for legal aid. Now only 48 per cent are. In April 1993 an estimated 12 million people have had their entitlement to legal aid removed. And court fees have escalated too, by 400 per cent in the last three years alone.

Access to justice is clearly about more than the scope of legal aid eligibility for traditional courts. But currently people have little choice but to go to court. Only 0.3 per cent of the legal aid budget is deployed through advice agencies and few systems for alternative dispute resolution (ADR) exist. It is vital that we look both at the role of ADR in promoting settlement of cases and the role of advice agencies in the delivery of more economical legal services.

Improving access to the law is not the only aspect of law reform. I have always believed that the legal system is not only a reflection of the social and economic situation in our country, but to a large extent shapes it. Law reform is as much about using the law to achieve social and economic reform as it is about simplifying legislation to make law more accessible to ordinary people. That is why this book addresses not only questions of reform of the legal system, but also areas such as environmental and planning law and defamation and privacy. It is also why law reform should be seen in the context of wider social and economic renewal.

Labour's goal of improving access to justice is an essential part of our commitment to social justice. That is why we published our proposals for extending access to justice in 1995. Paul Boateng MP, our House of Commons legal affairs spokesman and Lord Irvine, the Shadow Lord Chancellor, have outlined Labour's proposals. These include

- developing a community legal service which will be more responsive to the needs of the consumer rather than the lawyer
- expanding the provision of mediation services
- tackling restrictive practices in the legal profession
- improving the training and selection of judges

I hope that this book will move the debate forward. Of course, the Labour Party does not subscribe to all of the proposals that follow. Some will cause controversy. Others will be opposed. But, it is healthy to debate these issues and I welcome this book for that reason.

Introduction

David Bean

The Society of Labour Lawyers was founded by Gerald Gardiner and others in 1948 and has been affiliated to the Labour Party ever since. Its membership comprises Labour Party members who are solicitors, barristers, lay magistrates, law teachers or students of law. Its most celebrated member, Tony Blair, is Leader of the Labour Party.

The Society has published three previous books on law reform since its foundation in 1948. The first, *The Reform of the Law*, edited by Glanville Williams, appeared in 1951. The second, *Law Reform Now*, edited by Gerald Gardiner and Andrew Martin, was published in 1963, a year before Harold Wilson came to power. The third, *More Law Reform Now*, edited by Peter Archer and Andrew Martin, appeared in 1983.

Of these the most influential by far was *Law Reform Now*, because it preceded the election of a Labour government. Gerald Gardiner, its co-editor, became Lord Chancellor, and within two years of the book's publication Parliament had enacted one of its principal proposals — the establishment of the English and Scottish Law Commissions, charged with the duty of keeping the law permanently under review. Lord Scarman, Gardiner's inspired choice to chair the English Law Commission in its first years, wrote:

Contemporary society requires that it be given the opportunity to test its laws by its own criteria; it insists that laws are either to serve the needs of society or to be rejected. In other words, our fellows in society require first to understand, and then to evaluate the laws that

1

govern them. We demand, not only that the tablets be brought down from the mountain and their meaning made clear, but that we have the liberty to smash and replace them. (*Lindsay Memorial Lectures*, 1967.)

The three earlier books did not concern themselves greatly with the problem of access to justice. That was done in 1968 in the Fabian pamphlet *Justice for All*, written by a group of members of the Society of Labour Lawyers chaired by Morris Finer. The term 'charter' has been trivialised by John Major; but *Justice for All* can fairly be described as the charter for the law centre movement,and one of the most influential Fabian publications of the last 50 years. Eight years later there followed *Legal Services for All*, the Society's evidence to the Royal Commission on Legal Services; and, in 1991, *Legal Rights for All*, by a group including myself and three of the present authors.

The cost of the legal system, and the steady erosion by the Conservatives of eligibility for civil legal aid, are now dominant themes in any debate about law reform. So the present volume addresses these as well as substantive law topics. Its title pays tribute to the two traditions of *Law Reform Now* and *Justice for All*.

The chapters are the authors' own. They are not the official policy of the Labour Party, nor the collective view of the Society of Labour Lawyers. I do not agree with all of the proposals myself. But it is not an editor's job to be a censor. My responsibility has been to commission material which is worthy of consideration within the Labour movement and by the general public. I am particularly glad that one of the authors of the 1951 book, Ben Hytner, is a contributor to the present volume.

One chapter planned to appear in the book has been omitted. In early 1995 the government published a White Paper on disclosure in criminal trials containing some seriously flawed proposals. Vera Baird prepared a chapter containing stringent criticisms of the White Paper. Fortunately, and uncharacteristically for the Home Secretary, the Bill on this subject is very different from the White Paper and meets many of Vera Baird's points. It remains to be seen how the proposed changes will work in practice.

The great nineteenth-century law reformer Samuel Romilly was warned by his clerk that his professional clients

could never think well of a man who troubled his head with reforming abuses, when he ought to be profiting by them.

The authors of these essays, all members of the Society of Labour Lawyers, include men and women widely recognised as outstanding in their fields of work. They have troubled their heads about reforming abuses. Their proposals make a programme for law reform as radical as any in our history. The time when a Labour Government starts to carry out that programme cannot come a day too soon.

January 1996

Acknowledgments

On behalf of the Society of Labour Lawyers thanks are due to Tony Blair, for doing us the honour of contributing a foreword; to all the authors, who have written their chapters without financial reward; to Jenny Jeger and Robin White, each of whom cast an eagle eye over the proofs; and to Alistair MacQueen, Heather Saward and the staff at Blackstone Press, whose encouragement and energy has never flagged.

1

The Legal System and Law Reform under Labour

Lord Irvine of Lairg QC, Shadow Lord Chancellor

In this opening chapter I confine myself to three subjects of major concern to radical lawyers:

(a)   access to justice and the provision of legal services;
(b)   how the overweening power of government can be diminished by establishing enforceable, fundamental rights for every citizen; and
(c)   reform of the law.

Access to justice and the provision of legal services

Access to justice is an issue which stands high on the political agenda today. The claims that our justice system, and provision for legal aid securing access to that system, were the best in the world, were fashionable in earlier decades. They had some considerable plausibility in 1979, when Labour lost power. Then 72 per cent of households were eligible for legal aid. That proportion, however, has been reduced to 50 per cent by the recent eligibility cuts.

There is now a widespread agreement, and not merely by the consumer bodies, the voluntary sector (the Citizens' Advice Bureaux

4

(CABs), the advice centres and the law centres), the Law Society, the Bar Council and the Legal Action Group, that a crisis affects access to justice. Even the Lord Chancellor has been constrained to acknowledge that he does not regard as desirable any further reductions in eligibility.

Also there has always been a gap, which cannot rationally be justified, in the provision of legal aid. It is not available for representation before industrial, social security or immigration tribunals, or for coroners' inquests. A frequent excuse is that these tribunals apply simple and easily understood law in informal hearings. Both these propositions are false.

It is a pure myth that tribunal proceedings are informal or that they ever could be, so that experienced representation is unnecessary. Procedures are substantially the same as in the High Court and they always have been. There is examination and cross-examination of witnesses, indistinguishable from that in the ordinary courts; and much legal argument, rightly and unavoidably, because of the huge complexity of the legislation which Parliament has laid down, applicable Euro law, and case law. In fact there is often much more legal argument in, for example, the industrial tribunals than in the county courts, where legal aid has been available for decades, and very much more money is often at stake than in the county courts. It is disquieting to read the same old heresy trotted out in para. 8.14 of the 1995 Green Paper, *Legal Aid — Targeting Need* (Cm 2854):

These [tribunal] procedures are in general less formal and more simple than court proceedings. There is a risk that if legal aid were available for professional representation at every tribunal, the tribunal processes would become more formal and lawyer dominated and the benefits that tribunals can bring, such as informality and cost-effectiveness would be lost.

The truth is that there is no greater unfairness than the legally *unrepresented* applicant against the legally *represented* employer in industrial tribunals in cases about unfair dismissal, redundancy, sex and race discrimination and equal pay.

It is noteworthy that the Green Paper's proposal for a pilot scheme to test the merit of making legal aid more generally available for tribunals

5

has run into opposition from within the present government itself. The ostensible grounds are the informality of the proceedings; the real grounds are the cost. Yet it must remain irrational to exclude tribunal cases as a class from any call on the legal aid budget when the complexity of these cases is as great as any other class of litigation for which legal aid is automatically available, subject to means and merits.

The fact is, however, that no one, including the Labour Party, has any quick fix for the crisis besetting legal aid. Labour will have no new money to throw at problems whose solution calls for structural change. The figures are well known — in 1987/88 legal aid totalled £426 million. By 1993/4 it had risen to £1,020 million, of which £350 million went on civil proceedings. By 1996/97 the cost of legal aid is estimated to become £1,633 million, of which £685 million will go on civil legal aid. All lawyers are only too conscious of the sharp rise in recent years of the cost of legal proceedings.

The ambition of any Labour Lord Chancellor must be to restore legal aid to the status of a public social service which is so highly regarded for its economy and efficiency in securing access to justice that, with the support of the public, it can compete for scarce resources with the most highly regarded services such as health.

The ability of any Lord Chancellor to fight his or her corner for justice with the Treasury with success is dependent upon the courts and the legal profession, in cooperation, putting their houses in order. It is also dependent upon involving the voluntary sector to much more substantial effect in the provision of legal services generally. The voluntary sector would be likely to prove a popular candidate for the efficient targeting of scarce resources.

Labour's policy on access to justice is an essential component of its general commitment to social justice for all members of society. Legally enforceable rights and duties — enforceable in reality and not only in theory — underpin a democratic society under the rule of law. Rights without the means of enforcement make a mockery of social justice, just as hospitals which cannot deliver life-support systems make a mockery of the right to life.

An incoming Labour government cannot make money grow on gooseberry bushes; but it would pursue with relentless rigour an efficient justice system with access for all.

There is a major point which separates Labour's policy from that of the present Conservative government. Labour does not see the reform of legal aid as a distinct issue, hermetically sealed from the reform of the civil justice system itself. The best way to save money is not to exclude people from access to justice, but to cut the cost of litigation. The unacceptable cost of justice must be tackled at its source. So the reform of legal aid, and of the civil justice system, must go hand in hand. They are intimately bound up together. It is highly significant that Lord Woolf's remit for the interim report to the Lord Chancellor on the civil justice system in England and Wales, *Access to Justice* (June 1995) included no examination of the legal aid system, nor of the funding of civil litigation in general. It is bizarre that preparation of the 1995 Green Paper on legal aid and Lord Woolf's inquiries should have been conducted side by side yet entirely separately. The question of access to justice cannot be divorced from the question of funding. The point is emphasised by the way in which the 1995 Green Paper preceded by about a month Lord Woolf's interim report. I predict that under the Conservative government these two documents will prove to be ships which pass in the night.

Labour is acutely concerned by the relentless rise in legal aid expenditure in real terms over recent years. Current expenditure has, however, substantially stabilised, with modest recent underspends on budget. There is therefore no current imperative for cost capping the legal aid budget as the Green Paper proposes, independent of making a cost-benefit analysis of the gains that might be secured from as speedy an implementation as is practicable of the Woolf Report. What is required is prompt action to reduce the delays, the cost and, above all, the undue length of civil legal process: what is emphatically not required now is rationing of legal aid by cost capping.

The Green Paper has the fingerprints of the Treasury all over it. The Lord Chancellor has claimed that it is not about cuts, about spending less, but about spending better. We are all in favour of 'spending better'. But his claim has to be compared with this sentence in his Green Paper (p. 112):

Government policy is to reduce public expenditure as a share of national income over time.

Labour believes that, par excellence, legal aid is a form of public expenditure where that objective can be achieved by other means than cost capping.

The central point of the Green Paper is cost capping. It says:

The legal aid scheme must operate within an overall fixed budget to create a discipline for setting priorities (Summary, p. viii).

Capping signifies an abandonment of an entitlement basis for the grant of legal aid, based on merits (subject of course, to the highly restrictive eligibility criteria imposed by the government in 1993). Legal aid will cease to be a benefit to which the individual who qualifies is entitled. It will in practice become a discretionary benefit, available at bureaucratic disposal — a benefit which will have to be disallowed when the money runs out, or when another category of cases has been given funding preference. There is much sophistry about the contracts with the suppliers being for different periods, and long periods, so that no one in practice need be excluded. That is not persuasive. Capping is crude. Legal aid will cease to be a service available on an equal basis nationally. Cases will go forward in one region where identical cases in others, of equal merit, will not, because of capping.

In practice capping will lead at worst to substantial exclusion from justice and at best to long waiting lists. Typically legal aid is sought at a time of crisis for the individual. Its availability should not depend on the accident of where the individual lives or when application is made. It should depend on means and merits.

In his lecture, 'Access to Justice — towards the 21st Century' (given at the London School of Economics, 11 July 1995), Professor Michael Zander delivered a devastating attack on the Green Paper. His conclusion was that its implementation 'would cause incalculable harm to the legal aid scheme and would seriously diminish access to justice'. Professor Zander summarises the Green Paper accurately, thus:

The Lord Chancellor's proposal is that there should be an overall predetermined annual budget for legal aid expenditure. The money would be given, probably to the Legal Aid Board, for allocation according to priorities set by the Government and approved by Parliament. Priorities would be in general terms, indicating how resources should be distributed between different areas of law. The Board would enter into contracts with providers who might be lawyers or non-lawyers, who would agree to provide specified services over a specified period for a global sum agreed in advance. Block contracts would cover the type, quality, volume and price of services to be provided.

Among Professor Zander's twelve objections, I emphasise the first five:

(a) Legal aid has to be allocated to individuals as need arises: neither government nor Parliament could 'sensibly set priorities in regard to the allocation of legal aid as between different areas of law'.

(b) The rationing point made above. He adds tellingly that the Green Paper's exclusion of rationing of criminal legal aid, that is, that 'no case would be refused for lack of money alone', entails 'that in civil cases a shortage of money alone *could* be the basis for refusal of legal aid'.

(c) 'The possibility that a cap on legal aid expenditure might extend to criminal cases is a public scandal.' A denial of criminal legal aid, because a predetermined budget had run out, would be contrary to art. 6 of the European Convention on Human Rights. Professor Zander is plainly correct. He is also supported by a recent opinion given to Liberty by Michael Beloff QC and Murray Hunt. This holds that a cap on criminal legal aid could lead to breaches of both the European Convention on Human Rights and the United Nations International Covenant on Civil and Political Rights. The Green Paper refers to art. 6 of the European Convention, but nevertheless maintains that 'the government considers that the balance of argument is in favour of setting a predetermined budget for criminal legal aid'. The two are irreconcilable. Mr Beloff and Mr Hunt add that the same objection applies to 'the proposal that there be a cap on civil legal aid. At some point someone will be denied legal aid to enforce his or her rights, whether as spouse, consumer or otherwise ... for no other reason than that the money has run out'. Liberty has rightly warned that if these Green Paper proposals are carried into effect it will test the United Kingdom's compliance with the European Convention.

(d)   Sooner rather than later a cash-limited system would be used by the government 'to reduce the total amount of money available for legal aid'.

(e)   At present the legal aid authorities decide on legal aid applications on objective grounds of means and merits. Under the Green Paper proposals these decisions would be taken by solicitors, who would be tempted to favour cases that maximised their profit margin within their block grant, so giving rise to a potential conflict of interest between solicitor and client.

Labour favours *block franchising*, but opposes *compulsory competitive tendering*. Labour is against it because of the inevitable tendency to favour low-price against higher-quality bidders. Franchising will play a key role in developing the Community Legal Service that Labour proposes to develop. Compulsory competitive tendering, however, would be likely to undermine the whole franchising project, driving some firms away from the scheme and encouraging others to emphasise cost control, at the expense of quality assurance for the client.

Labour favours the delivery of publicly funded civil legal services on the basis of block franchises. It will, however, reform and improve the Legal Aid Board's franchising scheme by placing much greater emphasis on the quality of service and advice provided to clients. Quality control does not merely require transaction criteria to assess how well a case has been taken through a standardised procedure. Labour favours the introduction of more stringent and sophisticated quality control standards, together with improved assessment and compliance mechanisms.

Professor Zander pertinently observes on block tendering:

The tendency will be to accept the lowest bids. The Legal Aid Board will not be able to prevent corner-cutting by firms each naturally trying to make the best profit it can on its allocated budget. An example would be its use of a barrister. One would hope that the solicitor would bring in a barrister if the case requires one. But if the solicitor has a financial incentive in not using a barrister, how is the Legal Aid Board to know whether a barrister was not used for valid reasons or simply in order to maximise the solicitor's profit?

'No win, no fee' agreements have recently been sanctioned by Parliament. They will apply principally to personal injury cases. Uplifts of as much as 100 per cent on what would otherwise be payable in costs by the successful plaintiff are sanctioned. The operation of this new system will be closely monitored by a Labour government. It is not based on the amount of damages recovered, but on the costs the successful plaintiff has to pay to his solicitor. So the whole of the damages recovered could go to pay the solicitor his costs plus uplift. The present government declined to cap, say at 20 or 25 per cent, the proportion of damages that will have to go to the solicitor on uplifted costs. If the Law Society's recommendation of a 25 per cent cap is not adhered to in practice, and injustice results, Labour will not hesitate to revisit this issue. Litigation fought successfully, but in effect for the sole benefit of the lawyers, is unacceptable. That apart, in cases where damages are not consumed, or substantially consumed, by the uplifted costs, it very far from follows that a 100 per cent uplift is generally justifiable. In cases with a 50–50 chance of success, a 100 per cent uplift might in principle be justifiable. Labour, however, will require close monitoring of conditional fee agreements, in the consumer interest, to see that 100 per cent uplifts do not become the norm. That would be totally inappropriate in the very many cases where the prospects of success are very high and well in excess of 50–50. The success rate in personal injury cases is very high. Consumer protection requires that the maximum permitted uplift in cases that win should not be disproportionate to the risk of losing. Labour will also monitor to ensure that conditional fee agreements are in accord with that principle and will not hesitate to legislate if need be.

Lord Woolf's solution to the cost, delay and complexity of civil litigation is a decisive transfer of power and responsiblity for the management of civil litigation from the lawyers to the judges. No longer, if Woolf goes forward, will the judge be the boxing referee whose function is to see that the rules are kept and to count the points. The judge is not to be at the mercy of the contending sides. His function is to manage them, by restricting the ambit of their contest to what really matters.

The broad structure he proposes is for small claims up to £3,000; fast-track cases from £3,000 to £10,000 with fixed costs; and multitrack cases above that, with hands-on management by teams of judges for the heaviest cases. It has much to recommend it.

The recommendation that the small-claims limit be raised from £1,000 to £3,000 was accepted by the Lord Chancellor with alacrity, though all else remains undecided. It is difficult to resist the conclusion that the Lord Chancellor went on an instant exercise in cherry-picking from Lord Woolf: the effect of raising the small-claims limit from £1,000 to £3,000 is to remove cases in between these two figures from eligibility for legal aid. This is a good illustration of how the reform of the civil justice system and of legal aid are intimately bound up together and should not be addressed separately.

Over the long term there may be substantial cost gains to be secured from the implementation of Woolf, but there are clear resource issues in the shorter term, in terms of the burdens put on the judiciary by the fast-track cases; by judicial case management of the multitrack cases; and by the availability of sufficient judges for hands-on management; and their training for that purpose. There is also the critical consideration that major improvements in the civil justice system should not be made at the expense of the rest of the system. Lord Woolf now urgently needs to know whether his 'broad proposals for change are accepted in principle'. His intention is to submit his final report to the Lord Chancellor within a year of his Interim Report. Meanwhile he recommends 'the establishment of a Civil Justice Council as a continuing body with responsibility for overseeing and coordinating the implementation of his proposals' (Interim Report, p. 220).

Two steps should be initiated here and now: consultation in depth with the judiciary to assess the feasibility of implementation; and a cost-benefit analysis of the anticipated gains. Lord Woolf needs to be told where he stands — and sooner, not later.

There is much in Woolf that chimes with the policies that Labour has been advocating — the reduction of costs and delay; the encouragement of early settlements; and the promotion of mediation and alternative dispute resolution. A cost-benefit analysis, however, is indispensable.

There is, however, an important reservation that must be made about Lord Woolf's interim report. It is critical that the quality of justice is not a casualty of his urgency to shorten trials. He recommends (p. 179):

Cross-examination on the contents of witness statements should only be allowed with the leave of the judge. Such leave should not be given for cross-examination as to detail. Nor should it usually be necessary even when a more significant feature is relied upon. The advocate's comment will be all that the judge will usually require.

Read without major qualifications, I profoundly disagree. In all our efforts to simplify and reduce the cost of court proceedings, we must never lose sight of the sad fact that parties and witnesses in contested litigation often have an interest in being untruthful, or economical with the truth. The function of cross-examination is to expose untruths.

A *Practice Direction* of 24 January 1995, in the names of the Lord Chief Justice and the Vice-Chancellor, Sir Richard Scott, encourages judges in civil litigation to impose time limits on cross-examination. Unnecessarily lengthy or irrelevant cross-examination must always be prevented, but cross-examination for the purpose of getting at the truth, never — even if of unavoidable length. There should be no arbitrary time limits on relevant and concise cross-examination, for such limits can only operate in favour of the untruthful.

The modern practice of giving evidence-in-chief by way of a written witness statement — in practice drafted at great length by lawyers in a form in which it is inconceivable that it could conform to any oral evidence-in-chief that the witness could give in the traditional way from the witness box — increases rather than diminishes the need for thorough and relevant cross-examination. The preparation by lawyers of written witness statements for pre-trial exchange between opposing parties, has led to a whole new legal industry which front-loads excessively the cost of civil litigation. Lord Woolf should have proposed strict judicial control over the practice, so that what in substance is extensive legal argumentation is excluded from these statements — subject to severe cost sanctions if this is not done — in favour of the evidence-in-chief which witnesses might feasibly have given from the witness box in the traditional way. The way forward is emphatically not to permit the current abuses in the present system of exchange of witness statements, drafted by lawyers, to continue unchecked, whilst arbitrarily restricting cross-examination, the need for which is made the greater by these abuses. If the proper balance is not maintained by the judges, then un-cross-examinable pieces of paper drafted by lawyers will substitute for evidence tested by cross-examination in court.

In our search for simplified and economic procedures we must never overlook that a primary function of the justice system is to get at the truth. The Lord Chancellor has himself confirmed that the *Practice Direction* did not reveal an 'intention of in any way limiting proper cross-examination' (Hansard, HL, 25 May 1995, col. 1060). That position must not be imperilled by anything done in implementation of the Woolf Report.

A major plank in Labour's policy is the development of a Community Legal Service, within the existing legal aid budget. What is envisaged is a scheme much more broadly based than one which merely provides public money to purchase for individuals private commercial legal services. A scheme so limited cannot require solicitors to provide the full range of services that individuals require.

Labour intends to promote the rationalisation and revitalisation of the voluntary sector by deploying a much greater proportion of publicly funded services through CABs, law centres and the advice agencies. This could only proceed with the consent of the voluntary sector after the fullest consultation. The aim would be to secure a geographically fair network of CABs, advice centres and law centres across the country.

Finance for the CABs is essentially discretionary and therefore insecure. The story of the generalist advice centres is of serious, geographically based inequalities. The story of the specialist advice centres is that in very many parts of the country they simply do not exist. There is no policy for a geographically fair network of CABs, advice centres and law centres, nor is there a policy for their secure funding. The picture across the country is very fractured. There are overworked urban centres; in many rural areas centres do not even exist; and the geographic inequalities in advice provision are dramatic. In many urban areas, for example, long queues form outside the CABs before the doors open. The provision of specialist law centres is even worse: in very many rural areas there is simply no law centre or housing centre. The case for rationalisation is overwhelming and Labour will promote it.

Effective legal services are often best delivered by organisations that combine lawyers and paralegals working together. Solicitors' offices are such bodies. But so also are CABs. Law centres combine lawyers and non-lawyer advisers. For years the CPAG's Citizens Rights Office has combined lawyers with paralegals to great effect. All these bodies could in principle employ many more salaried lawyers. Since the introduction of legal aid in 1949, publicly funded legal services in the United Kingdom have been provided almost exclusively through fee payments to barristers and solicitors working in private practice. This has pushed costs up and has led to a bias in the type of service provided towards crime and matrimonial work and away from social welfare law (for example housing, consumer or employment disputes). In 1993/94, law centres employing salaried lawyers accounted for only 0.3 per cent of total legal aid expenditure. Other countries (for example, Canada, Australia and the Netherlands) make far greater use of salaried lawyers to keep costs down and expand access to legal advice. In Quebec, where 61 per cent of cases were handled by salaried public lawyers in 1989/90, the cost per case to the taxpayer is significantly lower for salaried lawyers than for private practitioners.

Labour's Community Legal Service will be coordinated by regional Legal Aid Board offices. Each regional office will first be required to assess the legal needs of its area and then to draw up a detailed strategy for meeting these needs in consultation with local authorities and new advisory legal services committees, so establishing priorities. The regional Legal Aid Board offices will both work in partnership with, and administer the entire legal aid fund through, lawyers in private practice and the voluntary sector. Labour intends to build on, and to coordinate, all the providers of legal services in the community. It believes that in the advice agencies there is a huge untapped potential. Labour will have a listening ear to every initiative proposed: for example, to mention only one, the suggestion currently being floated within the Bar that the direct access rules to barristers could be modified so as to enable the advice agencies to refer cases, in a state of preparation ready for a contested hearing in a court or tribunal, to barristers, for representation in tribunal or court for fixed modest fees. The advice agencies could do likewise to solicitors. Every proposal will be judged by its cost-effectiveness in securing access to justice. Labour's aim is to fashion out of all the disparate providers of legal services a rational system of low-cost access to justice worthy of public respect; and therefore worthy of support by the public purse, on which there are so many competing claims.

Constitutional change

The election of a Labour government will herald the opportunity for a major programme of constitutional change. On each issue for change which this section addresses, the Tories are opposed in principle to any change. It is Labour that is for the expansion of civil liberties.

Yet caution there must be. There are those whose affection for constitutional change in general, or for their own hobby horses in particular, is so great that they are blind to all the demands for legislation across every area of policy that an incoming Labour government will face. The highest priority of all for Labour will be to demonstrate its capacity to govern across the board in the interests of all the people. That will be the single greatest determinant of its capacity to win a second term and more.

Thus the danger of a constitutional overload of the Parliamentary timetable has to be recognised and resisted. Not everything that is desirable is achievable in a single Parliament. What follows therefore is a purely personal analysis of the targets for change. The manifesto representing the Party's priorities remains to be written.

Individual rights and freedoms

A major component in the democratic renewal of our country is to put the rights and freedoms of citizens centre stage, as their fundamental protection against an overweening State. The debate about constitutional reform is as central to the citizen, as bread-and-butter issues are to the consumer. So I start with the case for strengthening the rights of individual citizens.

The Labour Party has a long-standing and deep-rooted concern for the rights of the citizen. The Party was founded to protect the oppressed and underprivileged. Its traditions require it to protect the rights and interests of individuals against the power of the State, public authorities or private organisations, and vested interests of every kind. That is why the Attlee government of the post-war years took the lead in promoting the European Convention on Human Rights and Fundamental Freedoms. Britain was one of the first countries to sign the Convention in 1950. That is also why Labour governments in the 1960s and the 1970s passed successive Race Relations Acts and the Equal Pay and Sex Discrimination Acts.

Since 1979, Britain under the Tories has slipped behind the rest of Europe in the protection it gives to individual rights. Britain is alone amongst the major nations of Western Europe in failing to lay down in

16

legislation the basic rights of its citizens and in failing to give its citizens a direct means of asserting those rights through their own national courts.

The principal characteristics of the present government are that it is dogmatic, convinced of its infallibility and opaque to reason. Small wonder that there is a substantial flow of petitions to the European Commission alleging violation of the Convention by the UK. Britain's reputation in Europe is that it is one of the most consistent transgressors of human rights in the Council of Europe. The European Court has condemned our laws on contempt of court, on prisoners' rights, terrorism, telephone-tapping, on birching (in the Isle of Man) on homosexuality (in Northern Ireland), on detention and on freedom of association. It is unsurprising that the Tories are implacably opposed to our citizens enjoying their Convention rights directly in their own courts.

The argument for incorporation   The essential effect of incorporating the European Convention on Human Rights as part of United Kingdom domestic law is that its protections can be relied on in the ordinary courts, and directly against the national government. At present, unlike the citizens of almost every other European country, citizens of the United Kingdom have no such rights. If they want to seek the protection of the Convention, they must appeal to the Commission and the Court in Strasbourg. That process is intolerably slow: three years at a minimum, more like five years on average, and some cases have been known to take as long as nine years. Only the most determined, or those who are supported by outside organisations, are likely to stay the course. And while the process grinds on, the abuse of rights at home continues.

The failure directly to incorporate the Convention into British law has an adverse cultural effect. Although, at the end of the day, the British government is subject to the requirements of the Convention, the present set-up makes the protection of basic rights appear difficult, remote, even foreign. It reinforces an atmosphere that suggests that basic rights are not of much importance, and that our government regards them as a nuisance rather than, as it should, as a primary obligation. And that view is reinforced in the courts. The judges will take note of the requirements of the Convention when interpreting legislation that is ambiguous or uncertain. But, in the absence of Parliamentary instructions to the

17

contrary, they have, correctly under our present law, made it plain that, if a law exists that affects human rights in a way that clearly breaches the Convention, it will be that law, and not the requirements of the Convention, that they will enforce.

The Convention is not a vague, untested or uncertain code, but a mature statement of rights that has been interpreted and applied over many years by an expert court in Strasbourg. To bring the Convention directly into British law would not be to introduce some new or alien thing. Our law is already, and has been since 1950, ultimately subject to the requirements of the Convention. What is needed is to make that protection for our citizens a real one, and not something that is only available after years of effort and litigation.

The legislative steps: protecting the Human Rights Act from judicial attack   Incorporation could easily be achieved. Parliament should pass a Human Rights Act that incorporates the rules of the Convention directly into British law, and gives citizens the right to enforce those rules in their own courts.

Although technically a British Act of Parliament cannot be 'entrenched', effective protection of the Human Rights Act from undermining by the courts would be provided by a clause that requires that any other Act that is intended to introduce laws inconsistent with the Convention must do so specifically and in express terms.

That arrangement would have a number of benefits. First, if a government genuinely thought, say in a time of national crisis, that it had to curtail basic individual rights, it could still do so. But it would have to do so openly and expressly, as in a democracy ought always to be the way.

Second, however, it would in practice be almost impossible for existing or subsequent law to be interpreted as being inconsistent with the Convention. Judges would know that Parliament had to hand a means of making clear that it was derogating from the Convention, but did not use it. It should therefore in practice be impossible for the judges to hold that any legislation was intended to breach the Convention, unless the legislation stated that in express terms.

Third, the Human Rights Act would be expressly stated to apply to, and override, all law and legislation existing at the time at which it is passed. If the government wished to exempt any of that law from the provisions of the Human Rights Act, it would have to say so expressly, using the procedure just described. Here again, therefore, the government would have to be entirely open about what it is trying to achieve, and would have to justify what it is doing both to Parliament and to the public. In a democracy, Parliament decides what rights should apply, and should set them out in a manner that citizens can understand for themselves. Under these proposals, it would not be left to the discretion of the judges, or to archaeological investigations by legal and constitutional experts, to decide what protections citizens do and do not have.

The scope of protection: the rights of individuals, not of corporations The rights to be protected should be those of the individual against the State. The Human Rights Act should therefore provide that its protections can only be relied on by individuals, and not by companies or by organisations. There should not be repeated here the confusion and injustice that has occurred in some other countries, where companies and commercial organisations have tried to resist social legislation controlling their activities by claiming that it infringes their 'human' rights. And the Human Rights Act would not be designed to alter existing legal relations between individuals, but to protect individuals from State power. So the bodies that would be subject to the Human Rights Act would be State and State-related ones: national and local government, the police, and any organisation that exercises State power.

Subject to this, all governmental activity, and all existing and future law, would be subject to the human rights legislation.

The enforcement of human rights The rights that the legislation confers would be asserted in the first instance through the ordinary courts: either by applications for judicial review, to assert or confirm the existence and operation of a right in a particular case, or by way of defence in an ordinary action, should a State body try to use against a citizen a law that is inconsistent with the human rights rules.

This use of the ordinary courts is important in two ways. First, a specialist human rights tribunal, which dealt simply with human rights issues, would be vulnerable to incessant disputes between it and the ordinary courts over which body should be hearing a particular case or complaint. The result would be delay, confusion, and benefit only for the lawyers. Second, and even more important, it is essential that regard for human rights pervades the work of all courts, and is recognised as an integral part of their work, for which courts bear direct responsibility: whether they are, for instance, criminal courts dealing with claims of wrongful conviction or civil courts looking at government bans on free speech. That responsibility must be put on the regular courts: and the judges of those courts must be trained and be ready to respond to the challenge.

There should, however, be two further safeguards.

First, at the final appellate level, where points of fundamental or wide-ranging importance about human rights may have to be decided, there is a strong case for adding to the judges of the final court three non-lawyer members, drawn from a panel of persons with knowledge and understanding of society and of human rights in the broad sense. That would ensure that principles are not laid down from any narrowly legal perspective. The non-lawyer members would be full members of the court, whose vote would rank equally with that of the judges. They would best be appointed from a list to be drawn up, after wide consultation, by an independent Judicial Appointments Commission.

Second, to assist the courts, and also to assist individuals in asserting their rights, there could be established an independent Human Rights Commission, along the lines of the very successful Equal Opportunities Commission and Commission for Racial Equality that were instituted by Labour governments. The Commission would monitor the operation of the Human Rights Act; provide advice and support for those who wish to assert their rights; and where necessary itself institute cases to confirm or clarify particularly important issues. The Commission would thus act as a focus for human rights activities and ensure that the protection of the public was not left to the accident of individual enthusiasm or willingness to pursue cases.

The quickest and simplest route to achieving democratic and legal recognition of a substantial package of human rights is by incorporating the Convention by statute into our law.

The culture of secrecy

Tory governments from 1979 have been obsessed with secrecy. If Richard Crossman was right for his times when he said that 'secrecy is the British disease', over these last 15 years it has become a cancer. The authorities, throughout the GCHQ affair, the Ponting case and *Spycatcher*, made themselves ridiculous. After humiliating defeats in the courts, the Government turned to its majority in Parliament to bail it out.

The Security Service Act 1989   The Security Service Act of 1989 puts MI5 on a statutory basis for the first time. But its powers are so broad that it can do virtually anything. The service must not be used to *further* the interests of any political party. But there is no prohibition against *acting contrary* to the interests of a political party. The government, as Michael Supperstone QC observes (chapter 15 below), refused to accept an amendment, borrowed from Canada, which would have prevented surveillance of those engaged in lawful advocacy, protest or dissent.

This Act did not lead to the liberalisation of the security system. On the contrary, it gave huge statutory powers to the executive, without any effective system of scrutiny and accountability.

Official Secrets Act 1989   Then we had the Official Secrets Act of the same year. It was no liberalising measure. It provides no positive rights to information and no freedom of information. It fails to recognise the public interest to know of abuses by government of its powers. The government, as Supperstone (chapter 15 below) emphasises, rejected an amendment, in line with the common law, that would have allowed officials to reveal really serious misconduct, involving crime, fraud or other gross mispropriety. So there is no public interest defence for whistle-blowers. Newspapers could be prosecuted for disclosing an Irangate in this country. There is no defence for a newspaper, whose source is a civil servant on a security or defence issue, which reveals that a Minister of the Crown has not told Parliament the truth, or has wilfully withheld it, or been economical with it.

The categories of information protected under the Act do not, as the government claims, represent a narrowing of the scope, in practice, of official secrets. I agree with Supperstone that an Act which was becoming substantially inoperable in practice has been replaced by one capable of being repressive in practice. I would add '*more* repressive in practice' for the reason that Supperstone gives:

doubtless influenced by the *Spycatcher* affair, the Act imposes a lifelong duty of confidentiality upon all members and future members of the Security Service. It is an offence for a member of the Security Service to disclose confidential information, even if it causes no harm.

It is an offence for officials to leak information, however true, about unpreparedness in the military sphere, provided the truth can be shown to be damaging. It would be an offence to reveal in this country information given in confidence by our government to a foreign State, where the information has been leaked by that State, and even if the information has had the widest currency abroad, provided that the truth could be shown to be damaging. We retain a system well fashioned to conceal from public view any information embarrassing to government, whether bureaucratic error or, worse, deception. Our present laws do not reflect the balance a modern democratic society requires between the public interest to receive, and the State interest to withhold, information.

A public interest defence should be available to an individual charged with an offence under this Act, if the defendant can demonstrate that all avenues for prevention of serious misconduct were exhausted before the unauthorised disclosure was made.

In addition there is a strong case for putting into the Civil Service Code an obligation on civil servants to report to their permanent secretary instructions to them which would involve maladministration, abuse of official authorities or serious misconduct, including the misinforming of Parliament. The Permanent Secretary would be under a duty to investigate and if need be to report to an all-party Parliamentary select committee.

Intelligence Services Act 1994   This Act is criticised at length by Supperstone (chapter 15 below). It sets up for the first time an Intelligence and Security Committee to oversee the expenditure, administration and policy of the Security Service (MI5), the Intelligence Service (MI6) and GCHQ. This is made up of members of Parliament, though it is not a select committee, or a Parliamentary committee. It does not, therefore, have the power to call witnesses or demand documents. Information requested by the Committee may be denied because the Secretary of State is determined that it should not be disclosed. That power is far too sweeping.

There must be strong Parliamentary oversight and scrutiny, with reporting back to Parliament. Security services that operate in the world of espionage and counter-espionage cannot rationally be expected to distinguish adequately between lawful dissent and subversive conduct. This Committee should be given real teeth.

The way ahead   The way ahead is to create a new framework for national security and official secrecy. The Official Secrets Act 1989 should be amended by creating a public interest defence, and the Security Services Act 1989 and the Intelligence Services Act 1994 should be replaced by a single statute, establishing a charter for the Security Services and bringing them under an effective system of accountability and review by a select committee of Parliament.

The operational activities of MI5, MI6 and GCHQ must obviously live in secrecy. Terrorist organisations threaten British civilians and soldiers. London has had more than its share of international terrorist outrages. Information must be gathered about the organisations and individuals for whom violence is their way of life. But the limits to which this information may be used must be defined clearly.

A charter would define what the security services are properly about. Their role should be limited to threats to national security, designed to undermine constitutional government. Lawful political activities should be specifically excluded from their remit. Within these limits their day-to-day operations would be for them.

Interception of communications   All the legislation on interception of communications, e.g., by telephone tapping — the Interception of Communications Act 1985, the Security Service Act 1989 and the Intelligence Services Act 1994 — suffer from a common vice: the refusal of the executive to subject the interception of communications to any adequate scrutiny or control. Under the 1985 Act a warrant for interception can be issued by the Home Secretary in the interests of national security. There is no definition of what that means. The Home Secretary is judge. The model of other countries, requiring judicial authorisation, is rejected. There are so many of these warrants that it is obvious that they are authorised by officials under purely formal Ministerial approval. Judicial authorisation should become a requirement. If the security services cannot persuade a judge, sensitive to the needs of national security, that national security requires surveillance, then it must be doubted whether surveillance is truly required.

Freedom of information   The Human Rights Act incorporating the European Convention would be no more than a floor, not a ceiling, of rights. A general public right of access to official information by way of a Freedom of Information Act is urgently required. It would replace the Public Records Act 1958, as amended by the Public Records Act 1967.

A government that wants to act with the consent of the people must be open about its objectives, and expose the detail of its proposals to informed debate. A confident government working on the basis of well-thought-out policies should have little difficulty with public scrutiny of its thinking. Where the analysis is sound, the openness will help secure public acceptance. Where it is not, the process will help to identify and bring about the changes that are needed.

An unresponsive, inflexible government, on the other hand, which hastily commits itself to unworkable proposals, cannot tolerate such openness. Freedom of information merely exposes such a government to criticism which it is unable to answer. Then government strictly controls information. It severely punishes leaks. It consults minimally, or only amongst a highly selected privileged group. By restricting access to the decision-making process the government loses the benefit of outside expertise, whilst making itself more vulnerable to biased inputs from powerful lobbies with vested interests. This leads to poorer decisions and such decisions demand yet further secrecy, to suppress evidence that the promised benefits are not being gained. This is a vicious circle in which the government's attempts to sustain its credibility depend on public ignorance of what is taking place, while such ignorance frustrates any attempts to bring about change.

Freedom of information is also essential to communities. Without it people may be prevented from finding out about proposals that may affect their homes, amenities, services or safety until it is too late to have effective involvement in the decision.

To the individual, freedom of information is of most direct concern in relation to personal records. The file on an individual held by public and other bodies is the basis on which benefits are offered or withheld, the need for services assessed, or penalties imposed on those thought to have transgressed. A right of access for the individual is a fundamental safeguard. It allows the individual to check that information is accurate and judgments fair. But it also provides the basis for individuals to participate more effectively in decisions taken about them by caring agencies. Access provides the basis for a more equal relationship in which the agency works with the consent of individuals rather than standing in a position of unaccountable power over them.

The only exclusions should be where there exists an overriding need in the public interest to protect the confidentiality of the information. Supperstone (chapter 15 below) is right when he claims that

a British student of government will often learn more from a short period in Washington about the UK administrative process than he can learn from a lifetime in this country. This is because many of the documents withheld from the public in the UK, are sent, under bilateral arrangements, to other countries, where they become immediately open to inspection.

Discrimination

Labour is committed to the eradication of discrimination in all its forms. Labour governments were the authors of our race relations, sex discrimination and other equal rights legislation. The legislation is now in urgent need of strengthening. In particular a new definition of indirect discrimination is required. It would make unlawful any requirement, practice or policy, adversely affecting a racial group, which could not be demonstrated to be necessary.

There should be a statutory ethnic monitoring requirement on all employers. The only way in which the presence of racial discrimination, including covert and sometimes unintentional acts, can be routinely revealed is the ethnic monitoring of the decisions under question.

In the criminal law there should be express recognition of racially motivated violence as aggravated offences. The law of incitement to racial hatred should be strengthened. In all cases the prosecution should be obliged to put evidence of racial motivation before the criminal courts. And the judges should be obliged expressly to mark racial motivation as an aggravating factor in fixing sentences.

Immigration

Amendment of the Asylum and Immigation Act 1993 and the Immigration Rules to ensure the fair and humanitarian treatment of all persons subject to immigration control is required. Obviously stringent controls on bogus asylum seekers must be maintained. That said, we must maintain our country's tradition of ensuring fair and humanitarian treatment to asylum seekers fleeing from persecution. The 1993 Act removes effective rights of access to the courts from some refugees who may be sent back to persecution and even the death. Many asylum seekers are forced, under the fast-track procedures of this Act, to submit their appeal against refugee status within 48 hours. Then their appeal will be decided within seven days. These procedures sacrifice justice to expedition.

Also, the Act abolished the right of would-be visitors and short-term students to lodge an appeal against the refusal of any entry clearance. This retrograde step means that immigration officials make decisions about visitors to the UK without any form of accountability to the courts. There is a strong case for reinstatement of that right and for a major review of the provisions of this Act.

Conclusion

A large part of the malaise that grips our country stems from a profound disillusion with its system of government. The government is not trusted. Ministerial explanations are met with the deepest cynicism. Sleaze flourishes within a culture of secrecy. Citizens are denied in our courts basic rights against the State which are commonplace in the rest of Europe.

In this section I have not addressed the reform of the machinery of government itself, a crucial component of any major shift in the balance of power from the State in favour of the citizen. I have confined myself to one of the issues of greatest interest to lawyers: how the overweening power of government can be diminished by establishing enforceable, fundamental rights for every citizen.

Reform of the law

At the end of September 1994, the sad fact was that, of the 27 Bills published by the Law Commission since March 1989, only three had by then reached the statute book. The difficulties in finding Parliamentary time should not be underestimated. But for far too long non-controversial reports by the Law Commissions have been gathering dust in Whitehall. Lord Archer of Sandwell recently observed in the House of Lords:

> Between 1967 (when the Law Commission was established) and 1981, 40 Law Commission reports have been wholly or partly implemented — about half on the initiative of the government of the day and about half on the initiatives of private members in one or other of the Houses. Since 1981 only 33 have been wholly or partly implemented. Moreover, since 1989 there has been what Sir Henry Brooke has described as a grade one disaster area: only one Bill has been implemented on government initiative since that time.
>
> In 1981, 13 reports were awaiting implementation. That figure has doubled to 26 by 1985. The figure now stands at 36 reports and represents the hard work of some of our most talented people — hard work which has borne no fruit of any kind.

Since then there has been some improvement because three Bills, complex, though non-controversial in a party political, as distinct from a legal, sense, passed through the House of Lords in 1995 on the fast-track 'Jellicoe' procedure, where evidence is taken in committee, so obviating detailed debate on the floor of the House in the traditional way. The Family Homes and Domestic Violence Bill, however, after almost completing its passage through Parliament, was withdrawn because of ill-informed opposition from the *Daily Mail* and a handful of Conservative backbench MPs.

It was the Labour government of 1964 under its distinguished Lord Chancellor, Lord Gardiner, which set up the two Law Commissions.

It is only possible to keep increasingly complex and far-reaching law efficient, fair and up-to-date by making full and effective use of the Law Commissions. As the present Chairman of the English Law Commission recently observed: 'a nation which neglects the ordinary care of its laws is neglecting something which is very important to its national well-being'.

The Commissions have an impressive record in achieving clarification and reform of the law, but in recent years both Commissions have expressed increasing concern at the government's failure to implement their recommendations. Many much-needed reforms that have been fully reviewed and considered by the Commissions remain unimplemented. In many of those cases, the government has not even troubled to give a public indication of whether it accepts or rejects the Commissions' proposals.

The importance and momentum of law reform must be restored by enhancing the status of the Commissions and putting in place arrangements for the implementation of the Commissions' proposals. What is required is not merely *talk* about law reform, but the *action* that has been lacking in recent years. No government can, of course, be bound by the proposals of the Commissions, or underake always to implement them; but where government disagrees with these independent bodies, democracy demands that the reasons for that disagreement be stated openly; and be subject to public and Parliamentary scrutiny. To put law reform back with a high place on the political agenda, basic changes, as a matter of urgency, are essential.

The reports of the two Commissions are usually impressive documents, with proposals formulated after full consultation with all interested and informed parties. A Labour government would regard the Commissions' reports as the agenda for government response and action, and not as an excuse for delay through the government itself undertaking still more 'consultation'.

The important public status of the Commissions should be reinforced by government accepting an obligation to respond publicly within six months of the publication of any Commission report, giving full reasons for non-implementation or any delay in the implementation of the report's proposals.

This obligation of government to respond publicly to Law Commission reports could be reinforced by the creation of a joint committee of both Houses of Parliament, perhaps along the lines of the Ecclesiastical Committee, with a remit to oversee government action on law reform. This committee would draw on the combined legal expertise of both Houses of Parliament. The government's response to law reform reports would be monitored by the committee, and ministers would give evidence to the committee about that response. That would be an important obligation of government.

The Commissions would retain their present degree of freedom in selecting issues to consider for law reform, and would be encouraged to come forward with new proposals. However, in addition to their annual reports to the Lord Chancellor they would report publicly on a six-monthly basis to the committee, to give an account of progress, and of their use of resources, and (if the Commissions wished) to sound out the committee's opinion on suitable future projects.

Many law reform proposals will be controversial and need full Parliamentary debate. Many others, however, should not require that time-consuming and delaying process. One of the tasks of the joint committee would be to indicate which recommendations, and which parts of them, are in effect technical; and which raise issues of policy and substance. Active steps should be taken to expedite the implementation of proposals that the joint committee regarded as non-controversial and, fortified by the opinion of that committee, all parties in Parliament would be expected to cooperate in the rapid enactment of such proposals. That would leave more time for the full debate of law reform Bills involving issues of greater sensitivity, typically Bills concerning the reform of the criminal law.

Finally, although the Commissions would be the main engine of law reform, it is not practicable, or suitable, for the Commissions to undertake all of the work themselves. In recent years, however, too much use has been made of ad hoc committees, or of interdepartmental studies, without reference to the expertise of the Commissions. The position originally envisaged by Lord Gardiner should be restored: the Commissions should once again advise government as to the most suitable body to undertake any piece of law reform work, and where law reform is contemplated by other government agencies the Commissions should give advice on procedures and approach. That should avoid duplication; lead to a coherent programme throughout government; and ensure that all law reform work, wherever performed, is conducted to a high standard. It is vital that law reform be pushed significantly higher up the political agenda.

2

The Penal System in Crisis

Jack Straw MP, Shadow Home Secretary

There is now widespread agreement from those within the criminal justice and penal system, as well as outside, that there is a crisis in the system which needs our urgent attention.

Crisis of confidence in the criminal justice system

Let us look at some of the data. Recorded crime has doubled in the last 15 years. Yet during this period the total number of people formally identified by the criminal justice system as responsible for indictable offences has actually fallen by 7 per cent. By the phrase 'identified by the system as responsible' I include both those cautioned by the police and those convicted in the courts. If we take simply those pleading or found guilty of indictable offences we find that the numbers have fallen by a third since 1980. The court process is the only part of the system to which the public have any right of access, and to a growing number of them it no longer seems to be working properly. What people see is that the gap between the commission of a crime and its detection and punishment has never been greater.

Although most members of the public will not have the precise figures at their disposal, the fact that only 1 in 50 crimes results in a conviction will come as no surprise to them.

More and more spent doing less and less

The court process may only touch a very small percentage of all crimes but its proper functioning is crucial to the maintenance of public confidence. Increasingly, however, this process appears expensive, inefficient and outdated. More and more is spent doing less and less.

The costs of criminal legal aid have rocketed from £62 million in 1979/80 to £469 million in 1994/5 — a gross expenditure increase in real terms of 127 per cent per defendant or appellant in the higher courts. This may have something to do with an 80 per cent increase in the number of practising solicitors and barristers over a similar period.

The proportion of cases discontinued by the Crown Prosecution Service almost doubled between 1987 and 1994. Of course cases should be weeded out where there are strong evidential or public interest grounds. But as the 1995 Home Office Research Unit report on this subject points out, if appropriate cases were being filtered out one would expect there to be fewer acquittals. This has not happened. Indeed, there is a widening gap between acquittal and conviction. In 1986/7 the acquittal rate in the Crown Court where the defendant pleaded not guilty to all counts was 50 per cent. By 1994 acquittals had grown to 60 per cent of these cases. As the 1995 Home Office study states: '... the fact that the growth in terminations has not been rewarded with lower acquittal rates is disconcerting'. The study points out that: '... any increase in terminations carries a price both in terms of public perceptions and those of the police' (Home Office Research Study No. 137 (1995)).

Though the courts have fewer cases to deal with, they are taking longer to deal with them. The proportion of remand prisoners dealt with by the Crown Court within the statutory time limit dropped from 84 per cent in 1989 to 74 per cent in 1994. A recent paper, *A Future for Youth Justice Services*, published jointly by the AMA, ACC, NACRO, ACOP and the Directors of Social Services complained that: '... the time elapsing between offence and disposal is far too long ... final judgment can come many months after the original offence, and may have little meaning for the offender or victim'.

The years 1993 to 1995 saw a 25 per cent rise in the prison population — up from 41,561 in January 1993 to 51,807 at the end of August 1995. The public demand is in general for tougher, not more lenient sentences. But there is a paradox here, for I do not believe that the public feel reassured by the rising prison population. Rather, I believe it can heighten their anxiety about the prevalence of crime. For the public know the dismal truth that whilst prisoners cannot commit offences

31

outside — the tautology hidden in the claim that 'prison works' — more than half (53 per cent) of all prisoners are reconvicted within two years of release. This rises to 88 per cent for males aged 14–16 (*Prison Statistics 1993*).

Crime levels — good news, bad news

The Home Secretary makes a great deal of any drop in recorded crime. I welcome any reduction in crime, but even at the current modest rate of decline in recorded crime it would take the government another 15 years to get back to the much lower level which it inherited in 1979. The Home Secretary is fond of claiming that crime has been just as bad in other countries and that it has been no worse under his government than under previous ones. Between 1987 and 1993, according to the Home Office's own comparative international statistics, recorded crime in England and Wales rose by 42 per cent, compared with 35 per cent for the next highest country which is Portugal, and 22 per cent for France, 15 per cent for Canada and 5 per cent for the USA. What is more, Home Office figures show that the rate of increase in recorded crime since the War has always been higher under Conservative administrations than with Labour ones. The annual average rate of increase under the Conservatives was 8.1 per cent whilst with Labour it was only 3.4 per cent.

I recently visited Northumbria Police, who have worked hard to develop a partnership approach to tackling crime. A great deal of progress has been made. Even so, the Police Authority has recently put out figures showing that one in three residents in the area have been a victim of crime in the last 12 months, four in 10 households contain people who have been victims, and three in 10 residents have been a victim of burglary or car crime.

It is facts like these which have profoundly changed the experience of crime and therefore the politics of crime too. Crime used to happen to other people, now it happens to each of us — and the poorer you are, the more likely you are to be a victim.

The experience of crime leads to an ever wider fear of crime. The Northumbria Police survey found that four in 10 residents felt threatened at least a fair amount. A recent Norwich Union survey found that one in two women fears driving alone at night, and Barnardo's found that 70 per cent of parents refuse to let their children out unsupervised.

Fear of crime — the link between disorder and crime

It is not only crime that people fear: they fear disorder too. Much disorder and incivility goes unreported and unrecorded, yet it has a profound effect on the quality of life. This issue is of great importance. Fear on the streets and in the public spaces of our towns and cities inhibits and restricts people's lives, and undermines their sense of security and their ability to be active in the community.

None of us should have to put up with an environment in which public areas are scarred by graffiti; where walking down the street can lead to abuse and racial harassment; where families are unable to use parks because they have become the homes of the mentally ill and alcoholics, who have nowhere else to go for shelter and help; and where motorists, often women, feel intimidated into paying for having their windscreens cleaned.

I wholly disagree with those who argue that, if we tackle relatively minor disorder, such behaviour will be displaced into more serious offending. The *Guardian* put it like this: 'Stamping out windscreen cleaning at traffic lights will only divert [young people] into serious criminal avenues' (6 September 1995).

This was an astonishing comment which simply defied common sense. Indeed, the reverse is true. Stopping young people from being involved in antisocial behaviour can prevent that behaviour from escalating into more serious crime. What is more, as some of these young people are truanting from school, intervention at this point can give them a second chance in education.

Crime and disorder are linked in an even more profound way. Disorder and insecurity create a vicious circle of community decline in which those who are able to move out, do so, whilst those who cannot have to modify their behaviour and avoid the streets, squares and parks which they used to use. This leads to a breakdown in community ties, a reduction in natural social controls, and to the area tipping further into decline, economic dislocation and crime. As the American criminologist George L. Kelling has written, 'Poverty causes crime, but crime also causes poverty'. The truth is that crime and disorder are intimately linked.

What has caused this breakdown in community life? I am always hesitant about making claims that everything which has happened in the last 16 years is 'all the fault of the Tories', because plainly many other factors have been at work. But so far as the breakdown in community life is concerned, we may look no further than the policies of a Tory Party, which believes that 'there is no such thing as society', which has spent years denying the link between social conditions and offending, and which has constantly elevated private gain over public virtue.

When large mental hospitals are closed without adequate provision for care in the community; when the stock of public housing has been slashed; when young people leave school without any hope of proper training and employment or indeed any income; when a growing number of children are excluded from school; when the government reneges on its promise to ring-fence funding for residential care homes for alcohol and drug users, then is it surprising that the social fabric is damaged, individual lives are impoverished and communities disintegrate?

How do we get out of this mess?

So what needs to be done to get us out of this mess? We need a strategy which first tackles the underlying social and economic inequalities in which crime breeds; secondly, addresses directly the fear of crime, disorder and community breakdown; thirdly, aims in practical ways to prevent crime; and fourthly, deals more effectively with offenders, so that fewer of them reoffend.

Unemployment

Action is required on unemployment, especially that of young under-skilled males, the single most powerful factor in community breakdown. Senior Conservatives from Kenneth Clarke and Michael Howard to Norman Tebbit have now been forced to admit that unemployment, social deprivation and loss of hope have all been powerful causes of the record increase in crime since 1979. But while they are prepared at last to acknowledge this they are bereft of any ideas about how to tackle it. Cutting unemployment, particularly youth unemployment, will be at the heart of a future Labour government's economic policy.

Young people need quality education and training, with the real prospect of a job at the end of it, if despair is to be replaced with hope.

Homelessness

Action is needed too to tackle homelessness. The provision of a decent home is one of the most basic rights of all in a democratic society. It is a right which is being denied to all to many people in Britain today — with many now sleeping rough on the streets of our towns and cities. The number of homeless people is now three times greater than it was in 1979 — with more registered homeless families now than there were when 'Cathy Come Home' was first broadcast in the early 1960s.

What is required here is the provision of much more quality, affordable, public housing. The money is there for this in the form of local authority capital receipts, but government dogma would rather see these locked away in bank vaults than used to tackle Britain's housing crisis. This is economic madness and a Labour government would reverse this absurd policy.

Alcohol and drug abuse

Better preventative measures are also needed to deal with alcohol and drug abuse. Partnership at a local level is the key to delivering relevant education in schools, clubs, and the wider community. A range of better treatment facilities are also needed through the provision of wet as well as dry hostels for alcoholics and appropriate provision for drug addicts.

Care in the community

The crisis of confidence in the policy of care in the community for mentally ill people must be addressed. As Labour's policy statement, *Renewing the NHS*, says: 'The government has failed to apply in practice what we know are the requirements to ensure care in the community works: staffed accommodation, crisis services on a 24-hour basis and ensuring that every person leaving hospital is in touch with a mental health support team' (*Renewing the NHS* (Labour Party, 1995), p. 35).

Rights and duties

Rebuilding community life in Britain requires an approach which puts the emphasis equally on rights and duties. People have a right to decent housing, to proper training and fulfilling employment but they also have duties to the community they live in. The Conservative 'Me first, don't blame me' society has not only destroyed many of our communities, it has also undermined individual responsibility.

In conjunction with tackling the underlying causes of crime the community has a right to expect more responsible and less antisocial behaviour from all of its citizens. That means less intimidation, bullying and loutish behaviour on the streets and in our town and city centres.

But widespread police action is not the way to achieve this. Indiscriminately sweeping people off the streets would be neither an effective nor a humane response to the problem. What is needed instead are community-based management strategies for tackling disorder and reducing fear. A number of our towns and cities are already developing these for their own public spaces. These management partnerships bring together local authorities, licensing authorities, local business, voluntary organisations and the police.

The community management plan starts by analysing the local problem in consultation with all those affected. Then customised programmes of action are developed to address the problems identified. Towns and cities such as Coventry, Leeds and Nottingham have all successfully implemented management strategies to reduce disorder and encourage greater use of parks, squares and town centres, especially at night. It was one such initiative, the Lewisham community safety project, in south London, which I helped to launch in September 1995 when I spoke of the need to reclaim Britain's public spaces.

Disorder, like crime, can be tackled if we have both the policies and the political will.

Quiet life

People have the right to feel safe in their homes and streets. Sometimes new and imaginative approaches are needed where it is clear that the current system is not working. I have recently put forward proposals for dealing with the problem of the chronic, persistent, criminal behaviour of neighbours, which makes a misery of the life of its victims. New procedures are necessary because the system is ineffective in dealing with this kind of behaviour. This is because the current criminal justice system tends to deal with specific, 'acute', offences so that the cumulative impact on a family or neighbourhood is not apparent; and secondly because victims are all too often intimidated into remaining silent.

I have been consulting on these proposals in a series of 'crime hearings' around the country involving local councils, police, community groups, tenants' organisations and victim support groups. The response has been overwhelmingly enthusiastic. This is not surprising as my 'Quiet Life' proposals were developed out of local people's actual concerns about the problem of antisocial criminal neighbours. I am gratified that these proposals have met with the support of groups as diverse as the Commission for Racial Equality, the Police Superintendents Association and local authority associations, and received widespread coverage in the press.

Crime prevention

The third plank in our strategy is effective crime prevention. This must be at the heart of any serious strategy to tackle crime. The need for this is graphically underlined by the fact that 49 out of 50 offences do not result in a conviction.

The key to success in tackling local crime lies in partnership. This point was powerfully endorsed by the Home Office's own report on crime prevention, the Morgan Report, in 1991. The report recognised that crime prevention can all too easily be marginalised by different agencies. Its proposal to remedy this was that local authorities in conjunction with the police should be given a clear statutory responsibility for crime prevention. Ever since its publication the government has steadfastly refused to implement this most central of the report's recommendations.

The Home Secretary is now considering establishing a national crime prevention agency. Any form of plagiarism is flattery. Of course we welcome Mr Howard's conversion to the cause of crime prevention. But unless he is prepared to drop his dogmatic and blinkered opposition to the Morgan Report's recommendations then his proposals will be deeply flawed.

What businesses, victims' groups, and the police have all been saying to me as I go around the country is that local authorities must be the catalysts in developing effective crime prevention partnerships. It is simply perverse of the government to attempt to exclude the legitimate, elected voice of local communities from a formal role in any national or local crime prevention strategy. A Labour government will replace dogma with common sense by acting quickly to legislate on the Morgan Report and place on local authorities a statutory crime prevention duty.

Reforming the Crown Prosecution Service

The fourth plank in our strategy is action to improve the effectiveness of the criminal justice system in dealing with offenders, so that fewer of them reoffend.

Reform of the court system, and the formal processes of the criminal justice system, must now be an urgent priority.

Delays in the court process must be reduced. This is crucial for victims and very important too for those remanded in custody, waiting weeks for their trial, and for those on bail. The Howard League has highlighted the strain on remand prisoners. There are no winners when justice is delayed. Victims suffer dreadfully when cases are delayed, and the taxpayer has to foot the bill.

Delays in bail cases, particularly those involving young offenders, can lead to more offending and more victims, if the young person anticipates a harsh sentence and goes on an offending spree in the mistaken belief that he has nothing to lose.

Fuller use must be made of non-statutory as well as statutory time limits, courts should rigorously scrutinise requests for adjournments by prosecution and defence, and more use should be made of courtrooms with longer court sittings. I believe that a much more direct responsibility should be placed on the criminal courts to manage cases more effectively, in parallel with changes now being introduced in the civil courts.

The system of criminal legal aid should be reformed to cut out waste and inefficiency, and ensure that it operates in the interests of the public and not the legal profession.

The structure and administration of the Crown Prosecution Service should be changed. It is not working as effectively as it could, and this in part stems from its organisational structure. In my view the most recent reorganisation of the CPS only makes things worse. 31 CPS areas have been replaced by 13 regions, one of which now stretches from Chester to Windsor, covering five police areas.

The Stephen Lawrence case in 1995 was just one of a series of embarrassments for the Crown Prosecution Service. I called in a speech to the Police Federation (18 May 1995) for a thorough and external review of the CPS and everything which has happened since then has confirmed the need for this. We should return to the spirit of the 1981 Royal Commission on Criminal Procedure by creating a separate prosecution service for each police force. In this way accountability to victims and to the public at large would be strengthened and bureaucracy reduced.

Victims

The criminal justice system must give greater attention to the victims of crime. Confidence in the system as a whole is eroded when victims are treated in a thoughtless and insensitive way. They should be kept informed of the progress of the case against the accused, the charges brought, the dates of any court hearings, and the outcome. The CPS, when it is preparing a case, should ensure that it has all the facts about the impact of the crime on the victim. Such an understanding should imbue the prosecution case.

The courts should be more victim and witness friendly. Victims should not have to sit in the same waiting area as the accused.

And we should have a properly funded criminal injuries compensation scheme for the victims of violent crime. By cutting criminal injuries compensation by £700 million, the government is forcing the victims of crime to pay for its own inability to stem the rise in violent crime — up by 147 per cent since 1979.

Sentencing and treatment

Let us turn to sentencing and the treatment of the young offender in particular. Persistent and dangerous young offenders clearly need to be kept in secure accommodation. But local authority secure accommodation should be used for that purpose. We remain opposed to plans for secure training centres, since we believe that these large remote institutions are likely to become colleges for crime.

Once society has got to the point of locking up young people then the system has failed properly to prevent crime, since even in Michael Howard's plans for secure training centres such punishment can only apply to reoffenders. A range of community sentences must be available in every area to prevent the first-time offender from developing into a repeat offender. Speedy and effective intervention is needed to nip offending in the bud. This includes greater use of 'cautioning plus' programmes, which provide a swift and decisive response for the minority of young offenders who fail to respond to a first caution, the use of bail support and enforcement programmes which help to prevent offending on bail, and confronting offenders with some of the realities of their offending behaviour.

We have also proposed two new court orders for the minority of young offenders who fail to respond to warnings, help or punishment. Since the majority of young offenders do not reappear in court after a first court appearance, the second court appearance is a key time on which to focus policies to prevent persistent offending. Our proposed reparation order would be for a three-month period, and would involve reparation to the victim or the local community. The action plan order would be a highly focused three-month order, concentrating on the educational needs of the offender, providing support for the family to help parents fulfil their parental responsibility, and intensive activities in the young offender's free time.

All of us are concerned that the juvenile justice system should operate as effectively as possible. Existing projects must be rigorously monitored, and new ideas and proposals evaluated. For example, Crime Concern's new project in Dalston, in the London Borough of Hackney, for persistent offenders combines a week's residential course focusing on what the young offender wants to achieve in life, education and training to achieve that goal, and adult mentors from the community to provide continuous support. I shall be interested to follow the work of this and other projects focusing on persistent offenders.

Prison

It is prisons, of course, that have borne the brunt of the government's failure to produce effective policies for reducing crime and disorder. Prison numbers are going up beyond the capacity of the system to cope, so that prisons are finding it increasingly difficult to develop or sustain constructive regimes which provide any hope of preventing further criminality.

The futility of such an approach, is borne out by the experience of the United States. Between 1981 and 1991 the federal government cut its contribution to education by 25 per cent and increased its allocation for criminal justice by 29 per cent. Similar figures were brought to my attention on a visit to the US in 1995.

The government's policy towards prisons has been characterised by successive changes of direction, and accompanied by buck-passing and prison service demoralisation. A Government White Paper accepting the majority of the Woolf Report's recommendations has been tacitly abandoned. It has been followed in quick succession by prison privatisation, market testing, 'prison works' and austere regimes. It is hard, I believe, to expect prison governors to deliver consistent regimes, or indeed to be sure of the organisation's priorities in these circumstances.

Boot camps are now the flavour of the month with Michael Howard. But when I visited the USA to look at some of these in operation I found no evidence that boot camps were effective in reducing crime, and indeed I was told by the Commissioner in charge of New York's flagship 'Shock Incarceration Centre' that reducing offending was not part of their aim.

As the government lurches from one embarrassment to another with its ill-fated prisons policy, it is worth asking just what has happened to the Woolf Report. It is extraordinary that such an authoritative report, hailed as a masterly piece of work by everyone involved in the prison system, including the Conservative Home Secretary of the day, has been so quickly neglected. The Woolf Report offered us a unique opportunity to reform the prison system. We should return to its guiding principles of security, control and justice.

Let me reiterate that I regard privatisation of the prison service as morally repugnant. It is not appropriate for people to profit from incarceration, and we intend to take privatised prisons back into the public sector as soon as is contractually possible.

Conclusion

We can get out of this mess if we are prepared to reform the criminal justice system, to give far more emphasis to crime prevention, and to tackle a social fabric decimated by 16 years of Tory rule. There are few more crucial tasks. That is why tackling crime will be a major priority for Labour in government.

3

Legal Aid and Justice

Roger Smith, Director, Legal Action Group

Labour must enter government with a new vision of what can be achieved through a set of coordinated policies on law and justice. This requires the redefinition of the general objectives of policy allied with considerable attention to detail. In the run-up to the election, Labour needs to wrest back the initiative in this area of policy-making, which has been firmly held since his appointment in 1987 by the Conservative government's rather shrewd choice of Lord Chancellor, Lord Mackay of Clashfern. The Labour Party's recent policy document on access to justice is a good start but much of the detail needs to be worked upon before coming into office.[1]

Legal aid can no longer be defended in the form that it has developed since its inception in 1950. Non-lawyers are rightly sceptical of lawyers rushing to its defence. They know that, for lawyers, legal aid is big business, even if they are not aware that legal aid accounts for as much as 12 per cent of all solicitors' work and about 30 per cent of that of the Bar.[2] Furthermore, it is obviously true that the pursuit of due process in the law is different from seeking the achievement of social justice. The homeless, understandably, would prefer lodgings to lawyers.

---

[1] The Labour Party, *Access to Justice: Labour's Proposals for Reforming the Civil Justice System* (1995).
[2] See further R. Smith (ed.), *Shaping the Future: New Directions in Legal Services* (London, Legal Action Group, 1995), ch. 3.

The implication is not, however, that law is less important than substantive justice. Legal services and the justice system provide the context and the method for the enforcement of other substantive rights. The link needs to be acknowledged. One of the problems with the widespread use of the phrase 'access to justice' is the assumption that it is, in some way, self-explanatory.[3] Labour needs policies on access to justice which consider both the means of that access and the substance of the justice that is desired.

An adequate statement and sense of mission

Any effective statement of policy requires a clear statement of its basic principles or objectives. The current 'fundamental aim' of the Lord Chancellor's Department demonstrates how revealing such a 'mission statement' can be: 'to ensure the efficient and effective administration of justice at an affordable cost'.[4] This articulates the purpose as if justice were a business with neutral values. There are here, as elsewhere, alternatives. Labour should not accept uncritically such a managerialist approach.

Labour should be committed to the provision of legal services to the poor and others who are socially or economically disadvantaged because, and to the extent that, they aid the achievement of social justice. The purpose of legal services, broadly defined, is to level the playing field so that, for example, pensioners harmed by a defective drug have as fair an opportunity of a just determination of their case as its multinational manufacturer.

A number of subsidiary commitments follow from such a statement of basic objectives. First and foremost is the importance attached to enforceable rights as a defence against arbitrary decision, a general goal with consequences for almost every area of policy. Other subsidiary objectives are more specific to justice and legal services' policy. These include placing the needs of people first, rather than those of the legal profession or other providers of service; ensuring that all aspects of the legal and justice system reflect a commitment to a multi-ethnic and

---

[3] See *Shaping the Future* (note 2), p. 12.

[4] Lord Chancellor's Department, *A Programme for the Future: Strategic Plan 1994/95–1996/97* (London: Lord Chancellor's Department, 1994), p. 6.

multicultural society; easing the resolution of civil disputes by improving access to courts, tribunals and their alternatives; improving the process of policy-making by greater attention to research and the bringing together of currently disparate decision-making institutions and agencies; the provision of greater access to justice through reform of substantive law, procedure and legal services; increasing knowledge and understanding of legal rights and obligations; and improving the quality of the service currently provided by all those involved in the justice system, whether advisers, lawyers or judges.

Unfashionably, none of these objectives contains any mention of cost. This is deliberate. Labour must not follow the Conservative party's lead in limiting goals by expressing them only hedged about by restrictions on their cost. This is to surrender political ground. Obviously, cost is not irrelevant. On the contrary, there is widespread understanding that a Labour government will be limited in its expenditure plans. Ends must, however, be separated from means. Cost should be separated out as a restriction on how and by when goals will be achieved, not as a limitation on those goals themselves. Policy-making must follow a three-stage process: the investigation of demand; the prediction of cost; the planning of development. Need must, for Labour, always be the place where policy-making begins.

The justice context

An effective justice policy involves elements that are considerably wider than the law, lawyers, legal aid or the courts. Labour must be firmly committed to a society based on legally enforceable rights and obligations. To that end, it should seek to entrench the rights of members of society, particularly the poor and disadvantaged, to provide them with maximum protection against the interests of the powerful and wealthy.

An example of what can be done is provided by legislation on product liability. Rights in this area are obscure and, hence, litigation is costly. This is because domestic law remains largely based on negligence rather than on the principle of strict liability. The Conservative government failed to implement the full force of a European Directive on product liability[5] in the UK by the Consumer Protection Act 1987.

---

[5] 85/374/EEC.

A writer with experience of working for the National Consumer Council (NCC) explains the consequence of the Conservative government's approach over this legislation: '[It] took up, and — in the eyes of many — embellished, the development risks defence which the EC Directive allowed as an option. The decision to have the defence went against the advice of the Law Commission, the Bar and the Law Society — all of whom had seen it as a cause of fruitless litigation and of injustice to the innocent.'[6] The defence protects a manufacturer from liability if 'the state of scientific and technical knowledge at the relevant time was not such that [the] producer ... might be expected to have discovered the defect'.[7] The NCC opposed its inclusion on the grounds that: 'it would substantially erode the principles of strict liability and would be almost tantamount to a return to fault-based liability with the same difficulties of proof for claimants'.[8]

Labour should be committed to the introduction of strict liability in product liability matters and to removal of the development risks defence. More fundamentally, it should be committed to following the approach suggested by an analysis of this area of legislation. An effective legal services and justice policy must begin by looking not at lawyers and the courts but at the substantive law. Area by area, this needs to be reviewed to see how the rights of ordinary people can be clarified and improved, both as a desirable extension of justice but also as a way of saving the expense of legal aid, lawyers and the courts in overcomplicated litigation.

Integrated policies

The example of product liability is a fertile one for demonstrating the new element that Labour should introduce into legal services and justice policy — an integrated approach, deploying every available weapon in the elimination of injustice. It is noticeable that Lord Mackay has followed a disparate methodology with one judge providing a report on litigants in person, another on civil justice more generally and the government itself reporting on the future of legal aid.

---

[6] G. Deyn, 'Opren — problems, solutions and more problems' (1989) 12 *Journal of Consumer Policy* 408.

[7] Consumer Protection Act 1987, s. 4(1)(e).

[8] National Consumer Council, *The Case for Product Liability* (1987).

The clearest area of failure by the Conservative government in civil justice has been its inability or unwillingness to deal with the problems that arise when a large number of individuals have a common claim in relation to, for example, a disaster or product liability. These class, or multi-party, actions present problems for the legal system. These were demonstrated vividly by the Opren cases. Plaintiffs, many of them poor pensioners, required the philanthropy of an interested millionaire to attain any compensation as court procedures and legal aid rules broke down in the face of determined resistance by the government and the multinational drugs manufacturer involved.

The Legal Aid Board has examined class actions twice since it was created, most recently in 1994.[9] It concluded that: 'In our view, the range of measures available to the judge and the general arrangements for dealing with these cases are inadequate. They do not facilitate the manageable disposal of such claims and do not give the judge sufficient control over the action.'[10] Yet Lord Mackay has done nothing to implement reform.

Class actions and class rights admittedly present difficulties for an English legal system manifestly failing to adapt to one of the characteristics of modern society: the development of mass markets and collective obligations. Other countries have responded much more sensitively. A study by the Ontario Law Reform Commission in the early 1980s provides a coherent justification for adaptation of inherited legal procedures and concepts:

> ... the development of a highly complex, interdependent society ... has impeded the capacity of each person to vindicate his legal rights. No longer are we faced with only a single individual or small business against whom we have some grievance ... we live in a corporate society, characterised by mass manufacturing, mass promotion and mass consumption. The production and dissemination of goods and services is now largely the concern of major corporations, international conglomerates, and big government.... Inevitably, dramatic changes in production, promotion and consumption have given rise

---

[9] Legal Aid Board, *Issues Arising for the Legal Aid Board and the Lord Chancellor's Department from Multi-party Actions* (1994)
[10] *Ibid.*, para. 2.16.

to what may be called 'mass wrongs' — that is, injury or damage to many persons caused by the same or very similar sets of circumstances.[11]

The commission provided a powerful case for the introduction of class procedures and funding:

... a class action, in which many similarly injured persons join together, can provide an effective and efficient means of litigating such mass claims ... the presence of effective remedies must contribute to a sharper sense of obligation to the public by those whose actions affect large numbers of people. This is the case whether the obligation is owed by an aircraft manufacturer, a pharmaceutical company, a financial institution or even a government.[12]

Labour must implement reforms to facilitate actions by groups of plaintiffs. This requires the integration of new procedures and new funding methods. Ontario followed its Law Reform Commission report by implementing a scheme originally established in Quebec in the late 1970s. British Columbia and Australia have introduced aspects of similar procedures without the attached funding mechanisms. Class actions are, of course, well established in the United States. There are, therefore, plenty of precedents in other jurisdictions to examine.

For Labour, class litigation provides not only a specific area where reform is required but which Conservative politicians have avoided. More importantly, it shows the sort of integrated working model that is required to bring together substantive law, procedure reform and funding changes into a coherent overall policy.

Legal education of the public

Another issue must be considered before looking at the nuts and bolts of how legal services are provided, the usual focus of debates on legal

---

[11] Ontario Law Reform Commission, *Report on Class Action* (Ministry of the Attorney-General, 1982), vol. 1, p. 3.
[12] Attorney-General's Advisory Committee on Class Action Reform, *Report* (Ministry of the Attorney-General, 1990), pp. 16–17.

48

aid policy. A distinctive element in Labour's approach should be a commitment to legal information and education so that people, particularly those often marginalised by society, understand their rights and duties as well as being helped to deal with problems as they arise. As the Legal Action Group argued in its programme for reform in 1992, *A Strategy for Justice*: '. . . education and information on legal rights and duties should be identified as a priority in the context of increasing concern with the concept of citizenship and the context of the Citizen's Charter'.[13]

Legal education should become part of Labour's development of the idea of citizenship taken over from the Conservatives. As a result, Labour should strongly support the work of bodies like the Citizenship Foundation which have worked to increase acceptance of such a broader definition.[14] Labour should look, for instance, at how legal information might become more available in public libraries. There are exciting examples of what can be done in other countries, for example, the legal information and access centres established in the public libraries of New South Wales. New technology offers enormous opportunities, in particular in the use of interactive video. People could explore how to bring a small claims action or the consequences of divorce by using interactive ways of informing themselves available in advice offices, courts, lawyers' offices, public libraries or, even, their own homes.

The failure of governments in the UK to take an interest in the role of public legal education and information contrasts strongly with the position in Australia and Canada. LAG discussed the role played in Quebec by the equivalent of the Legal Aid Board in *A Strategy for Justice* and published contributions on similar sorts of work in British Columbia and New South Wales in *Shaping the Future*, which also contains a contribution describing the information work undertaken by some law centres in this country.

A Labour government should lead an offensive towards greater knowledge and understanding of the law and, more widely, the social obligations and aspirations that underlie it. Again, the key to a successful policy is integration and coordination. More elements of law

---

[13] Legal Action Group, *A Strategy for Justice* (1992), p. 150.
[14] See J. Newton, 'The Citizenship Foundation and publicly funded legal education and information', in *Shaping the Future* (note 2), ch. 7.

could be included within the national curriculum. Much of the development of public legal education and information will require much greater liaison between the Lord Chancellor's Department and the Department of Education.

An element of the legal aid budget should be earmarked for legal information and education activity. Some of this might be given to specific organisations, such as law centres or CABs involved in educational activity, and another part might be used to finance particular initiatives and projects.

Serious fraud: an example

Another specific illustration can be given of the benefit of looking with a new sense of vision and in detail at different areas of policy. Legal aid for those who are apparently rich has become an issue because of recent media concern and a consequent consultation paper issued by the government.[15] Unfortunately, both the media and the government have tended to conflate two separate issues. One is the protection of the legal aid scheme from abuse; the second relates to the representation appropriate in very large criminal cases, particularly those relating to serious fraud where, ironically, the deprivation of legal representation for defendants can actually impede successful prosecution. Cutting back on legal aid can, even in pure expenditure terms, be the equivalent of cutting off one's nose to spite one's face.

Serious fraud cases constitute a distinct group. They often concern allegations of dishonesty in complex financial transactions involving large amounts of money by defendants who were, at the time, extremely well off. The ultimate sanction in the usual type of legally aided case, i.e., denial or withdrawal of legal representation, is not effective. The prosecution, the court and the defence all have an interest in effective legal representation. As a result, it might be better to see these cases as part of the unavoidable cost of regulation of the City of London and the financial dealings that it represents. The City requires these cases to be brought in order to preserve its integrity and its international reputation as an honest centre of business. Hence, it too has an interest in the successful determination of such cases.

---

[15] Lord Chancellor's Department, *Legal Aid for the Apparently Wealthy: a Consultation Paper* (1994).

It is sometimes argued that, because of the cost of serious fraud trials there should be fewer criminal prosecutions and more use of regulatory offences. This is, however, the equivalent of arguing that armed robbers should be charged with breaches of firearms regulations. There is no reason why City fraudsters should escape criminal sanction.

Labour should consider whether the defence of all cases of serious fraud involving defined aspects of financial services and transactions — perhaps even the costs of their prosecution — should be paid out of a special fund. The resources of the fund would not come from the taxpayer but from the City's regulatory bodies. They would be reimbursed through subscription by those whom they regulate. The costs would, thus, fall upon those with the closest interest in the issues under investigation. This would have the advantage of providing an incentive for both regulators and the bulk of those regulated to stamp out fraud. There seems little reason why the cost of regulation of the City of London should fall upon the general taxpayer.

The savings from implementation are likely to be large. No reliable figure exists for expenditure on legal aid in serious fraud cases but it is rising fast. In 1993/94, 14 cases cost over £1 million in legal aid. Most of these are likely to have been serious fraud cases.[16].

Legal aid

Labour must consider its legal aid policy only in the context of the broad approach, combining new vision and attention to detail illustrated above. The government has encouraged policy discussion of legal aid to be obsessed by its cost. This did, indeed, rise sharply in the late 1980s and early 1990s, see table 2.1.

Table 2.1 Net legal aid expenditure in £millions (including administration)[17]

1989/90	1990/91	1991/92	1992/93	1993/94
569	685	906	1,090	1,257

[16] D. Newnham, 'The cold shoulder', *Guardian*, 6 May 1995.
[17] *The Government's Expenditure Plans 1993/94 to 1995/96: Departmental Report. The Lord Chancellor's and Law Officers' Departments* (Cm 2209) (London: HMSO, 1993), p. 8 and LCD press office.

The causes of this rise were essentially twofold. The number of legally aided cases rose at the same time as the cost for each one. Fixed fees have successfully dealt with the rising cost per case and the Lord Chancellor's Department recently reported that 'the unit cost growth in legal aid remuneration should be contained so that by March 1996 it does not exceed inflation'.[18]

That leaves the rise in numbers of cases. A widely publicised paper from the right-wing Social Market Foundation has suggested that the reason for increasing numbers is 'supplier-induced inflation', i.e., the effect of solicitors chasing more business.[19] However, the truth seems different. Increased use of lawyers, the courts and legal aid follow a trend more widespread in society as a whole than is often acknowledged. People are reaching out for help in ever-increasing numbers, in relation to both the material and the psychological aspects of their problems, as can be seen from table 2.2.

---

[18] *Departmental Report of the Lord Chancellor's and Law Officers' Departments: the Government's Expenditure Plans 1995/96 to 1997/98* (Cm 2809) (London: HMSO, 1995), p. 5.

[19] G. Bevan, A. Holland and M. Partington, *Organising Cost-Effective Access to Justice* (Social Market Foundation, 1994).

Table 2.2   Numbers using various sources of assistance[20]

Organisation	1971	1981	1991
Alcoholics Anonymous	6,300	30,000	45,000
Citizens Advice Bureaux	1,500,000	4,514,600	7,648,900
Relate	21,600	38,300	70,000
Young People's Advisory and Counselling Service	89,000	314,700	470,000
Samaritans	21,600	38,300	70,000
Civil legal aid	201,072	174,795	256,000
Crown Court criminal legal aid	52,575	100,720	137,175
Magistrates' court criminal legal aid	71,618	296,134	477,170
Legal advice	n/a	649,496	1,230,000

The rise in legal aid has, thus, paralleled the increased use of a wide range of helping organisations over the last 20 years.

Another frequently ignored factor is the changing pattern of wealth. Over the last decade and a half, there have been major shifts in income between different sectors of society. Confirmation of the relative drop in income for the poor and growth of income for the rich comes from the recent Rowntree inquiry into income and wealth. This was reported as proving that 'Britain is now a more divided society than it has been

---

[20] *Social Trends 23* (London: HMSO, 1993), table 11.22; *Criminal Statistics: England and Wales 1972 and 1981* (the figure for Crown Court legal aid in 1971 is in fact the number of certificates given in 1972); *Judicial Statistics 1991; Legal Aid Report 1971/72 and 1981/82* and *Legal Aid Board Annual Report 1991/92*. All legal aid statistics except those for the Crown Court are in fact for 1991/92. The figure for civil and Crown Court criminal legal aid is for certificates granted. The other figures are for bills paid. The apparent drop in civil legal aid grants in 1981 is due to reclassification of categories. There was, for example, no advice scheme 10 years earlier.

at any time since the Second World War ... [with] divisions between the bottom tenth of the population, who are 17 per cent worse off than they were in 1979, and the top tenth, who are more than 60 per cent better off'.[21] Will Hutton, influential *Guardian* financial correspondent, argues that changes in relative prosperity are bringing about a 'thirty, thirty, forty society': '... the first 30 per cent are the *disadvantaged* ... the second 30 per cent are made up of the *marginalised* and the *insecure*.... The last category is the *privileged*'.[22]

Such a context helps to explain the rise in the use of legal aid. It is not surprising that, although eligibility on financial grounds has been cut by around one third since 1979, the numbers claiming assistance rise every year. Increasingly, legal aid is becoming a benefit available only to the very poor, a fact which emerges clearly from the ever-rising proportion of legally aided litigants who are eligible for free legal aid. In the 1960s around half of all recipients of civil legal aid for cases in the civil courts paid a contribution. In 1993/94, that proportion had fallen to 14 per cent. Thus, the essential character of legal aid is changing: it is no longer a benefit for which the majority of the population is eligible. Cuts have limited it to the poorest section of society, a group which is itself increasingly detached from those who pay for it through taxation.

Franchising

The Conservative government has approached the problems of legal aid by capping the legal aid budget and developing contracts with legal providers in a way that will drive down prices, thus obtaining more coverage for the same amount of money. By the time of the next election, the Legal Aid Board is likely to have extended its franchising arrangements to most major legal aid providers. It may also have completed its pilot schemes with the use of non-solicitor advice agencies. Franchising contracts impose quality conditions on the general running of franchised practices and on the quality of casework undertaken by franchised firms. This is the first attempt to impose quality conditions in legal aid. Potentially, it makes the Legal Aid Board

---

[21] 'To have and have not', *Independent on Sunday*, 12 February 1995.

[22] W. Hutton, *The State We're In* (London: Jonathan Cape, 1995), pp. 106–8.

a more powerful force in controlling the quality of solicitors in their day-to-day work than the Law Society. It is a significant advantage of franchising in England and Wales over its implementation in some other jurisdictions, such as the Australian state of Victoria, where no quality standards have been imposed.[23]

There are, however, significant problems with how the Legal Aid Board has approached the question of monitoring quality. It has placed great weight on procedural judgments, having developed transaction criteria which assess how well a case has been taken through a standardised procedure. Franchising has been resisted by some conservative elements within the legal profession. In addition, some enlightened practitioners, who have supported the principle of franchising, are questioning its practice. Labour should take up the argument on quality assessment and not accept assertions from the Legal Aid Board or the Lord Chancellor that this issue has been solved. On the contrary, it needs considerably more work.

Labour should, therefore:

(a)   support franchising in principle as the basis of its proposed Community Legal Service;

(b)   resist any call for franchising to become exclusive, i.e., that legal aid be restricted only to franchised practitioners, until it can be shown that franchised practitioners alone can provide an adequate level of service throughout the country;

(c)   oppose any move to compulsory competitive tendering, as an unwanted restriction both on client choice and market forces;

(d)   conduct an external review of the Board's use of transaction criteria and other quality mechanisms within a year of coming to office, in order to improve the provision of quality services, the encouragement of best practice, and the professional independence of service providers from State control;

(e)   extend the franchising concept, with the development of better quality control mechanisms, through the whole range of legal services provision; and

(f)   consider how franchising might be applied to the Bar.

---

[23] J. M. Giddings, *Franchising Arrangements and the Quality of Legal Aid Services* (1995), unpublished.

In *A Strategy for Justice*, LAG argued that:

> ... advice, assistance and representation require comprehensive services provided by:
> (a)   legal aid private practitioners;
> (b)   law and legal centres;
> (c)   advice agencies;
> (d)   enforcement agencies, such as the Health and Safety Executive and the Commission for Racial Equality;
> (e)   directly salaried services.[24]

Franchising contracts provide a mechanism for a desirable diversification according to local and individual circumstances. For instance, LAG argues that 'social welfare law' areas of work, like housing, are ideally suited for services delivered by lawyers and advisers working together within voluntary sector organisations such as law centres or CABs. There are, however, significant numbers of excellent housing practitioners in private practice. Franchising allows the growth of an integrated network of provision involving many different types of delivery which are similar in only one way: they meet defined quality criteria.

Labour should oppose capping as contrary to a rights-based approach. Legal aid has always been demand-led in recognition of its link with the enforcement of rights. The demand may be managed through open and transparent eligibility criteria but the element of randomness introduced by capping must be resisted. The Social Fund provides a grim example of the consequences of capping a social benefit. So, too, do other jurisdictions that have capped their legal services budgets.[25]

Labour should be committed to ensuring that legal assistance reaches all for whom it is intended. A Labour government should mandate the Legal Aid Board to provide an annual or biennial review of those who receive its services, concentrating in particular on groups within the community — for instance, the elderly or those from ethnic minorities, particularly those with language difficulties — who might be expected to have difficulty in obtaining access. This would serve to emphasise the

---

[24] Legal Action Group, *A Strategy for Justice* (1992), p. 150.
[25] See *Legal Action* (May 1995), p. 3.

client-orientation of the service and would follow the practice of most Australian legal aid commissions. Representative examples of the work undertaken might also help to dispel media criticism of the level of expenditure.

Alternatives

A number of alternatives are sometimes suggested for legal aid. None of them are likely to prove very effective. Poor people are unlikely to find legal expenses insurance attractive and, in any event, most policies exclude criminal charges and matrimonial work precisely because they are the two largest groups of cases. Conditional fees, recently introduced by Lord Mackay, are unlikely to have much effect. The danger is that such fees will actually benefit only lawyers, rather than their clients. The indemnity costs rule, under which losers pay the costs of the other side, means that such fees could play only a limited role in increasing access to justice. The main disincentive to litigation is often precisely this potential liability. The Law Society has organised insurance to deal with this but it is likely that, in fact, this will be available only in cases where, currently and in technical breach of professional rules, solicitors act 'on spec', totally waiving their own fees. Contingency fees play such a large part in the United States precisely because the indemnity costs rule does not usually apply. Labour should launch an inquiry into the operation of the limited conditional fees permitted under regulations introduced by Lord Mackay.

Any alternative, or supplement, to legal aid has to deal with the costs rules. Labour could encourage certain types of litigation by amending these in specific cases. For instance, legal assistance in employment cases could be encouraged by allowing industrial tribunals to award costs to employees where their cases were successful but not against them where they lost. This would allow trade unions and solicitors to provide representation in cases that they reckoned would be successful. This would, however, be vulnerable to later attack by the introduction of costs rules against employees.

The benefit of litigation brought *bona fide* in the public interest should be recognised. Public interest litigation, certified in some appropriate way, could be exempt from awards of costs if cases were lost. In this way, certain environmental challenges, for instance, could be encouraged. Legal aid rules should be changed to make it explicit that public interest criteria are relevant in the grant of legal aid.

The way forward

There are no easy choices left in the field of legal services policy. The restriction on spending more money means that, after a point, the options run out. It is important to recognise that the problems are international. Many developed countries are experiencing the clash caused by rising expectations and increasing 'legalisation' meeting declining economies and greater political resistance to government expenditure.[26] Many have responded by establishing reviews of their civil justice systems that differ from Lord Hailsham's civil justice review or that initiated by Lord Woolf at the behest of Lord Mackay precisely by their acceptance of the kind of integrated approach argued for above. For instance, an official Australian committee has just produced a 500-page *Action Plan* on access to justice.[27] The Canadian province of Ontario is in the midst of a major civil justice review, the 400-page first report of which was published in March 1995.[28]

Labour needs a similar global review of its justice policies. The fragmentation of the Conservative approach is currently very evident. April, May and June 1995 saw the publication of a White Paper on divorce, a Green Paper on legal aid, Lord Woolf's first report on access to civil justice and proposals from the Court Service for a considerable rise in court fees.

The next election will take place at a critical point in a fast-evolving legal services market. Decisions of government can still affect events to a major extent. Labour has an enormous opportunity to give impetus to reform that will be beneficial for the widest range of people. Labour must be ready with policies over a wide range of issues because an unprepared administration will find it difficult to respond with sufficient speed.

---

[26] See further, *Shaping the Future* (note 2), ch. 2.
[27] Access to Justice Advisory Committee, *Access to Justice: an Action Plan* (Commonwealth of Australia, 1994).
[28] Ontario Civil Justice Review, *First Report* (1995).

4

Delivering Civil Justice: Alternatives to Legal Aid

Professor Ross Cranston, London School of Economics

A system of civil justice must be judged by the way it treats those at the bottom of society. Wealth and power buy privilege in the arena of civil justice, as elsewhere. We see this in the excellent legal services available to commercial interests, notably through the large commercial law firms and leading sets of barristers' chambers. If commercial interests are enmeshed in litigation it is most likely to be handled by judges of outstanding calibre. This is not to gainsay the problems: even commercial interests complain about the high cost of civil justice, the hazards created by our rules of civil procedure and the long-windedness in getting contentious matters to a final resolution.[1] Compared with the obstacles those at the bottom face in obtaining access to justice, however, the position at the top is rosy.

Building on existing mechanisms

Historically our system of civil justice has been adversarial. This has much to commend it but it assumes that the different parties will be equally matched. That is hardly ever so when an individual without

---

[1] The interim report on access to justice (1995) by Lord Woolf addresses these problems; it also reports on some of the matters dealt with in this chapter.

assistance faces a corporate or governmental opponent. This being the case we need somehow to adjust the system so that the balance is redressed. There are already some mechanisms for doing this. One is legal aid. Since Labour's post-war revolution in legal aid, many have obtained access to justice from a private practitioner who has received a state subsidy to provide advice and assistance to them. But it is now clear that it will never be possible to deliver justice for all in this way. A major wrong turning was the failure to implement those parts of the Legal Aid and Advice Act 1949 which contemplated a salaried legal aid service.[2] But irrespective of the history, the plain economic fact is that no government, including a Labour government, can fund without limit a system which is largely driven, as is traditional legal aid, by market forces. That does not justify cutting traditional legal aid — the involvement of private practitioners provides powerful political support for publicly funded legal services — but it does make it incumbent on Labour lawyers to foster and devise additional mechanisms for providing justice for all.

Law centres have been the real success story of the last 25 years in delivering legal services to those at the bottom. The Society's pamphlet, *Justice for All*, in 1968 was a significant factor in putting law centres on the political agenda. The justification for public funding of law centres is that they make legal services available to people who might not otherwise enjoy them through traditional legal aid. They do so by going beyond the narrow concerns of the latter to an interest in the wide range of decisions affecting ordinary people made by employers, businesses and government. Their location in deprived communities also means that they are readily accessible physically and geographically to the poorer sections of society. Yet the coverage of law centres is patchy and their hold on life sometimes tenuous.

In ch. 18 of his interim report, Lord Woolf was favourably impressed by the system of ombudsmen in both the public and private sectors and recommended more extensive use of the concept. The ombudsman system performs two broad functions. The first, and obvious, function

---

[2] The first version of this present volume, *The Reform of the Law*, edited by Glanville Williams (London, 1951), seemed to recognise this; it opined that the legal aid legislation of 1949: 'goes some way to alleviate the worst evils of the present sitatuion, but it can hardly be regarded as more than a stop-gap measure. The legal service will still be far behind the new national health service' (p. 32).

is to handle individual grievances. Generally speaking people must exhaust an organisation's internal complaints procedures, but having done that can have a matter taken up by the relevant ombudsman. In this sense the ombudsmen are an alternative to the courts, although in an important respect their jurisdiction is broader in that they can decide a matter on other than legal grounds (for example, maladministration or good practice). By the same token not all complaints about a particular institution fall within the terms of reference of the relevant ombudsman. Some jurisdictional limits on ombudsmen have been surprising and have been criticised both by the ombudsmen themselves and outside bodies. The second function of an ombudsman is to establish benchmarks of good practice within a sector and to raise standards. Courts are not especially adept in doing this, even if they wanted to: they have a general, rather than a special, jurisdiction, and so do not have a sufficient caseload to acquire a detailed knowledge of, or to monitor, changing practice within a particular sector.

New mechanisms for delivering justice for all

The remainder of this chapter sketches some approaches to delivering justice to all which are capable of much further development. A first approach is to empower individuals so that even without traditional legal assistance they are no worse off; a second is the collective approach whereby individual interests are coalesced; and a third is to sidestep the civil justice system entirely.

Empowering individuals

Delivering civil justice for those at the bottom need not necessarily involve lawyers in private practice, or even the courts. There is no reason in theory why the quality of civil justice offered through other mechanisms should not be comparable with what can be obtained in more conventional ways. Moreover, these other mechanisms are as likely to be as efficient, possibly more so, if this is measured in terms of minimising cost (but at the same time avoiding error and achieving the

61

desired quality of justice).[3] It is an arrogance of lawyers to assume that they and the existing machinery are somehow indispensable for the fair administration of civil justice.

There are a number of examples of resourceful individuals, perhaps with limited assistance, litigating successfully in person. During the anti-poll tax campaign the Court of Appeal confirmed that a litigant in person can be accompanied as of right by a person — the so-called *McKenzie* friend — giving quiet and unobtrusive advice. Self-help in the legal system, it can be argued, is a form of empowerment; it can:

> bring more people into close (and understanding) contact with legal processes, thus making those processes more responsible to people's needs; and increase people's self-confidence and sense of social responsibility by allowing them to participate in the resolution of their own problems.[4]

What is needed if self-help is to work, however, is a simplification of the law and legal procedures. Individuals must have access to easily understood manuals, specimen forms and assistance in specific matters. Much can be done through new technologies. The public education work of the People's Law School in British Columbia, which the Legal Action Group has done much to publicise in this country, is illustrative of how individuals can be given knowledge and confidence to operate more effectively in the civil justice system. But as far as many individuals are concerned, self-help is overly romantic when they come up against institutional power or are involved in traditional litigation. For most, self-help will be a last resort, through a lack of alternative. While with some help ordinary people might be able to present simple matters before tribunals or in the small-claims jurisdiction, it would otherwise seem too much to expect.

---

[3] Evaluating quality is, of course, a difficult issue. Its dimensions include individual satisfaction (whether the individual is satisfied, in terms of the experience and outcome); individual autonomy (whether the mechanisms strengthen the capacity to deal with one's own problems, minimising institutional control); social justice (whether social and economic inequalities are neutralised, or possibly ameliorated); and social solidarity (whether the mechanisms generate common values etc.): see R. Barush Buch, 'Defining quality in dispute resolution' (1989) 66 Denver ULRev 335, 347–8.
[4] Legal Action Group, *Life without Lawyers* (1978).

Legal assistance for individuals, however, does not necessarily mean the traditional lawyer. In some contexts skilled non-lawyers can be just as effective — indeed more so — than lawyers.[5] There is a long tradition of such paralegals in this country. Traditionally the law clerk — now the legal executive — was the backbone of the solicitor's office. In the CABs, and later the law centres, non-lawyers have provided legal advice, assistance and representation (before tribunals). Indeed, there is a strand of thought which values paralegals over lawyers:

> ... they tend to be more accessible than lawyers, more capable of understanding and working with ordinary people ..., less likely to distort the informal procedures of tribunals and more capable of providing a broad and flexible range of assistance, going beyond the immediate (and possibly superficial) 'legal' problems.[6]

The Civil Justice Review saw an enhanced role for lay representatives.[7] Following their recommendation, s. 11 of the Courts and Legal Services Act 1990 empowers the Lord Chancellor to remove restrictions on rights of audience and rights to conduct litigation in specified proceedings in the county courts. A limited order has been introduced. Systematic training for paralegals is, of course, essential.

In ch. 17 of his interim report, on litigants in person, Lord Woolf lent his support to court-based duty advice and assistance schemes, in particular that there be permanent advice centres in the larger courts. Coupled with these Lord Woolf has recommended trying out information kiosks (an idea borrowed from the United States), the simplification of substantive law in areas such as housing, and the 'unbundling' of legal work — in other words a division of tasks and a sharing of responsibility for doing them between adviser and client.

Public intervenor actions; the office of public advocate

The term 'public intervenor action' describes appearances before a court or an official inquiry by government agencies, or more probably

---

[5] H. Genn and Y. Genn, *The Effectiveness of Representation at Tribunals* (Lord Chancellor's Department, 1989), p. 70. The empirical work of the Royal Commission on Legal Services reached a similar conclusion.
[6] Legal Action Group, *Life without Lawyers* (1978) pp. 3–4.
[7] Cmnd 394 (1988).

non-government organisations (NGOs), acting in the public interest. The remedy sought is non-compensatory in nature, primarily that someone act or be prevented from acting in a certain way. We already have limited examples in this country in the applications for judicial review and support of test cases by groups such as the Equal Opportunities Commission, the World Development Movement and Greenpeace. Equally such groups have appeared before official inquiries, notably planning inquiries.

Procedurally, the key issue about the public intervenor action is standing. Standing seems no longer to be a major problem with judicial review or many government inquiries. Otherwise there must be a specific statutory authority. In this country that is rare, even non-existent. By contrast legislation in civil law systems empowers agencies and groups to take various types of legal action in the name of the public interest. For example, in Germany under the Law on General Terms and Conditions 1976, consumer groups, trade associations and chambers of industry and commerce can sue to prohibit specific enterprises from using invalid standard terms. Similarly in France environmental groups are authorised by statute to take action against specified violations of environmental law. Professor Cappelletti has written of such devices:

> The advantages of this solution vis-à-vis the isolated litigator are clear: on the one hand, they are 'specialised' in the area they represent. However, unlike the 'specialised governmental agencies', they are better suited to preserve the 'zeal' of the private persons involved, while at the same time representing the *entire* interest and not merely a fragment of it. They can also multiply the resources of isolated individuals. The shortcoming of this solution ... is that usually only associations duly 'registered' (*certifiées*) and, quite frequently, only associations in existence for one or more years are entitled to bring actions as the representatives of the entire group or category. Furthermore, a statute is also usually necessary to define the requirements for such power of representation.[8]

Cost is also an obvious problem if NGOs are to be intervenors. In 1988 Ontario enacted its Intervenor Funding Project Act, to finance

---

[8] M. Cappelletti, 'Alternative dispute resolution processes within the framework of the worldwide access-to-justice movement' (1993) 56 MLR 282, 286.

interest groups appearing before certain administrative agencies in the province. (Indeed it is an accepted feature of Canadian public life that government agencies fund interest groups and others wishing to intervene in the administrative process, especially in the environmental area.[9]) The Act sets out criteria that intervenors must fulfil to be eligible for funding, primarily that the issues affect a significant segment of the public and the public interest, and that the intervenor be representative, relevant, potentially helpful etc. In its first three years $25 million was awarded as intervenor funding and intervenors, administrative agencies and others expressed overwhelming support for the idea. Criticisms that it primarily benefits lawyers and consultants, that it creates a disincentive to industry to proceed with worthwhile projects, and that it lengthens hearings were not widespread.

There should be an office of Public Advocate. At one level this would be an Equal Opportunities Commission, Office of Fair Trading or Commission for Racial Equality writ large. It would be a government department with power to represent the public interest before courts, administrative agencies and other bodies. The idea is along the lines of Lord Woolf's Director of Civil Proceedings, who could initiate civil proceedings whenever required in the public interest and could act as *amicus* in all relevant proceedings.[10] One of its functions would be to seek a compensatory remedy on behalf of a group of the public. There are few examples in this country, although the action of the Parliamentary Ombudsman in obtaining compensation for the Barlow Clowes investors is one. I first wrote about this in the 1970s in the context of consumer protection:[11]

The mass restitution suit ... allows a [public advocate] department to bring a suit for damages or injunctive relief on behalf of all the consumers affected by 'multiple or persistent' breaches of the law. There is no need for consumers to have complained before the action is commenced. The department bears the burden and the cost of

---

[9] See the many examples in M. Valiante and W. Bogart, 'Helping ''concerned volunteers working out of their kitchens'': funding citizen participation in administrative decision making' (1993) 31 Osgoode Hall LJ 687.
[10] Sir Harry Woolf, *Protection of the Public — A New Challenge* (London, 1990), pp. 110–11.
[11] *Consumers and the Law*, 1st ed. (1978).

instituting the proceedings although it can recover this amount in a successful action plus the costs of investigation leading to judgment. The advantage of mass restitution suits is obvious in that they can guarantee recovery to consumers who might not bring an action themselves. At the same time the possibility of a mass restitution suit would act as a deterrent to businesses which would ordinarily have to compensate only a few of the consumers adversely affected by a trade practice in breach of the law. Individual consumers need not be identified before a judgment is given, although the court might establish measures to notify potential recipients. To participate in any judgment consumers need only convince an officer of the consumer protection department of their entitlement.

Clearly the idea can be refined and extended to other areas.

Sidestepping the civil justice system

It is a fixation that ultimately rights can only be guaranteed by courts. With social rights, for example, the courts can only ever have a marginal role. To the reformers of the nineteenth and early twentieth century, government was the pathway to a better society, and social change was seen as a matter of electing reforming political parties, of making representations through influential contacts and of generating a public awareness about issues. Involvement of the courts in social change was far from the minds of the Benthamite reformers, for they could see how ill-suited the courts were to matters such as factory, poor-law and lunacy reform. Their approach is summed up in Jeremy Bentham's own view: 'an amendment from the judgment seat is confusion'. 'New liberals' such as Joseph Chamberlain demonstrated the efficacy of government reform. Legislation and State action were also hallmarks of the approach of the early socialists to social change, and it was never considered that the courts should have anything to do with matters such as nationalisation, municipalisation, the redistribution of wealth, the regulation of the economy to stem unemployment, and the establishment of national minimum standards below which no person would be permitted to fall.

The paradox of the bureaucracies established by the reformers has been that they develop their own agendas: although ostensibly devoted to the wider public interest and to the interest of intended beneficiaries, they sometimes appear to neglect these interests in their action. External review by ombudsmen, auditors and inspectorates is a means of keeping them on the right track.[12] While not denying the importance of external review, however, what is essential is to influence the ethos of these bureaucracies. Partly this turns on the institutionalised control of their behaviour. Partly also it involves integrating desirable trends into the everyday practices and training of officials. Participation of a bureaucracy's clientele in its operation has some role here.

We need to question the existing pattern of rights and their enforcement. Debt provides one example. Why should the courts simply rubber-stamp the claims which creditors bring against debtors (and rubber stamp it is, since most cases are undefended)? Although most debtors owe the amount claimed, the Civil Justice Review research discovered that some one third of debtors disputed the cases against them.[13] Indeed, why should creditors be able to invoke the power of the State to sue debtors at all if they have irresponsibly advanced credit? And why in particular should the privatised utilities have the added clout of being able to disconnect essential services such as gas, water and electricity when customers are behind with their payments?

Accident compensation is another area where we must look beyond the existing civil justice system. It is a historical accident that those injured at work and on the road are able to claim compensation through the courts. That would not be a fatal objection to the tort system if it were not so capricious in determining who obtains compensation through it or in the grossly inefficient way it operates (in particular, the high legal costs).[14] The last Labour government appointed the Pearson Royal Commission, which recommended reducing the incentives for accident victims using the courts by increasing the comparative attraction of social insurance.[15] In 1974 a Labour government in New

---

[12] In this respect judicial review is largely beside the point: see my 'Reviewing judicial review', in G. Richardson and H. Genn, *Administrative Law and Government Action* (Oxford, 1994).

[13] Touche Ross, *Study of Debt Enforcement Procedures* (1986), pp. 63–5.

[14] And now research for the Law Commission also demonstrates that the tort system cannot adequately calculate for victims' long-term needs: H. Genn, *Personal Injury Litigation: How Much Is Enough?* (Law Com. No. 225, 1994).

[15] *Royal Commission on Civil Liability and Compensation for Personal Injury* (Cmnd 7054, 1978).

Zealand was much more radical and replaced the tort system with a comprehensive compensation plan for accident victims. This is not a complete answer but it does place a large question mark over the present approach.

Conclusion

In reforming the civil justice system our concern must be not only with access to justice, but with equal access to justice — access in the hands of the many, not the few. At present, equality before the law is contradicted by the way our civil justice system works. Those at the bottom get an especially bad deal.

What can be done? First, we can build on existing mechanisms such as law centres, advice agencies and ombudsmen. With law centres, as well as a sideways expansion, there needs to be a deepening. National support centres are one possibility — taking account of the work already done by specialist bodies such as Shelter, CPAG and MIND — to conduct research, disseminate information and to act as a base for coordinating national campaigns. Advice agencies also need strengthening: more law-related training for generalists is one aspect, so that legal problems are spotted; more specialist law-related back-up is another. For some time LAG has advocated as well a statutory duty on local authorities to provide an adequate advice service. The concept of ombudsmen has much to commend it, although in the private sector it needs statutory underpinning.

We also need new mechanisms which facilitate access to justice for the many. Empowering individuals through education and training will enable some to navigate the shoals of the system, although only a small number will benefit without fundamental adjustments such as procedural simplification and an interventionist approach by judges. Collective mechanisms can advance the interests of those traditionally unrepresented before decision-makers (including courts) and allow intervention in the decision-making process where this has never previously occurred. One approach is to generalise the work of bodies such as the EOC and CRE by establishing an Office of the Public Advocate. Finally, it is as well to recall that procedural and institutional reform cannot be divorced from reform of the substantive law. We need to review the legal rights to which the civil justice system gives effect:

subtracting from and adding to those is also a necessary step if equal access to justice is to become a reality.

5

Judges

Lord Williams of Mostyn QC

Any survey of the judiciary in England and Wales produces a rich collection of paradoxes. On the one hand the intellectual quality of the High Court judiciary and its reputation for being politically and financially incorruptible are universally applauded. On the other hand the system of selection, training and monitoring of judges generally is lamentably amateur. About a century has passed since the last significant reforms, namely, the setting up of the Supreme Court in its modern form and the entitlement of a defendant in a criminal case to give evidence on his or her own behalf. What we see at the moment is piecemeal reform which deals with the structure of the legal system and to a lesser extent the content of law with very little lateral debate on what the judiciary ought to be, what it ought to offer and whether it delivers what is reasonably required.

English lawyers criticise the system in the United States of America where a judge may sit full time for 10 years or so and then return to practise at the Bar. I share that criticism. But in England and Wales we have what is potentially an infinitely worse system, namely a dangerous over-reliance on part-time judges. The usual focus of criticism is that rightly made about the use of deputy High Court judges. Very often there are more part-time than full-time judges sitting in the Royal Courts of Justice. This is a serious criticism, but not I think the most important. We rely far too much on assistant recorders and recorders whose only commitment is to sit for a minimum of four weeks per year. In 1992 there were 538 assistant recorders and 786 recorders compared with 467 circuit judges. The relationship between those figures has barely altered in the succeeding three years. In addition there were 2,470 part-time appointments to tribunals.

The public generally have a feeling that they want a 'proper' judge to try their case. There are serious arguments in principle and in practice against this over-reliance on part-timers. In principle it seems to me that a job of this power and importance should be carried out mainly by full-timers. The public find it very difficult to understand, as I do, to rationalise and explain, the fact that a barrister (normally) or a solicitor may simply act part-time for one month a year, given the nature and scope of the powers which are exercised. Some of the power is absolute, that is to say, not subject to any appeal in the majority of cases. A refusal to grant bail is virtually incapable of being appealed. As long as a sentence is within recognised parameters no appeal will succeed. These powers are given to part-timers sitting a fortnight at a time. We would not tolerate this from a surgeon or consultant physician. Why is it acceptable in the judiciary?

The true answer lies in the unplanned growth of the system, which has barely been subjected to critical scrutiny. The recommendations of the Runciman Royal Commission about the judiciary were hardly commented on.

It is often said that service as a part-time assistant recorder or recorder is a useful indicator to the Lord Chancellor's Department in deciding who shall have permanent appointment. Indeed the present Lord Chancellor's policy is not to make permanent appointment except from the ranks of those who have served as part-timers. This has a superficial attraction in some cases. However, the truth is that many practitioners continue to sit part-time either beyond the age of a sensible prospect of full-time appointment or in the sure and certain knowledge that they would not accept an appointment even if it were offered. A recorder or assistant recorder who has been sitting for 20 years part-time has surely demonstrated capacity or incapacity at the end of the first five years.

The truth is that the system depends on part-timers because it is obliged to do so. The meanness of the Treasury, to which unfortunately the Lord Chancellor's Department conforms, means that sufficient High Court and Circuit judges are simply not being appointed. Yet they are not expensive to provide. If one takes the High Court judge's salary of £100,000 a year together with, say, a £50,000 annual contribution to the pension component, a total sum of £150,000 is about what it will cost to keep a single child in a secure training centre under the government's present proposals. We ought, I believe, to move to a system where the use of part-timers is genuinely used simply to assess judicial capability and quality on a full-time basis.

The present system is grossly inefficient. If a sentence has to be adjourned or a case runs over a fortnight, frequently a fresh judge will have to read the papers and sentence or try the case. Listing is constrained if the part-timer only has a two-week commitment. As far as I am aware no management audit has ever been carried out on a systematic basis to find out the true costs of those inefficiencies. Such a management audit ought to be the first step to the reform of the judiciary in this country.

In any event, despite the recent cosmetic improvement by way of advertisement for the lower judicial appointments, the present system of appointment remains inefficient. What is the intellectual justification for demanding application for circuit judge appointments and their advertisement, but declining to advertise for applications for the High Court appointments? There is, simply, no sense in it. This is particularly so with senior circuit judges commonly trying the serious criminal cases such as rapes and murders; indeed many of them have much more experience of that type of crime than High Court judges who process on circuit. How can it be justified in 1995 that a silk who has practised entirely in commercial work or, it may be, family and matrimonial work, is let out to try serious criminal cases? It simply does not work; and learning on the job cannot be an acceptable substitution for training and monitoring judicial performance.

There will be no improvement unless the structure is altered. The structure needs to be the consequence of a recognition that selection, promotion, training and monitoring should be done by a single body, namely, a judicial college. It is essential that a college should be kept free of political interference. The great glory of the present judiciary is its political independence. It is noteworthy that in the last 25 years an increasingly supine and passive Parliament has done infinitely less to control an overweening executive than the process of independent judicial review. It was not a freak that brought both the UDM and the

NUM to the High Court to protest against the closing of the mining industry in this country. Both believed that their rights could only be asserted by the court rather than protected by a whipped House of Commons.

The head of any judicial college ought to be either the Lord Chief Justice or a senior designated Lord Justice of Appeal. Funds are needed. The present Judicial Studies Board does good work but it is hopelessly underfunded and under-resourced. The judicial college to be set up by the next Labour government ought to deal with all appointments from stipendiary magistrates upwards.

Runciman recommended that there should be retraining on a regular basis. The present commitment, as is well known, is simply one week every five years for a Circuit judge. Runciman's modest proposal is one week every three years. We should be moving as quickly as possible to one week's retraining every year. The retraining needs to be done on a more flexible basis. We need to look at judicial practices and experience in other countries. Remarkably little is provided for United Kingdom judges by way of information about how judges work in other jurisdictions. There is no systematic monitoring of judicial performance.

There is no satisfactory open disciplinary process available either by way of guidance, assistance or reproof for judges who simply get things wrong. A rude, offensive or incompetent judge is well known to practitioners but unless he makes the headlines of the tabloid press he is rarely detected by the Lord Chancellor's Department. We all too readily forget that most people come into contact with the legal system once or at most twice in their lifetime. The impression given by the judge matters enormously. Not least, the training should give guidance in how to deal with people in a courteous and decent way. These are elementary steps which we simply overlook.

There ought to be a proper disciplinary procedure. If a serious complaint is made against a judge it should be tried by a judicial complaints commission which ought to be under the control of the judicial college. It should be staffed by judges in the majority but should have practitioner and lay representation. In the worst cases removal from the bench ought to be available as a sanction. There are other cases where a reprimand might need to be made public. But the most important aspect might well be assistance, guidance and advice for those who have simply got things wrong through ignorance or thoughtlessness. The work, properly done, is so difficult that it is well worth every support mechanism that we can offer.

Every judge on appointment should have a one-month training sabbatical. It struck me particularly that when the present Lord Chief Justice was appointed he had little opportunity to set out his plans for the next ten years or so and was simply pitched into sitting in the Court of Appeal virtually at once. The same is true of all full-time appointments — announcement on Friday, start sitting on Monday. The judicial college, being residential, could offer part of the training. A further part at least should include in depth knowledge of other systems whether on the Continent or in the United States. It is remarkable and noteworthy how few full-time judges have any knowledge or curiosity of other judicial systems.

The investment of public funds in court systems building (plant and equipment) is enormous. Yet no judge has any training in simple management skills nor any assistance in the management of these very expensive resources. We still have the cultural overlay that the judge must not be kept waiting even if judicial time is the cheapest component of the daily running cost of any Crown Court. Many judges train themselves and provide their own computer systems. Most do not. We cannot lurch on in this way any longer. If the Woolf reforms are to work at all then the judiciary will have to be properly trained. At the least any case, whether civil or criminal, that enters the system needs a computer number with a designated judge appointed to manage that case throughout its progress in the system.

We need to set and stick to sensible retirement ages. This should not be more than 65 for first-instance judges nor 70 at appellate level. Retirement should mean retirement. There should be no return to sit part-time. The Lord Chancellor made a very serious mistake in insisting on a 20-year period of judicial service before a pension is available. Fifteen years is a long time to be a judge and anyone who feels that he has given his best work after 15 years ought to be entitled to have his pension and go.

We need a proper review of stipendiary magistrates. I fully understand that they are not popular with all magistrates' courts. There is a serious case for providing more stipendiary magistrates sitting, not alone, but with two lay magistrates to form a more sensible compromise between the magistrates and the jury system of trial.

The appellate system in crime needs a complete overhaul. The delays are not acceptable. Many judges who have to deal with the workload in the Court of Appeal Criminal Division say quite openly that they feel uneasy about the volume of work with which they have to cope. One senior Lord Justice wrote to me saying that he did not feel that he was complying with his judicial oath because the volume of casework was so great that he was not conscientiously able to give his full attention to every case that he was hearing in the Court of Appeal. There are two remedies here. The first is to have the Court of Appeal Criminal Division staffed entirely by Lords Justices. The present system of the presiding judge in a particular Division being a Lord Justice with two High Court judges sitting on an ad hoc basis is no longer acceptable. It tends against a coherent development of sentencing policy and raises the reasonable question in the public mind as to what a High Court judge is doing sitting on an appeal from someone who is his equal in the judicial hierarchy. I believe that the introduction of senior circuit judges to sit in the Court of Appeal Criminal Division was a mistake. It is an inefficient use of manpower since they are forbidden to sit on appeals from High Court judges and it simply compounds the lack of cohesion. There is no sensible back-up provided for the Court of Appeal Criminal Division. There are insufficient research facilities. Surely we can learn from the example of the United States and provide a law clerk for every Lord Justice who wants one. This would be a secondment for perhaps two or three years for the brightest and the best, whether barristers or solicitors, and it would provide the bare minimum of assistance which any appeal court is entitled to look for. I do not believe there is any similar appellate court in the world which is so badly treated.

The same lack of research facilities is true of the Civil Division of the Court of Appeal and even more so in the House of Lords. Most foreign lawyers and judges are quite disbelieving when they are told that the Lords of Appeal in Ordinary do their own research without structured assistance of any sort.

Do we cast our net wide enough? There is no doubt at all that women and ethnic minorities are grossly under-represented among the judiciary. There is no woman Law Lord. There is only one woman in the Court of Appeal, and very few female High Court judges or circuit judges. There is no ethnic minority judge above circuit judge level. It is a foolish parrot call to expect a perfect representation of all sections of the community on the bench. It is, however, reasonable to require that the judiciary at least reflect the wider community that they serve.

Is there not a reasonable argument for appointing academics at least to the Court of Appeal or House of Lords? I see entirely the disadvantage of an academic being appointed to try cases at first instance; but it is reasonable to suggest that if, say, Professor Glanville Williams had been in the Court of Appeal Criminal Division or in the House of Lords dealing with criminal appeals many errors and oddities might have been avoided. Should we not be more willing to appoint suitable candidates directly to the Court of Appeal and in rare cases to the House of Lords? There are a number of names which spring to mind who would not be willing or (it may be) equipped to sit at first instance but would be strong candidates at appellate level.

New Labour will only win the next election if the public regard it as the party of demonstrated efficient management. The reforms which I have set out briefly are simply a reflection of the proper management of the judicial system.

6

Tribunals

Rt Hon Lord Archer of Sandwell QC

Until the 1950s, transferring power to the people was a cornerstone of Labour doctrine. And 'the people' meant government ministers and statutory bodies. The need was real enough. Conservative dogma equated freedom with the right to enjoy one's property without restriction, and without regard to the consequences for others. Planning, environmental protection measures, safety legislation, employment rights and taxation were all seen as 'interference'. Provision for the disadvantaged distorted the natural working of private charity. On this view, freedom was endangered only by civil servants.

For the first half of the century, the reply of the political Left was that a measure of freedom must be sacrificed in the interests of fairness and of compassion for the underprivileged. It was not suggested that the transfer of power was concerned with freedom itself, and that freedom may be in greater danger from the abuse of economic power than from statutory regulation. This failure to recognise the nature of the issue led to two disastrous consequences. First, it left much of the moral high ground to the Right. Secondly, it meant that in Socialist theory, questions of accountability were marginalised. It was an initiative from the Left which established the National Council for Civil Liberties (now Liberty) in 1931, but that was addressed to specific pragmatic issues. Probably the earliest attempt within the Labour movement to point out that bureaucracies, too, need to be made accountable was in 1955, when the Fabian Society published Dick Crossman's pamphlet, *Socialism and the New Despotism.*

Before and immediately after the Second World War, therefore, it was the Right which emphasised the rule of law. And they located it rigidly within the traditional courts. In 1929 Lord Hewart, then Lord Chief Justice, wrote *The New Despotism*. He alleged that there was a conspiracy by the executive (consisting partly of ministers, but more particularly of officials) to destroy the separation of powers, and (among other themes) to divert from the courts the function of deciding disputes in which the government had an interest. He could hardly bring himself to mention tribunals, except in the context of *droit administratif* which, although un-British, was at least a system, while our tribunals were totally unsystematic.

The ensuing debate led to the Committee on Ministers' Powers (the Donoughmore Committee) which reported in 1932.[1] Their views on tribunals were more temperate. They recited the advantages offered by tribunals over the traditional courts: cheapness, accessibility, freedom from technicality, expedition, and specialist expertise.

'But', they went on, 'while we recognise these advantages we repeat that such Tribunals should be set up only in those cases in which the conditions beyond all question demand it. It is in the ordinary courts, higher or inferior, that justiciable issues, whether between subject and subject or between Crown and subject, ought as a rule to be determined'. And their terminology was a give-away. The word 'tribunal' hardly ever appeared without the adjective 'ministerial'. Tribunals were really an arm of the executive. Yet it was the executive which needed to be controlled.

It was a quarter of a century later, in 1955, when the Crichel Down scandal led to the setting up of the Franks Committee on Administrative Tribunals and Enquiries,[2] which reported in 1957.[3] The world had changed. The existence of tribunals was not questioned. The adjective 'ministerial' had disappeared, although it was replaced by 'administrative'. Tribunals were no longer a front for the executive. Certainly they were not an affront to the rule of law, but they remained part of the administration, and not really of the judiciary. The need for systematic thought on the subject was evidenced by the 95 recommendations in the

---

[1] Cmnd 4060 of 1932.
[2] In the Committee's title, 'Enquiries' was spelled with an 'E'. In the title of the subsequent Act, the 'E' became an 'I'.
[3] Cmnd 218 of 1957.

report, all directed to achieving the three objectives of openness, fairness and impartiality, themselves elements in the rule of law.

In the 38 years since Franks, it has become common ground politically that an increasing number of activities require statutory regulation, and that someone must regulate the regulators. The proliferation of tribunals, therefore, arises from the victory of the Left in establishing that freedom requires a measure of regulation and that, far from regulation being inconsistent with the rule of law, the rule of law is part of the process. Indeed, the Deregulation and Contracting Out Act 1994 itself produced a range of regulations and of new rights of appeal.

The Franks Committee recommended the establishment of a Council on Tribunals to keep under review the constitution and working of tribunals. This recommendation was implemented in the Tribunals and Inquiries Act 1958, with two subsequent revisions in 1971 and 1992. The Council's remit is to keep under review the constitution and working of the tribunals specified in sch. 1 to the Act (as amended from time to time), to consider and report on matters referred to the Council in repect of any tribunals, and to consider and report on matters relating to statutory inquiries. The Council is an advisory body, and it is a matter for departments whether they accept its advice. There is a statutory requirement that ministers shall consult the Council on procedural rules for tribunals falling within its responsibility,[4] and it is normally consulted about all other procedural rules, but its influence depends on its relations with departments and on such public support as it can evoke in the annual reports which it makes to the Lord Chancellor and the Lord Advocate, together with any special reports which it feels impelled to issue. Nevertheless, the influence of the Council has been out of all proportion to its statutory powers or its resources.

There are, however, a number of simple additions to its powers which would greatly increase its effectiveness. Regulations which require consultation with the Council recite that the Council has been consulted. This may be taken to mean that it has approved the Regulations, but in fact its recommendations may have been ignored. If, when subordinate legislation is before Parliament, the Council were empowered to require the appending of a statement, setting out its criticisms, Parliament would be aware of the options.

---

[4] Now Tribunals and Inquiries Act 1992, s. 8(1).

Again, the Council relies largely for its awareness of problems on the visits which its members make to tribunals, not as inspectors but in order to gather information. Visits include attendance as silent observers at the deliberations between members, where it may become clear that the proceedings have failed to make available all the necessary information, or that a member has not received sufficient training. Usually the visits are welcomed by tribunals, but occasionally a chair[5] declines to admit the visitor to the deliberation stage, and the right to attend may depend upon the specific legislation or regulations applying to that tribunal. It would be relatively simple to clarify the position comprehensively.[6]

In its annual report for the year to 31 July 1994, the Council observed that in one year, four new tribunals had been added to its supervisory jurisdiction (bringing the total to 70) and that the workload of existing tribunals is increasing. A citizen is six times more likely to encounter the judicial system as a party to tribunal proceedings than in proceedings before the traditional civil courts. Inevitably, in view of the disparate activities on which they adjudicate, the composition and procedures of tribunals follow little by way of a common pattern. Some consist of a single individual, some of a number of members. Some include (by statute or practice) a legally qualified chair, some a legally qualified clerk, and some simply dispense with legal training. Some are scarcely less formal than the courts; some are more reminiscent of a case conference. Some are administered by the Lord Chancellor's Department; some by the department against which they hear appeals.

This tangled jungle has attracted many calls for rationalisation. But the most important common factor is that tribunals adjudicate on rights, and are firmly established as part of the judiciary and not of the executive. Even Franks insisted, 'We consider that tribunals should properly be regarded as machinery provided by Parliament for adjudication rather than as part of the machinery for administration'. Indeed, not all tribunals decide cases between the citizen and the executive. Industrial tribunals include in their jurisdiction claims between employers and employees; the Lands Tribunal hears disputes between private citizens; and Traffic Commissioners decide issues in which the Department of Transport has no policy interest.

---

[5] Although the term 'chairman' continues to appear in statutes, the expression 'chair' is used throughout this book.
[6] See generally the Special Report on the Functions of the Council on Tribunals, Cmnd 7805 of 1980, and Annual Report of the Council, 1988–89.

There are certain principles, therefore, which are common to tribunals and to courts. First, their existence and jurisdiction ought to be decided by Parliament, and not by the executive. Tribunals established by ministerial regulation include industrial tribunals, service committees of family health service authorities, meat hygiene appeal tribunals, police pensions appeal tribunals, vaccine damage tribunals and valuation tribunals. And Bills continue to be introduced conferring on ministers power to establish tribunals by subordinate legislation. Most recent are the Antarctic Act 1994 and the Activity Centres (Young Persons' Safety) Act 1995. In its report for 1992–93, the Council on Tribunals commented:

> Establishment of a tribunal by Act of Parliament emphasises the tribunal's independent standing, which is appropriate for a body exercising adjudicative functions in relation to the statutory rights of individuals. It is appropriate also to include the principal constitutional provisions of tribunals in primary legislation. Regulation-making powers should be confined to detailed matters, including the tribunal's procedures.

Secondly, tribunal members, and particularly Chairs, ought not to hold their appointments at the pleasure of the department involved in the disputes which they hear. While this principle has secured general acceptance, appointments to education appeal committees are made by local education authorities or school governors, who have an interest in the outcome of appeals.

But it does not follow that it is immaterial whether a new forum is designated a court or a tribunal. The name 'tribunal' evokes a culture which differs in important respects from that of the courts, and which, in appropriate cases, deserves to be encouraged. First, tribunals do not normally feel the necessity for wigs, witness boxes and bowing. Of course, informality is not to be confused with sloppiness. Rules of evidence are less rigidly observed, but fairness and accuracy are no less important than in more traditional jurisdictions. The purpose of informality is to induce a user-friendly ethos, which does not discourage people from pursuing their entitlements, and which helps them to articulate their case. Secondly, tribunals frequently consist of three or more members, of whom at least a majority are not lawyers, but are broadly representative of the community, and sometimes of the groups who are likely to use the tribunals, and who have experience of the activities which are the subject-matter of the jurisdiction. This may encourage confidence in the tribunal among those who appear before it. Thirdly, there is at least an aspiration to decide cases expeditiously, not always associated with the traditional courts. Fourthly, those who appear are less at risk of orders for costs.

Probably most important of all is that tribunals usually deal with a specific subject or group of subjects, and so acquire an expertise with which no all-embracing jurisdiction could or should seek to compete. If all the issues now dealt with by tribunals were decanted into the undifferentiated jurisdiction of county and magistrates' courts, not only would the quality of expertise suffer, but the bulk of cases would be beyond the capacity of any administrative machine to cope.

An overzealous attempt to amalgamate jurisdictions, therefore, would destroy the most important advantage of the tribunal system. What is required is not to impose a single pattern on all tribunals, since they must differ according to subject-matter in relation to the nature of their procedure, the length and nature of hearings, the status of the chair, the need for lay members, the expertise of the clerk, the amount at stake (and consequently the amount which it is worth spending in costs) and many other factors.

But it does not follow that all attempts at coordination are pointless. First, there is scope for rationalising the plethora of jurisdictions. When a new right of appeal is created, it makes sense to explore whether there is an existing tribunal which could sensibly include the new jurisdiction. In its annual report for 1969–70, the Council on Tribunals insisted, 'We are increasingly impressed by the need to avoid undue proliferation of tribunals by, wherever possible, organising them into fewer and stronger units and to ensure that each group has a proper structure and, where necessary, adequate arrangements for appeal'. The Justice report on Administrative Justice in 1988 commented, 'In our view the Council on Tribunals have this matter well in hand; the cause for concern is that too little attention appears to be paid to their recommendations'. Since housing benefit review boards were established to hear appeals from local authority determinations of benefit, they have been the subject of much criticism, on the ground that they are not independent of local authorities. A research report in 1990 argued convincingly that the problems would have been avoided had the jurisdiction been conferred on the existing social security appeal tribunals. As long ago as 1973, a Fabian pamphlet proposed the establishment of a Social Court, to hear appeals from all decisions relating to welfare benefits, and providing an appeal on law to a Social Division of the Court of Appeal.[7]

Secondly, there is scope for establishing a more attractive career structure among legally qualified chairs. It is only in recent years that a tribunal chairmanship has been perceived as other than an interruption in professional practice. The Justice report of 1988 recognised that tribunal chairs have to be independent. It considered that appointments for less than three years might compromise this and, somewhat inconsistently, suggested that independence could be secured by appointing for a single term. It is now recognised that a full-time chair in certain tribunal systems is equivalent in status, salary and promotion prospects to a district judge, and in some cases a circuit judge. Circuit judges are sometimes appointed as presidents of tribunal systems. Usually return to practice after a full-time appointment is no longer an option, and a tribunal chair should expect security of tenure, subject to competence and good conduct. Already, social security commissioners, presidents and chairs of the various social security tribunals and of industrial tribunals, and members of the Lands Tribunal, participate in the statutory pensions scheme for judges, provided that their appointments are full-time.

Inevitably most systems will make use of some part-time appointees, or deputies, as do the courts. A sudden onset of work need not necessarily lead to more full-timers, who may not be needed when the wave is past. And some who are not available on a full-time basis may nevertheless give good service. But no system should rely as of course on a substantial proportion of appointees without security of tenure, and more efficient use can be made of chairs who are wholly at the disposal of the system. There are, however, those whose time, while occupied fully within tribunals, is shared among different tribunal systems. At present their whereabouts on a given day depend on who invites them first. Some thought should be given to organising their time more rationally, and to including them within a coordinated career structure

---

[7] Fulbrook, Brooke and Archer, *Tribunals: A Social Court?* (Society of Labour Lawyers).

and a superannuation scheme. This would facilitate full-time and secure appointments, while preserving flexibility within each individual system.

There is scope, too, for a review of clerks and support staff. Naturally, clerks vary widely in status and duties. In some systems they work on a full-time basis; in others a clerk may be seconded for a particular hearing from staff normally occupied in other duties. Clerks to general commissioners of income tax are legally qualified, with a lay bench dependent on them for administration and advice, very much like magistrates' clerks. At the other end of the spectrum are clerks whose duties resemble those of ushers, and whose role in relation to case files is to deliver them to the appropriate room.

But there are principles which should apply universally. First, a clerk, and particularly one who is seen to advise the tribunal, should be, and be perceived as being, independent. It is not satisfactory that clerks should be seconded from the department or authority whose decision is under appeal. Secondly, many last-minute adjournments could be avoided if it were someone's responsibility to look in advance at the file, and to assume a proactive role in warning appellants acting in person what they will need to establish and what documents they should bring with them. Thirdly, it is rarely if ever that a tribunal should have neither a chair nor a clerk with legal training. Educational appeal committees do not lack common sense or a concern for fairness, hopefully supplemented by some training, but when questions arise of excluding a child for a disputed offence, these assets may not suffice. Coordination among different systems might enable them to share the services of clerks of various grades, whose qualifications might be standardised. And resources might well be employed to greater advantage if thought were given to sharing administrative staff and office accommodation on a regional or area basis.

Indeed, tribunal accommodation offers further scope for coordination. Premises should be reasonably accessible, adequately signposted and with comfortable waiting accommodation, not least because it is in the interests of justice that parties should not be unduly stressed before embarking on the hearing. The Council on Tribunals has issued a code of practice on access for disabled people. And where a tribunal meets irregularly, this can create problems. Not all premises are in use by the same tribunal all the time. Yet it is not unusual to find a tribunal sitting in a draughty and totally unsuitable village hall, while in the same area a suite controlled by another tribunal system stands vacant. With responsibility for tribunal accommodation spread over at least 12 government departments, coordination is not easy. Following an initiative by the Council, after enlisting the support of the Comptroller and Auditor General, Property Holdings, who manage government property, were persuaded in 1993 to establish a register of tribunal hearing accommodation, to distribute information between those in need of accommodation and those who have it to spare. But it would make both administrative and financial sense to go further, and consider providing tribunal centres in a number of major cities. This might also facilitate the sharing of information technology, library provision and research among tribunal users.

Training is an area where provision varies greatly. Training in the law relating to a particular subject is usually best provided by the specific tribunal system exercising that jurisdiction, if there is a central agency capable of making the necessary arrangements. But training in the nature of judicial work, particularly for new lay members, may well be shared. The Tribunals Committee of the Judicial Studies Board is anxious to seek out where the need is greatest, but lacks adequate resources.

One problem common to virtually all tribunals is that of making available advice and, where necessary, representation. This is a subject dealt with by Roger Smith and Ross Cranston in chapters 3 and 4. The research of Professor Hazel Genn and Yvette Genn has established that applicants are substantially more likely to succeed if they are adequately represented, whether or not by lawyers. What is of more immediate concern for this chapter is that a high proportion of appellants 'had little idea about what ''appealing'' or making an application actually meant. They certainly had little accurate knowledge about the powers of tribunals or what the possible outcome of their hearing could be.'[8] Tribunals could learn much from one another about simplifying appeal forms and making available leaflets explaining simply the purpose of the hearing and the order of proceedings.

---

[8] H. Genn and Y. Genn, *The Effectiveness of Representation at Tribunals* (Report to the Lord Chancellor) (1989).

There has been much searching for a common appeal structure. For the claimant, dissatisfied with an initial departmental decision, it is sensible that there should first be an opportunity for an informal conversation with a sympathetic official, in order to ensure that no obviously relevant circumstance has been overlooked, so that the matter may be rectified before further time and expense have been incurred. This elementary observation usually evokes agreement, but in many under-resourced departments, there is rarely an official with the time, the patience and the training to listen and discuss.

Some structures make formal provision for an internal review, if requested. In some cases (notably child support, disability benefit and housing benefit) invoking an internal review is a necessary condition of proceeding to a tribunal at the next stage. It has been suggested by Dr Roy Sainsbury and others[9] that this may entail a double disadvantage. First, it may extend the time consumed before the issue is ultimately resolved. Secondly, it may be perceived by many applicants as one more appeal, and if this is unsuccessful, the applicant may be discouraged from initiating yet a further appeal to a tribunal. There is need for further research on the question, but the Council on Tribunals has drawn a distinction between providing for an internal review which, if unsuccessful, automatically triggers a tribunal hearing, and one which when notified to the claimant leaves it to him to initiate an appeal. The latter is generally to be discouraged.

There has been much discussion whether, from a first-instance decision of a tribunal, there is room for an appeal procedure common to all or most tribunals. As early as the Donoughmore Committee, Professor W. A. Robson proposed in his evidence a general administrative tribunal, which would hear first-instance appeals from administrative decisions for which no tribunal already existed, and appeals from the tribunals which did exist. The Justice report, *The Citizen and the Administration* (the Whyatt report) in 1961 echoed the proposal for a general tribunal of appeal, citing a Swedish precedent. The Commonwealth of Australia established in 1975 an Administrative Appeals Tribunal, to hear appeals on the merits from a wide range of administrative decisions for which no appeal was previously

---

[9] Social Policy Research Unit of York University, September 1990. And see *Annual Report of Council of Tribunals, 1990–91.*

provided. But the Justice report of 1988 considered that a similar institution in the United Kingdom would not be practicable, because of the much larger caseload.

Indeed, the Franks Committee was less ambitious. It suggested that there should be an appeal from a tribunal of first instance on fact, law and merits, except 'when the tribunal of first instance is so exceptionally strong and well qualified that an appellate tribunal would be no better qualified to review its decisions'. But it did not argue for one general appeal tribunal. It further recommended that all decisions of tribunals should be subject to review by the courts on points of law. The three-stage model of first-instance decision, appeal on fact, law or merits, and further appeal on law only, is generally desirable, but not essential in all circumstances. When in 1993 the Law Commission issued its consultation paper, *Administrative Law: Judicial Review and Statutory Appeals*, the Council on Tribunals warned in its annual report for 1992–93, 'We reiterate that the pursuit of uniformity for its own sake is undesirable'.

In summary, therefore, there is probably little to be gained by attempting to impose a uniform structural and procedural pattern on all tribunals, but there are many areas where tribunal members, tribunal administrators and tribunal users would benefit from some imaginative coordination. The difficulty is that there is no single executive authority which can initiate them. Some tribunal systems are administered by a president, notably the industrial tribunals and the system of welfare benefit tribunals now known as the Independent Tribunal System. These have demonstrated the advantages of a single authority who can make optimum use of members' time, accommodation and equipment; arrange for shared training; offer a lead on standardising procedures; rationalise administration; and monitor standards. Of course, there is room for argument over the borderline between standardising judicial policy on the granting of adjournments and trespassing on judicial independence. And there are no clear guidelines on whether, constitutionally, a president should act as the budget-holder. It is arguable that since the president should have power to decide questions on which justice may depend, such as the maximum length of sittings, he should control the judicial resources necessary to implement his decision. Yet not all presidents wish to have budgetary responsibility, with the prospect of being examined by a Parliamentary committee. But the existence of such problems only emphasises the need for reflection.

Some tribunals have themselves responded valiantly to the challenge. Members of valuation tribunals have formed their own national committee, as have the clerks to valuation tribunals. And representatives of a group of tribunals sponsored by the Department of the Environment are now meeting on a regular basis.

But none of this addresses the need for the overall direction and drive of a co-ordinated tribunal service. Some initiatives have emerged in recent years. The Tribunals Committee of the Judicial Studies Board sponsors a half-yearly journal, *Tribunals*, to serve as a link between the various systems, and to ventilate common problems. In 1991, the Council on Tribunals published a set of model procedural rules for the guidance of those responsible for procedures, in the hope of introducing a degree of uniformity. At about two-yearly intervals, the Council convenes a seminar for heads of tribunals, to discuss topical problems, and it is now exploring with tribunal heads the possibility of establishing a Council of Tribunal Heads.

But if there is to be effective overall coordination, the need is twofold. First there will have to be a permanent standing unit with a mandate and the time to reflect on policy. And secondly, it will need access to the muscle and the resources to override departmental empires on the one hand and departmental inertia on the other. An obvious candidate may be the Lord Chancellor's Department, which is responsible for most appointments of legally qualified chairs. In recent years, the Lord Chancellor's Department has absorbed the administration of a number of tribunal systems, but it would require a substantial expansion in personnel and resources for a wholesale takeover of all tribunals.

The Council on Tribunals is not an executive body and, since its role is that of a watchdog, it would be wrong to combine that function with being a government policy unit or a controlling administration. The most hopeful model may be a small policy unit with power to convene meetings of departmental officials for the administration of various tribunals, and to make proposals to Cabinet committees. Hopefully it would cultivate good relationships with the Council on Tribunals, the Tribunals Committee of the Judicial Studies Board, and similar bodies. And it should be accountable either to the Lord Chancellor, or to a Cabinet committee. The cost would almost certainly be more than recovered in savings achieved by coordination.

What is essential is first, that those who use the various tribunals, professionally or as litigants, should have channels for making known causes for complaint, to those who can sift, reflect and recommend; and secondly that those who administer should have the time and the concern to listen and act. And that depends at each step upon motivation. In the last resort, that must stem from a government which cares about people.

7

Magistrates

Jenny Jeger JP

The responsibility for implementing the pledge from a Labour government to be 'tough on crime' will largely fall on the shoulders of the
nearly 30,000 lay magistrates who deal with over 97 per cent of all cases
which appear in court. The work covers both civil and criminal matters
ranging from routine traffic and licensing issues to the frequently
harrowing care cases in the family court. Almost every aspect of human
predicament may be dealt with in the local magistrates' court yet
members of Parliament seem to be singularly unaware of this fact.
Politicians of all parties, policymakers and influential members of the
judiciary too often rely on outdated anecdotal evidence to a dangerous
extent when forming their views about the Bench. A well-remembered
visit to a magistrates' court in 1965 bears little relation to the
modern-day equivalent. It is instructive and alarming that during all the
legislative upheavals over the past few years neither the Home Secretary
nor any junior minister felt it necessary to spend any time in a
magistrates' court before introducing any of the six Criminal Justice
Bills since 1985.

The 1980s were at least marked by a consistent view of penal policy
— that community-based punishment worked better than imprisonment. The sudden wild swing in the opposite direction, from the same
government, has had a disturbing impact on the Bench. Magistrates do
not impose a prison sentence without proper consideration of all the
options. The problem now is that those options have been dramatically

reduced and benches are being encouraged to send people to prison for lack of any alternative. Sentencing is becoming a debate about deciding the least inappropriate variable. Further proposed changes in sentencing powers may provoke more vocal rebellions as witnessed over unit fines in the early 90s.

The Labour Party has not given much thought in recent years to the role of either the lay or stipendiary magistracy, partly through ignorance and also from an innate suspicion of the whole system. The Labour Party has always been diffident about encouraging lay participation in the judicial process. Problems experienced by Labour magistrates in court over the poll tax and the miners' strike fuelled these suspicions. It is, however, ironic that the only government department which positively welcomes Labour Party members for public appointment is the Lord Chancellor's Department.

The need for balanced benches is important, although personal political opinion is not a relevant factor in ultimate selection. It counts neither for nor against appointment. Extremist prejudices towards the police, racism and social circumstances can emerge alarmingly from any candidate at interview, regardless of political preference. The perception that most magistrates are Conservative is based on insubstantial information which takes no account of change in voting habits, although in some more rural areas it is hard to find a range of candidates to balance the bench. More serious factors are relevant in attracting candidates from wider areas in the community.

Recruitment

It is frequently assumed that the magistracy is some secret organisation like the Freemasons, and that likely members are tapped on the shoulder and invited to join in a mystical ceremony. This may indeed have been the case when the local magistrates were appointed through social connection, without interview and with no training.

These days anyone can apply to become a magistrate in their local area. Individuals can put themselves forward or be encouraged to do so by a political party or other community-based organisation. The only disqualifications would be age (over 60), serious criminal offences, certain occupations connected with courts such as the police, some social service employees or some other conflict of interest. Literacy and command of English are clearly essential but formal educational qualifications are not. The intention is an open process of selection and there is no rejection at this stage, apart from the reasons stated above. Application forms request full details about personal as well as professional circumstances and two referees are required. Everyone who has sent in the completed application form (subject to the above criteria) is interviewed. This procedure is standard practice around the country. Variations occur at the next stage — the interviewing process.

Local advisory committees have been encouraged to adopt the two-stage interviewing process but there is no conformity of view about the nature of the first stage — the second being a rigorous interview to test suitability. Stage one may be a day at court for a group of potential magistrates under the supervision of the clerk and the presiding justices with plenty of opportunity for asking questions. This stage eliminates basic ignorance and enables the candidate to withdraw from the process if desired. The court visit is compulsory before interview as are a number of visits to observe in magistrates' courts run by lay and stipendiary magistrates where possible. The candidate will be tested at interview on impressions from the court visits and the nature of the judicial process.

Although court visits are essential for everyone prior to interview, some areas have also adopted the 'home visit' as the stage-one process. Apart from the invidious social judgments which arise, this is a time-consuming process which cannot be done in a large city area — nor should it be contemplated. It creates discomfort and embarrassment on all sides and smacks of paternalism in a fashion which can be avoided in an interview in impartial surroundings. Professional methods of interviewing and evaluation of criteria should be uniform in all commission areas. The nature of court work in Gloucestershire will never be the same as in Inner London but the qualities required in a magistrate should not be different nor assessed differently.

Advisory committees

The Lord Chancellor delegates the interviewing and recommendation process to local area advisory committees who are also responsible for disciplinary matters. The committees are composed of magistrates and lay members with most frequently the Lord Lieutenant of the county in the chair, except in Inner London where for some reason the chairmanship alternates between a judge and a lay member.

There has been an increase in the number of lay members on advisory committees, with mixed results. Some have appeared through the mysterious process of patronage and have no experience of any aspect of court work, even as a defendant. They are frankly bemused by the whole process and never reach an understanding of judicial aptitude or the famous retiring-room test.[1] This places a large burden on magistrate members who often face critical decisions regarding interview and selection processes or a considered response to consultation from the Lord Chancellor. Local benches require direction from advisory committees on a number of issues and the advisory committee needs to be credible in the eyes of the bench.

Advisory committees need to be given firm guidelines about recruitment to the committee according to expertise, age range and general suitability. The time commitment is a major factor, as it is with magistrates' duties, with up to eight days a year in interviewing time in Inner London. It would seem right to make some payment for this service. The secretariat should be adequately provided according to the needs of the area and the workload of the committee. Each committee should be allocated an annual budget to cover necessary expenditure on recruitment leaflets, advertising or other appropriate methods of communicating the work of the magistracy and encouraging new applicants. City areas have the greatest responsibility in encouraging participation from ethnic communities.

The time commitment

Concern about job security, or the potential for promotion are deterrents for many, mostly male, potential magistrates. Employers for the most part are not keen on public service and consider a day in court to be

---

[1] The 'retiring room test' should be some acute questioning from the interviewing panel to the potential magistrate regarding his or her liability to be swayed by the arguments of colleagues, the acceptance of a majority decision and determining a sentence when in the minority.

For example, the magistrate in the chair is a forceful personality, your other colleague is uncertain — how would you persuade them to your point of view? You have lost the argument and must now decide on a sentence. Would you argue for a lesser penalty because you believe the defendant to be innocent?

skiving and not a useful contribution to the employee's skills portfolio. Although the potential magistrate must discuss an application with the employer, and a letter is sent from the advisory committee explaining the responsibility and the commitment, the Employment Protection (Consolidation) Act 1978, s. 29, is largely ignored by the private sector, unless the organisation has a positive attitude towards public service. A strengthening of the provisions, currently 18 days a year, plus some public incentive, such as a community service award similar to the Queen's Award to Industry, might persuade more employers to be public spirited and 'put something back' into the community. Part-timers, the self-employed and the intermittently unemployed frequently have difficulty fulfilling sitting commitments. There is a danger that the well-to-do independent business man or the prosperous housewife will dominate benches because they have the time. Greater flexibility in sitting commitments is possible to arrange whilst maintaining the minimum requirement without losing experience, otherwise talent will be lost.

Training

Magistrates have received compulsory training since the 1960s. Apart from basic compulsory training, there is a constant need for training every time there is a change in legislation. There have been six Criminal Justice Acts since 1985 as well as the Children Act in 1989. Training also means keeping up to date with local treatment initiatives, community alternatives to custody programmes and visits to remand centres and prisons. Formal training varies in quality and needs serious professional review in order to present a uniform standard throughout the country. It should also include regular briefing on the changes in the State benefit system. Even the most socially aware magistrate has difficulty in keeping up to date. Such ignorance in court widens the gulf between the bench and the defendant.

Monitoring of new magistrates during their first year should be compulsory in all areas. This should include the option of resignation. A magistrate may perform very well at interview, pass the training sessions, yet be a disaster in court when faced with decision-making in real cases. There is currently no 'get-out' point at which a magistrate can decently resign. Similarly there is seldom any feedback on individual performance. Magistrates who do not have qualms about sending someone to prison are singularly shy when it comes to passing judgment on their colleagues. Appraisal of longer-serving magistrates at regular intervals tied in with the greater use of the fixed period of appointment as a sacking device would ensure the tactful removal of magistrates who do not fall within the need for disciplinary procedures.

Fair procedures for performance assessment, resignation and sacking are not hard to enforce. All voluntary organisations now demand high standards of professionalism and the lay magistracy should not be exempt.

Lay versus stipendiary

Any debate about the future of the lay magistracy usually centres on its abolition and replacement by stipendiaries — an argument often fuelled by the stipendiaries themselves.

In truth there is a need for both varieties. The legally qualified stipendiary magistrate is recognised for working fast and often sitting alone in court. These may be considered virtues in a political climate which encourages value for money and a 'pack 'em in, pile 'em high' philosophy towards the courts but does little to further the notion of justice in the eyes of the defendant. Any lay magistrate who has sat with a stipendiary knows well the difficulties which can arise. There seems to be no strong reason why the requirements for the lay magistracy cannot be the same for stipendiaries. They are not required to live anywhere near the area in which they sit, therefore they have little or no knowledge of local crime patterns, familiarity with the local resources, the operation of the court, or even the local criminals. A fleeting visit between ten and four to salubrious Camberwell from a resident of the comfortable Home Counties does not go down too well with the local bench.

Given that most defendants have no idea what is happening in court, lay magistrates are trained to explain proceedings and are used to speaking in plain clear English. Stipendiaries speak law and seldom address the defendant in terms which are understood. The selection process for stipendiaries does not seem to expose prejudice or lack of social awareness, often with alarming results, particularly in youth courts.

A more permanent relationship between a stipendiary and a lay bench would ease some of the difficulties. Lay colleagues can learn from a good stipendiary and a stipendiary can benefit from the more day-to-day experiences of lay colleagues in a community.

Serving the community

The precarious nature of employment, child-minding, and the whims of employers frequently make it difficult for defendants in both the adult and youth court to attend court. The requirement for an adult to attend the youth court is an added difficulty for younger juveniles. If a responsible parent does exist and is in paid employment, there is often an embarrassed reluctance to reveal the reason for time off for fear of dismissal. There is clearly no excuse for deliberate time-wasting but there may well be a better use of the courts if they were open for early evening sessions and more regularly on a Saturday morning to deal with routine guilty pleas and emergencies. Time wasting is not only the prerogative of the defendant. Many a magistrate has debated a suitable punishment for the absent solicitor or barrister who has failed either to appear or has not prepared for the case to proceed. Building contractors pay large penalties for failure to complete projects on time. Magistrates should be given the power to impose daily penalties on lawyers who waste court time and fail to complete a case by an agreed timetable without good reason. Time might also be better used if each court had a manager to work with the clerk in order to check at least a day in advance with all parties that a case is ready to proceed to the next stage with the necessary papers, witnesses, police and defendant.

Idle thoughts in the retiring room perhaps, but all magistrates swear an oath on appointment to dispense justice without fear or favour. It would be nice if we felt able to do so.

8

The Legal Profession: Two Views

Henry Hodge OBE

Lawyers are mostly pretty privileged. They need a reasonable academic background to get into the profession. Once trained and qualified the vast majority can expect secure working conditions, above average pay, public recognition and interesting work. Lawyers have secured for themselves a number of monopolies which support and enhance their status. At the core of these monopolies are the lawyers' rights to be the only people who can be paid to litigate on behalf of others in our courts. Lawyers have traditionally been regarded as professionals. So, in addition to various monopolies, they have created, and to a large extent retained, the right to group themselves into professional bodies and to regulate themselves.

There has been significant Parliamentary intervention in the legal profession. Solicitors in particular have always had the right to hold clients' money. Hence the regulatory framework for the larger branch of the profession is tighter than for barristers.

The legal professional bodies

The lawyers' professional bodies — the Law Society for solicitors and the General Council of the Bar for barristers — have retained a number of core tasks. They set admissions standards for new entrants. This includes academic standards as well as practical training requirements in articles or pupillage. They administer admissions. All lawyers are subject to professional rules and codes of conduct. The Law Society has led the way in setting standards for practice, for client care, for the development of skills and for in-service training.

Both the Bar and the Law Society monitor their members' activities. They deal with complaints and discipline. In addition to providing services to their members, they lobby and liaise with the government and with other professions and other bodies. They attempt to help their members to react to competitive challenges.

But the public identify the legal profession as essentially in the business of looking after themselves. Are the professional bodies really regulating in the public interest? Most studies show that voters have a pretty poor opinion of lawyers generally. Solicitors' clients, while not having a particularly good view of the profession as a whole, do, however, generally feel well served by their individual solicitors. The professions purport to regulate themselves in the interests of the public. The challenge for Labour is to make sure that happens.

Professional numbers

Over the last 20 years the number of solicitors with practising certificates has doubled as has the number of barristers working in independent practice. The numbers increase each year. The availability of a wide range of properly trained lawyers must contribute to the availability of legal services and to holding the price of those services at a reasonable level.

The way to keep the price of such services up is to restrict the points of access. There are signs that the solicitors at least want to do that.

The Law Society had its first presidential election for more than 40 years in July 1995. The winner ran a Poujadist, put-solicitors-first campaign which had at its core the call to limit entry into the profession. The way to greater profitability, those who now lead the Law Society claim, is to cut the numbers coming into the profession. The Bar may go the same way. There is less work, particularly for young barristers, because of heavy competition between them and from solicitors. A Labour government will have to intervene if restrictive attempts are made by the professional bodies to limit entry into the profession artificially simply to preserve the position of those who are already licensed to practise.

Client service

Many users of the legal system are frustrated by delay and the slow pace at which their case progresses. The regulatory system used by the professional bodies must properly address these difficulties. Solicitors and barristers should be required to publish and adhere to service standards. These should be provided to clients and be generally available and accessible to potential users of legal services.

So lawyers will provide information to their clients about how their case will be run at the start of the case and at periodic intervals during its conduct. Clients should know within what period to expect a response from their solicitor or barrister. They must be told how long the case will last.

Similar rules need to be made, or, where made, complied with, about costs. Business and in particular private clients, all want to know how much their lawyers are likely to charge. Failure to provide this information at an early stage leads to numerous complaints about lawyers' services. The regulatory regime for solicitors and barristers must require all lawyers to give clear information about costs and penalise those who fail to meet this demand.

There is an increasing trend within the professions towards specialisation. Clients in particular want their lawyer to specialise in the particular field where their problem lies. The professional expertise implied in being either a solicitor or a barrister is no longer enough. Clients need to know they are dealing with somebody with special skills. It is vital therefore that the professional bodies develop systems of specialisation accreditation. These can be subject-based or relate to a range of potential services. There needs to be some further external pressure on the professional bodies to ensure that the public's demand for specialist services is being met by accreditation systems approved by the professional bodies.

It is no longer acceptable that lawyers should simply rely for their continuing professional expertise on their initial training and their practical experience. This has been recognised by the Law Society with the requirement for solicitors admitted in the last 10 years to be involved in continuing professional education. The Bar must introduce a similar scheme. The right to practise within a restricted system must carry with it the obligation to keep abreast of changes and developments. Compulsory continuing education is an appropriate way to achieve this.

In particular, continuing training and education must include both legal and skills training. Updating and refresher courses on legal issues are at the core of legal education. But lawyers need wider skills. They must be familiar with management and business-based techniques. Communication skills must be kept up to date. The Labour Party should promote the relevant changes required to achieve this.

Systems of practice

Traditionally solicitors practise in partnership or alone. They have for some years been entitled to incorporate with unlimited liability but few have done so. Barristers continue to practise alone. Neither profession allows its members to be involved in multidisciplinary partnerships. But both solicitors and barristers can work as employed lawyers within commercial and similar organisations.

The public are attracted by one-stop shopping. Virtually the only professional organisations which have an absolute bar on their members practising together with other professionals are solicitors and barristers. Solicitors are not allowed to practise in partnership with accountants, surveyors, barristers or other similar professionals. They may give profit shares to people employed by them who are not in fact solicitors but the ownership of the practice has to remain wholly in the hands of solicitors.

Barristers have always practised wholly on their own. Virtually all barristers in independent practice operate from sets of chambers where the groupings are often as big as many medium-sized solicitors' partnerships. Members pay chambers expenses and meet the general running costs of the properties they work from. However, they do not share fees. At its most extreme this has the odd effect that two barristers who work in the same room in the same set of chambers can appear on different sides in a case before the courts. They are not regarded as being in conflict with each other despite the wholly opposing interests they put forward for their clients.

The system should be freed up. Professionals need an open choice as to how they practise. If they want to join with professionals from other disciplines they should be entitled to do so. Labour must therefore remove all restrictions on solicitors' and barristers' practising systems. Multidisciplinary partnership should be allowed. Solicitors and barristers can then practise together if they choose. They can equally join together with other professions so clients can benefit from a range of professional expertise provided within one organisation.

Labour should require more public accountability from lawyers and should promote the removal of restrictive practices. There is no reason why the model of partnership practice should be left untouched. Solicitors in private practice must join a compulsory insurance scheme. Barristers should be required to do so as well. Compulsory insurance and the Solicitors Compensation Fund protect clients in the last resort from theft by lawyers. Systems of practice should therefore be freed up so that legal businesses can incorporate with limited liability.

Client access

Clients have unrestricted access to any solicitors who are prepared to assist them. Direct access to barristers is more restricted. I have proposed that barristers and solicitors should be allowed to practise together. But it is likely that many barristers will wish to continue to practise alone, or in partnership only with other barristers or in sets of chambers as at present. I see no reason why access to barristers should be restricted.

Hence Labour should promote the removal of the professional rule which prohibits general direct access to barristers. Client service standards will need defining. A regime for the holding of costs on account, or indeed clients' money, will have to be developed. Barristers will be able to enter contracts with their clients under which barristers may sue and be sued.

A fused profession?

The removal of the various restrictive practices which separate methods of practice by solicitors and barristers must be in the public interest. Equally, substantial sums of public money are spent on funding legal education. Grants remain widely available for degree courses and, despite significant reductions, grants can still be obtained for pre-qualification professional training courses. Unversities are, in addition, all in receipt of public funds in one way or another.

Hence the public have an interest in ensuring that legal pre-qualification training is provided in the most cost-effective way. The legal knowledge and skills required to be a solicitor or barrister are the same. Each branch of the profession develops its particular skills further once lawyers start to practise. Labour must ensure that common professional training is in place for all lawyers. I can see no reason why all lawyers should not qualify via the same training programme. Individuals can then choose where their particular interests lie. I think it likely that those who wish to specialise in advocacy and join sets of barristers in independent practice may make such a choice later than they now do. It may become the norm for all lawyers in independent practice to start their careers in legal firms which provide a range of services to the public. Those who want to be specialist advocates may join the Bar later. There is no need for the profession to fuse. Barristers and solicitors will work more closely together. There is no reason why an individual should not be both a barrister and a solicitor. But the two professions can retain their separate professional identities.

Regulating the professions

It is in the public interest to have a properly regulated legal profession. Solicitors have been subject to greater Parliamentary controls because they hold clients' money. But, even then, the power to make subordinate legislation has been delegated to the Law Society, the solicitors' professional body, subject originally only to the agreement of the Master of the Rolls. Otherwise the legal professions have been left to regulate themselves.

The Courts and Legal Services Act 1990 introduced a significant change. It attempted, not very successfully, to reduce various legal monopolies. Under that Act some new professional rules and regulations which the professional bodies want to introduce are subject to scrutiny. The Advisory Committe on Legal Education and Conduct (ACLEC) has to be consulted on some proposed new professional rules. Rule changes have also to be approved by the four senior judges who head the Supreme Court Divisions and the Lord Chancellor has the final say.

This system was created to help deal with the Bar wars that broke out in 1988. Most barristers and many judges regarded the idea of extending rights of audience in the higher courts to solicitors as the end of the civilised world as they knew it. The self-interest of barristers was described as the public interest. The Conservative government backed away from confrontation with a hostile Bar and judiciary. The result has been a messy compromise. Since the Act, simple regulatory changes for the professions get bogged down in ACLEC's ludicrously slow procedures. Changes which threaten existing monopolies take years to be dealt with. Key issues such as those on rights of audience are ducked until decisions must be taken and are then decided on the thinnest of majorities.

But Labour needs something like ACLEC as a back-up to enable its professional regulatory changes to be promoted. ACLEC needs reconstituting. The veto of the heads of divisions should be removed. The Lord Chancellor or his political successor must retain a role.

A regulatory framework for the legal professions needs a new Legal Services Act. The professions would be expected to trigger most new delegated legislation. Only where there was a public interest element need the regulations be subject to comment by an advisory committee. That committee should advise the Lord Chancellor alone on the issue. Any veto by the Lord Chancellor should be the subject of automatic Parliamentary debate. The advisory committee might also be given a residual right to call for regulatory change from the professions if they were thought to be operating against the public interest.

Benet Hytner QC

In 1948, at the heady age of 20, I was asked to contribute, together with Professor Harold Laski and others of similar standing, to *The Reform of the Law*, edited by the great Professor Glanville Williams. With that quality which mothers call self-confidence, but others arrogance, I agreed and wrote a section urging the abolition of the distinction between misdemeanours and felonies. It took three years for the book to be published, and a further 16 before Parliament succumbed to my advocacy. Such is the normal pace of law reform.

In 1952, when I was called to the Bar on the Northern Circuit, the legal professions did not consider themselves candidates for reform; each was sure of its own perfection. Indeed each had abundant virtues. Although statistics may prove an ageing memory defective, my recollection is that it was rare for a solicitor to defraud a client, and the standard of honesty was extremely high (the exception being that many solicitors, otherwise impeccably honest and thoroughly honourable, considered it perfectly permissible not to pay counsel's fees).

The standards of honour at the Bar were also of the highest. There was, certainly on circuit, almost total trust between opponents. This state of affairs had been developed over decades partly as the result of traditions which out of context appeared quaint and indefensible. Above all, barristers and solicitors regarded themselves as professional people, adhering to professional standards of conduct, which at the end of the day overrode the profit motive.

There was a darker side to both professions. Snobbery was rife. Whilst it was always possible for a barrister of 'lower-class' origins to come to the Bar, some chambers, often those with the best work, were closed not only to them but also to Jews and, in the rare cases where applications were made, to other ethnic minorities. This snobbery was even more endemic among solicitors. Well into the 1960s I was told by a partner in a well-known Manchester firm that they only gave articles to applicants of 'good family'.

It need hardly be said that discrimination against women was rife, often led by clerks whose power was awesome, and invariably excused on the ground that they 'would only go off and get married and leave a hole in chambers'.

Probity also had its limits. Each profession clung jealously to its restrictive practices and beyond doubt the ultimate *raison d'être* of these practices was to ensure high standards (thus, the 'special fee' and circuit junior demanded for an invasion of an alien circuit were intended to preserve the circuit system which was seen, justifiably, as a means of encouraging those standards) but no thought was given to balancing the trivial damage which might be done to the system by abolition of the practices against the extra cost and inconvenience to the litigant of maintaining them.

Furthermore, the litigation game was more often than not pursued with scant regard for the litigants, and little sympathy or support was offered to those who wished to simplify procedures.

This picture, I am aware, is of course that still painted of the professions, particularly of the Bar, in our national newspapers, both tabloid and broadsheet. It is, however, hopelessly out of date. Enormous strides have been taken by both sides of the profession to clean up their acts. Both have in recent years been in the forefront of attempts to reform procedure; both have fought to attack discrimination on the grounds of race, religion, sex and marital status; greater success has been achieved in these fields in the past decade than in the previous half century. Snobbery has markedly diminished and there is a greater awareness that restrictive practices, however valuable their ultimate goal, must be weighed carefully against the wider public interest.

Is there a role for a Labour government in pursuing further success in these fields?

I turn first to consider the social make-up of the professions, and consequently of the judiciary which springs from them. Much cant is uttered — some regrettably in the Labour movement — on this topic. By definition, professional judges can never be regarded as 'working class': having been to university and worked for 20 years as solicitors or barristers they become 'middle class' whatever their family origins. Furthermore, experience does not lead to the conclusion that a judge of working-class origin is of necessity better or more understanding of the problems of the deprived or under privileged than one from a more affluent background, nor is it necessarily true that a woman is a sounder judge of a case involving attacks on women than a man (particularly bearing in mind that such cases invariably also involve men).

However, most judges are indeed white middle-class males. Most people accept that this is wrong, but many believe that the introduction of more women or judges from ethnic or working-class backgrounds will improve the quality of the Bench. I do not believe for one minute that this will be so. I recall from my early days at the Bar in Manchester that the local county court judge from whom it was hardest to obtain damages for a plaintiff was the one from the most socially deprived background, whilst in more serious cases plaintiffs used to await eagerly the return to the assizes of the upper-class Mr Justice Barry.

I do, however, fervently believe, as an old-fashioned socialist, that it is a social outrage that the Bench is not more representative of society as a whole. Unless a career judiciary is to be introduced (which it is to be hoped a Labour government would never countenance) the judiciary will be a reflection of the entry to the professions 20 years and more before. On that basis the number of women and those from ethnic minorities coming 'on stream' in the next few years should enable a

Labour Lord Chancellor to make the Bench more representative without lowering its quality (a temptation to do which in the interests of populist acclaim he or she must resist).

That, however, does not deal with class. In dealing with the class origins of the judiciary it must of course be emphasised that any comparisons with other jurisdictions must take account of the magistracy which, dealing as it does with over 90 per cent of all criminal cases, is more representative of society (in sex and social origin and even — though to a lesser extent — class terms) than are the civil servants who comprise the career judiciaries in Europe.

Nevertheless, the pool of barristers from whom the bulk of the higher judiciary will continue to be drawn remains of overwhelmingly middle-class origin.

This is a scandal. Who is to blame and how can this obvious social evil be redressed — for evil it is that the opportunity to belong to one of the greater professions appears to be minimal for those coming from what is loosely called 'the working class'?

The thoughtless and prejudiced take the easy way out, and blame the Bar. It is, of course, undeniably true that some barristers and corporately some sets of chambers are snobs. In recent years, however, particularly under pressure from the Bar Council, the selection procedures for pupillages and tenancies have undergone fundamental changes in most sets of chambers. The problem is not that applicants of 'working-class' origin are in general discriminated against (though I am sure that there still are isolated examples of this happening) but that such applicants are relatively few in number.

Without adequate statistical research it is of course impossible to form reliable conclusions, but it would certainly appear from experience that disproportionately few of such students actually reach university in the first place. If true this means that our primary and secondary education systems have failed the majority of pupils, since innate academic ability must be evenly spread among the population and the advantages of home background (i.e., books, a home environment conducive to study and parental motivation) can only be partly significant.

A Labour government ought to tackle this problem. It is one for an Education Secretary, not a Lord Chancellor to solve; but without a solution there will continue to be, well into the next century, a higher judiciary drawn from a middle-class background.

There is, however, a problem intermediate to schooling and the Bar. There is abundant anecdotal evidence that secondary school teachers and lecturers at universities (particularly the 'new' ones, that is, the old polytechnics) actively discourage those from 'working-class' or ethnic minority backgrounds from going to the Bar on the ground that it is a middle-class profession (as late as the 1980s one of my own sons was somewhat surprised, at a law lecture at his poly, to hear that all barristers were upper class and Tories).

Allied to this problem is another — again based, alas, on anecdotal evidence, namely, that students at the 'new' universities (whose degrees are in truth rarely accorded the same weight on a CV as an equivalent degree from, e.g., Oxbridge, Nottingham, Manchester or Birmingham) are not necessarily failed entrants to the Oxbridge, redbrick or plate-glass establishments, but are often from deprived or ethnic minority backgrounds who have applied only to their local 'new' university because they believe that they would be socially more comfortable there.

I believe that a Labour government should set out to discover, by a proper enquiry, what the true facts are, and additionally whether (as I believe to be the case) local authorities are reluctant to give grants to less affluent graduates who wish to read for the Bar. It should then be in a position to provide such remedies as are in the power of a government. The Bar and Law Society must also give their support to measures aimed at encouraging those from less affluent backgrounds to fulfil their potentials and not to be scared off the legal professions.

Race and sex discrimination are in a different category. Such discrimination originates in minds and hearts, and from these organs must ultimately be eradicated. Legislation and strict professional codes of conduct have their roles. The fewer discriminatory practices that take place due to legal or professional coercion, the sooner such practices appear not to be respectable. And the sooner they appear disreputable the sooner will they diminish further. They will not, however, disappear until people cease to *think* in a prejudiced fashion.

I personally doubt whether in these areas more can be realistically achieved by legislation or professional codes. There is, of course, a strongly held contrary view; if it prevails, it is crucial that further proposals for legislation or extended codes of conduct should be scrutinised sensitively to ensure that they are not counter-productive by causing undue resentment. However, the main responsibility for further progress must lie with the Bar Council and Law Society to continue monitoring, and to provide constant reminders to their members that discrimination, apart from being a breach of professional codes of conduct, is uncivilised.

I would also add in relation to sex and marital status discrimination that every female barrister or solicitor who returns to work shortly after having a child strikes a blow against discrimination; every woman who, whatever the hardship of the circumstances, leaves practice on those occasions, hands a weapon to the discriminators.

Lastly on this subject, complaints are from time to time made about sexual harassment in chambers or in the office. It is right that when circumstances justify it, a complaint should be made where those involved are of unequal status. It is right because this is an old problem, but in the past has been ignored, to the detriment of women, because it has never been acknowledged as a problem. The request for (or, it must be emphasised, the *offering* of) sexual favours for a place in chambers or an office is, above all else, a form of corruption, and, as I see the development of the professions, one that will diminish as the power to grant a pupillage, a tenancy or a job is taken from the head of chambers or senior partner and handed over to committees with recognised procedures.

Thus far, my review has dealt with areas where much progress has been made but where a Labour government could directly or indirectly encourage further progress. Some 'progress' in the past decade has however not been beneficial to the public.

Seventeen years of Thatcherite philosophy and legislation have created a climate encouraging the belief that chasing a fast buck is the highest form of morality, and, to be more specific, in which any professional rule inhibiting the unbridled pursuit of profit is deemed to be a restrictive practice, a term universally adopted as a pejorative.

Until relatively recently, touting and ambulance chasing were pejorative terms. These activities — now euphemistically described as 'practice development' — are now regarded as the norm. Advertising has plumbed depths of taste and accuracy which would have shocked practitioners 10 years ago. Barristers speak blithely of 'running a business' to describe the organisation of their practices.

Undoubtedly, the growth in size of chambers and partnerships has been inevitable, granted the increase in the cost of sophisticated equipment, of accommodation and salaries; of course such organisations need to be run in a businesslike fashion. However, essentially, barristers and solicitors are not running a business, but providing services for the public within a framework of rules of conduct designed to protect the public from mischief and to enhance standards of integrity and skill.

Again, advertising of services is not merely harmless, but is of benefit to the public. It is the advertising, whether crude or sophisticated, of claimed skills that constitutes a vehicle for fraud on the litigant. The listing of 12 or so 'specialities' in a directory seems to me to be a contradiction in terms; the phrase 'field of practice' does not to some, however accurate it may be, have the same ring about it. The boasts of clients worked for does not reflect how they were obtained nor the quality of work done; a list of successful cases has an echo of the notorious league tables of hospitals and schools so beloved of Tory governments, in which a school struggling with pupils from a deprived catchment area, and notwithstanding a high quality of teaching, is at the bottom of the table and is thus excoriated in relation to a school at the top, doing not as well as it might with the best of talent.

Trust between practitioners is in the interests of litigants and the public in general. It is the lubricant that enables litigation, both in and out of court, to run smoothly and swiftly. Touting and advertising of alleged skills destroys that trust. The professions in these regards have regressed.

I doubt whether a Labour government could (or would) intervene directly in these areas of professional codes of conduct. What it can do, however, linking these activities with its concern about standards in public life, is to create a wholly different atmosphere in which the legal professions will be under pressure to revert to their former higher standards. As I write, however, proposals are being mooted advocating multidisciplinary partnerships to provide 'one-stop shopping'. One-stop shopping is a Thatcherite device which, by cloaking conflicts of interest, provides a vehicle for fraud. Those who, for example, buy a house and seek a mortgage are entitled to independent legal, independent financial and independent property advice, rather than advice on the value of a house from the same source as has an interest in lending the money and doing the conveyance. It is sincerely to be hoped that this further erosion of professional standards will be abandoned.

So far as skills are concerned it is clear to me that legislation has now, in many fields, developed in detail and amount to such an extent that the existing trend towards specialisation will inevitably strengthen. However much I, as an old-fashioned circuit knockabout, may regret this, the trend is in the public interest in both branches of the profession. Barristers should, however, never forget that their basic skill is advocacy, and that whatever the nature of their specialisation, they must possess and have those skills — the ability to absorb and analyse large quantities of documents, the development of good judgment to distinguish between the good and bad point (or more accurately between those which will attract a judge or jury and those that will not) and the ability to articulate clearly, concisely and eloquently the arguments to be advanced.

It is abundantly clear that the ability to make submissions concisely will become more and more important, and it is to be expected that a Labour government would press forward with procedural changes which, whilst preserving the oral tradition, will cut down on time-wasting and verbosity.

On the whole the public are better served today by both branches of the profession than when I was called to the Bar, and I confidently anticipate that five or more years of a Labour government will ensure further progress to that end.

9

Legal Education and Training

Professor Peter Jones, Nottingham Trent University School of Law

In his book *The Age of Unreason* Professor Charles Handy describes how a frog will allow itself to be boiled alive. Place a frog in cold water. Gradually increase the temperature. The frog will not stir; it will die. Handy's point is that the frog is so comfortable with continuity that it does not realise that a point is reached when a dramatic change in behaviour is required. Why, when I recently reread this passage in Handy's book, did I think of lawyers, and law teachers in particular?

The world of practising lawyers is changing rapidly. Clients, be they commercial, private fee-paying or the government through the Legal Aid Board, are demanding higher levels of service and competence from their legal advisers. The outcomes of legal advice are being scrutinised as is the performance of practitioners; standards of service are being defined. The tighter control of the legal aid budget, conditional fees, the fee sensitivity of commercial clients and the Woolf proposals all demand greater value for money. The system is becoming, to use the jargon, more client-driven and more transparent. Whatever mechanisms are adopted by the future Labour government, this trend is set to continue.

And practising lawyers must respond — or like the frog they will die, at least professionally. We see significant changes in organisation of legal practice on both sides of the profession. For example, there is a shift towards greater reliance on paralegal staff; many are already well qualified law graduates who cannot get training contracts. With the advances in information technology, for example, in the use of expert systems, paralegals will be able to do the work previously reserved for solicitors and barristers.

One thing is clear. Whatever happens to the legal economy, there will be a permanent reduction in the demand for fully qualified solicitors. For the same reasons the Bar will suffer a similar reduction, particularly as it can no longer rely on its monopoly in the higher courts.

It is against this background that we should consider the future of legal education. For all its worthy deliberations the Lord Chancellor's Advisory Committee on Legal Education and Conduct has failed to analyse the shape of the legal profession to come. It is not as if legal education is special. It should be seen within the framework of higher and continuing education generally, particularly when we require graduates to be far more mobile and flexible than we have before.

Let us now look at particular aspects of legal education.

Undergraduate legal education

The law teacher – frog will say: 'We've never had it so good — jump right in; the water's lovely'. Young people are clamouring to enrol in undergraduate law degrees; many want to practise law. This pleases the university authorities. With student fees now a major source of institutional income, low-cost legal education produces high yields.

But for the individual law student it may all end in tears. The mismatch between graduates (in law and in other disciplines) who wish to practise and the number of training places will become worse, not better.

So the temperature of the water is rising. Well, the university law schools say, there really isn't a problem. We all know that many of our law graduates do not end up practising law. The law degrees have always been a good grounding for other occupations; law graduates have 'transferable skills'. But do they really? In truth many law degrees have been designed only with the professions in mind; indeed 'designed' is overstating it. There is little systematic analysis of what undergraduate legal education is trying to achieve — what outcomes are sought. Just as the lawyer (rather than the client) has dominated the agenda in law practices, so in legal education it has been dominated by law teachers. Law teachers claim to be responding to the requirements of the professional bodies, the Law Society and the Council of Legal Education who in turn claim to be responding to the needs of the professions. So we have seen prescription of the content of law degrees. Despite their protestations to the contrary, law teachers feel comfortable with this; they can concentrate on the ninth of the ten exceptions to the rule of which they have made a special study. It does not require much thought. So much emphasis has been placed on coverage that law students have been force-fed with black-letter law.

A change of focus

With some notable exceptions, law schools are producing the educational equivalent of pâté geese (with large livers but little brain). The undergraduate legal education system should be producing free-range chickens. There needs to be a change of focus. Law schools must determine what they are seeking as the outcomes of academic legal education. Whilst the acquisition of legal knowledge is important, they must look afresh at the skills, competencies and knowledge that the modern law graduate should possess. Indeed it is wider than this. We should be joining in the current debate about the core skills that modern society should expect from its graduates. Therefore, it would be wrong for outcomes to relate only to what is needed to be a good practising lawyer, whatever that may be. This is too narrow a prescription. For the future, the majority of law students may well end up (whether willingly or not) seeking work in areas other than the law. Law teachers must be able to market law graduates as possessing skills which they can apply not only in the legal profession but elsewhere.

Prescription from the centre?

It sounds as if there must be central control of the form and content of undergraduate legal education. But this would be disastrously over-prescriptive.

We must question the legitimacy of professionals exercising the influence that they have in the past. This may have been easier to justify when the law degree was such a heavy 'breeding ground' for the practitioner but as the proportion drops so the legitimacy of that role reduces. The Law Society and the Bar Council should adopt a minimalist position. They may inform the debate by assisting in the determination of standards and outcomes which should be achieved in undergraduate legal education: apart from that, their role in course content and specification is counter-productive.

Indeed, any attempt to control the form and content of legal education from the centre will be counter-productive. The Lord Chancellor's Advisory Committee on Legal Education and Conduct is a marvellous forum for the interplay of sectional interests; worthy of academic study in itself. It comes up with findings that academic lawyers see as defending professional interests and the professional bodies think do not go far enough. Anyway, it is extremely difficult to determine the forms of learning likely to produce the best practising lawyers — indeed the best practising anything. There are too many variables. Much time and energy can be spent for little reward.

The major failing of law degrees is the lack of transparency in the outcomes sought. With some exceptions, it is very difficult to determine what a particular law degree seeks to achieve, other than in the most general terms.

The future Labour government has a legitimate interest in ensuring that there are minimum standards which undergraduate legal education courses should maintain. The emphasis should be on the word 'minimum'. Against that backdrop, university law schools must have the freedom to determine the outcomes they seek. However, these must be properly specified and be transparent to the intending student and future employer. There should be variety: universities should be able to offer degrees with a vocational bias provided this is clear from the outcomes of the course; there should be degrees with outcomes that are substantially non-vocational and which may provide the student with more flexibility in the job market. There again, a degree that places an emphasis on the economic, business, social and political context in which law operates followed by shorter more focused vocational outcomes may be a winner; as may be a degree which has outcomes concentrating on legal skills in a clinical context. One could envisage a far more flexible structure involving different entry points and exit points, incorporating part-time and distance learning elements and perhaps building upon paralegal qualifications so as to provide a much broader system of entry into the legal profession than traditional programmes.

114

Legal educators will do well to remind themselves of boiled frogs when determining outcomes that best fit the aspirations of the modern law student and the needs of legal practice. For reasons articulated later, there is a need for a co-ordinating body to oversee those standards and outcomes not only in undergraduate legal education but also throughout the 'legal education continuum'.

An outcome-driven approach: the Legal Practice Course

The Legal Practice Course (LPC) is a significant development in legal education. Although it is a vocational course it provides a model of what can be achieved elsewhere. The Legal Practice Course builds on a system of standards and outcomes that seek to define the competencies and skills required by someone entering the profession as a trainee solicitor. The standards do not set down course content or the number of hours that a particular element of the course should take. This is for the providing institution to determine.

There are early indications that the standards-driven approach taken by the Law Society is producing variety and experimentation by course providers. It is a far more dynamic system which can respond more easily to changing needs in the legal profession. The standards can be adapted and amended in the light of experience. The Law Society validates new courses against the standards and outcomes, and monitors each course to ensure that the standards are being achieved. On the whole universities are declaring their enthusiasm for the LPC. They are in charge of developing the course content to deliver the prescribed outcomes; it is the university's course, not the Law Society's.

In the long term, the central administration of the system will be comparatively inexpensive because the regulatory hand can be applied with a lighter touch.

Joint vocational training

The decision by the Bar Council to devolve responsibility for the Bar Vocational Course is to be welcomed. But the idea that the existing course should be franchised in its current form is misplaced. Other providers of the course will not feel that they have ownership of it and this will stifle innovation. It will slow the progress towards common

115

vocational training, which is inevitable anyway and in the public interest. There should be a similar approach to the LPC with standards and outcomes being defined. This will enable the best features of both regimes to be combined in common elements of study.

Professional development of practitioners

Various recent developments are welcome. Barristers will undergo compulsory continuing education in the first three years after qualification. The emphasis placed by the Law Society on management training recognises this as a 'pervasive skill' for all lawyers concerned with the delivery of a high-quality service to clients.

But the system of compulsory education (which is soon to be extended to the whole of the solicitors' profession) has its dangers. First, the notion that practitioners have to 'clock up' hours of education can produce absurd results with lawyers attending, courses with little relevance to their practices; second, although such an à la carte system can produce an occasional meal of exceptional quality, particularly in some of the in-house courses now available, the system is essentially aimless and unstructured.

On the other hand, LLM programmes are often highly academic and theoretical and lack relevance for the practising professional. Furthermore, even where they are part-time, the commitment involved does not suit the practising lawyer. There are, however, interesting developments. Bristol and Cardiff Universities run LLM programmes where the 'taught' element takes place over weekends of study. More recently there have been significant developments particularly in the area of 'practice masters' degrees' in which the writer has been heavily involved. These are designed to acknowledge the intellectual skills of the advanced, reflective practitioner. Experiential learning techniques are employed enabling practitioners to learn through simulation and role play. The LLM in Advanced Litigation at Nottingham Law School represents this development. As with the LPC it is based on standards and outcomes. These define the process involved in the management and practice of advanced litigation and dispute resolution. The educational programme is designed to meet those outcomes, to enable the individual student to become an 'advanced practitioner'. The programme draws on the experience already acquired by the practitioner. Learning is interactive in nature, organised around weekend schools, which themselves are structured around extended simulations and case studies.

The standards define the process engaged in by practitioners working at the forefront of the process of dispute resolution. The course is delivered by practitioners and academics. Real clients also attend the weekends to act as tutors as do senior members of the judiciary. The programme bridges the unproductive divide between the practice, teaching and study of law. The students are experienced practitioners, solicitors from a variety of practice backgrounds from the large City firm to the specialist legal aid firm, and barristers. Early evaluation of the LLM shows that the students are using the skills acquired on the programme to considerable effect in practice. Many report that they have been able to reflect upon practice and devise more effective ways of managing the process and resolving disputes.

The MBA in legal practice, another programme delivered by Nottingham Law School, recognises the need for training practitioners in management disciplines. It reflects the particular problems and issues affecting professional firms, in particular the increasing complexity and sophistication of the management of legal practice. It seeks to address the lack of management education among lawyers, particularly in the area of service delivery to clients.

These programmes satisfy the continuing professional development requirements of the Law Society several times over. They are rigorous. The standards and outcomes of the courses are clearly defined and transparent. They are geared to the concept of the advanced practitioner. There are considerable similarities to the approach through the National Vocational Qualification system though at a master's level. Though it will sound like special pleading, it would be a comparatively inexpensive measure for the Labour government to introduce an element of tax relief for individuals who take such programmes especially when they are seeking excellence in the practice of law.

Judicial education and training

Despite the creation of the Judicial Studies Board in 1979, the system of education and training for judges is inadequate. There is little involvement of professional educators. The system compares unfavourably with most other EU countries as well as other common law jurisdictions such as the United States, Canada and Australia. This is still due to the notion that the integrity and independence of the judiciary would in some way be compromised by professionalising the system of judicial training.

Yet why should judges be immune from the move towards a more outcome-driven approach to training in which competence to perform the task defines the educational objectives?

We need to ask a number of searching questions. What sort of person will the post-Woolf judge be? As lawyers are encouraged to be more client-driven should judges not be as well? Is the modern judge more than someone who can listen to and evaluate argument and evidence, and what skills are needed to do this? What skills does the judge need for judicial management, particularly when the judiciary are required to be guardians of the public purse as never before? How about managing a caseload in a multi-track system?

Are we beginning to ask the unforgivably radical question, What makes a good judge? If we are, then we may soon take the equally radical position that it is possible to design an outcome-related selection and training system whereby a judge is not necessarily someone who is old, white and male and who was once a jolly good advocate at the Bar. Even leaving selection to one side, the time has come to look again at the system of education and training both for new and established judges. Many of the recent developments particularly in vocational and professional training could be applied profitably in judicial training as they are in other parts of the world. Who knows, we may end up with an MBA in judicial management!

The legal education and training continuum

I have already characterised the advisory function of the Lord Chancellor's Committee. It is far too cumbersome. It has now produced two consultative documents covering the initial stage and vocational training and continuing professional development. In neither document does it address the fast-changing needs of practice. There appears to be an assumption that things will carry on much as before.

Although it will deny it, the committee also has a regulatory function, for example, in regard to the Rights of Audience Course currently administered by the Law Society. Here its operation is marked by delay, procrastination and nit-picking. The central problem has been its approach to course design. The committee did not consider the role of solicitor advocates devised by a system of functions, skills, knowledge, and understanding of law and procedure — a system of outcomes in other words. Rather a course model was imposed through detailed content and the dreaded 'class contact hours'. The process has been very conservative and stultifying and has led to the perception of unequal treatment.

And it is this characterisation which is at the root of the difficulty in regulating legal education. The Labour government should abolish the Lord Chancellor's Committee. It should be replaced by a committee whose function is to set standards throughout the legal education continuum rather than impose control. And that there will be a continuum, rather than a series of stages, should be central to the operation of such a body. It should be astute to detect the influence of monopolies on the legal education and training system and recognise and encourage as much variety as possible in routes to qualification including through part-time study.

The new committee's standards-setting function can apply (as I have tried to illustrate) across the whole field of legal education. This does not prevent different standard and outcome-setting bodies such as the Law Society, the Bar Council and universities continuing to operate within this framework as long as they are enabling and coordinating rather than controlling. Above all, there must be a recognition by legal educationalists of the fast-changing world in which we live.

10

A Bill of Rights

John Wadham, Director, Liberty
(the National Council for Civil Liberties)

The movement towards a Bill of Rights in this country is gaining strength. The converts to the incorporation of the European Convention on Human Rights into domestic law have infiltrated the establishment and include the Master of the Rolls[1] and the Lord Chief Justice.[2] Lord Lester QC's Bill to incorporate the Convention has also attracted widespread support amongst senior members of the judiciary.[3] The late John Smith also supported the incorporation of the Convention in a keynote speech organised by Charter 88.[4] Of course there remain many people yet to be converted. Nevertheless I wish to concentrate in this chapter not on the necessity of a Bill of Rights but on the content and on the mechanisms for enforcement. Liberty has set out its arguments for a Bill of Rights elsewhere.[5]

The Labour Party conference in 1993 adopted a policy supporting a two-stage process to implement mechanisms to enforce rights. The first includes the incorporation of the European Convention on Human Rights, entrenching this set of rights by the use of a 'notwithstanding

---

[1] *The Independent*, 3 March 1993.
[2] *The Independent*, 2 December 1992.
[3] Hansard, Lords, 25 January 1995, col. 1136; 15 February 1995, col. 762; 29 March 1995, col. 1692 and 1 May 1995, col. 1271.
[4] *The Guardian*, 2 March 1993.
[5] *A People's Charter: Liberty's Bill of Rights* (Liberty, 1991).

120

clause' procedure[6] and setting up a human rights commission to monitor and promote human rights. The second stage was for a Labour government to set up an all-party commission to consider and draft a home-grown Bill of Rights for future implementation. Graham Allen MP, when he was the shadow spokesperson on constitutional affairs, promoted a Bill which set out these aims in legislative form.[7]

Tony Blair MP set out his agenda for change in July 1994 and included within it the need for strengthened incorporation and the idea of a 'notwithstanding clause'.[8] The call for a Bill of Rights was again raised at the 1994 and 1995 conferences.

The incorporation of the European Convention on Human Rights has been supported by the Liberal Democrats for some time and perhaps is no longer controversial. However the Conservative government continues to oppose the incorporation of the Convention.[9] Interestingly part of the government's proposals for Northern Ireland include the commitment that, 'Protection for specified civil, political, social and cultural rights would be reinforced'.[10]

This chapter will deal with issues concerned with civil and political rights and not with the arguments for or against the inclusion of social and economic rights. Even with such restrictions there remain two very controversial issues. The first is whether the Convention is any longer an appropriate vehicle for a Bill of Rights for this country and the second is what mechanism there should be to enforce a Bill of Rights. It is to these issues that I wish to turn.

Content

The origins of the European Convention on Human Rights and Fundamental Freedoms go back even before the establishment of the Council of Europe.[11] The Convention was partly based on the United

---

[6] This mechanism is described further below.

[7] Human Rights (No. 3) Bill, 19 October 1993.

[8] Speech on 15 July 1994 in Cardiff.

[9] Even the 'weak' version of incorporation contained in Lord Lester's Bill is opposed by the government (Hansard, Lords, 29 March 1995, col. 1696).

[10] *A Framework for Accountable Government in Northern Ireland* (1995), para. 20.

[11] See, for example, A. H. Robertson and J. G. Merrills, *Human Rights in Europe: A Study of the European Convention on Human Rights*, 3rd ed. (Manchester: Manchester University Press, 1993).

Nations Universal Declaration of Human Rights and the text was finally agreed in 1950. The Convention is now 45 years old and in many areas that age is apparent.

Omissions

First, a number of rights are missing from the text of the Convention. There is for instance no right to information from public bodies.[12] There is also no duty on the State to provide rights of due process in the extradition process or before deportation.[13] The right to a fair trial contained in art. 6 of the Convention does not apply because the deportee has no pre-existing civil right for the article to bite on. One obvious protection that could be provided for those at risk of deportation would be a duty on the State seeking extradition to demonstrate a prima facie case in court before extradition is ordered.[14]

The Convention also provides no assistance to those held in detention pending deportation or extradition because art. 5(1)(f) allows detention in such circumstances and there is apparently no limit to the length of detention or any restriction on the legal justification for such a detention.[15] In fact the rights of 'aliens' are further and specifically restricted by art. 16 which states that the rights of freedom of expression and assembly and the anti-discrimination article shall not: 'be regarded as preventing the High Contracting Parties [the States] from imposing restrictions on the political activity of aliens'.

The only restrictions on removal from a country are imposed by other articles such as the right to family life or freedom from torture.[16] Even

---

[12] Article 10 does protect the right to impart information.

[13] The right to submit reasons, the right to review (not necessarily before a court) and the right to representation, before an expulsion is effected are contained in Protocol 7, art. 1, but this has not been ratified by the United Kingdom. The article also permits expulsion without those protections where it 'is necessary in the interests of public order or is grounded on reasons of national security'.

[14] This was the position before the Criminal Justice Act 1988.

[15] But see *Chahal* v *United Kingdom* (27 June 1995), App No. 224/4/93.

[16] *Soering* v *United Kingdom* (1989) 11 EHRR 439.

in family life cases the European Court of Human Rights has held[17] that if the family life can take place in the country to which the person is being deported then there is no breach of art. 8.

Of course the Convention does not include a right to enter a country, either to take up residence or as an asylum seeker, and furthermore provides no due process rights for those who allege they have substantive rights to enter and remain.

The right to be free from discrimination contained in art. 14 is flawed because, being drafted 45 years ago, it does not refer, for instance, to a person's sexual orientation or to disability.[18] It is also flawed because, unlike, for instance, the United Nations International Covenant on Civil and Political Rights,[19] it applies only where another right under the Convention has been violated. This has led to the provision being treated inadequately by the Commission and Court in Strasbourg, who often prefer to give judgment on the breach of the substantive right and ignore art. 14.[20]

In the context of minimum standards within the criminal justice system the Convention does not contain any equivalent of art. 14(3)(g) of the International Covenant on Civil and Political Rights which

---

[17] *Abdulaziz, Cabales and Bakandali* v *United Kingdom* (1985) 7 EHRR 471. It has taken particularly extreme circumstances for the Court to uphold a violation of the right to family life in such cases. For instance the Court decided that in the case of a Moroccan who had lived in Belgium since the age of three and whose close relatives, including his parents, his seven brothers and sisters, all lived in Belgium, deportation following a sentence of 26 months' imprisonment for a number of offences (none of them grave) was disproportionate (*Moustaquim* v *Belgium* (1991) 13 EHRR 802).

[18] However, it does make unlawful discrimination based on 'other status'.

[19] See art. 26.

[20] There are some important judgments, however. See, for instance, the *Belgian Linguistic Case (No. 1)* (1967) 1 EHRR 241.

provides that in the determination of any criminal charge, a person shall not 'be compelled to testify against himself or to confess guilt'.[21]

Although there are restrictions on the lawfulness of detention in the Convention, outside the provision against torture and inhuman or degrading treatment or punishment, no minimum conditions are set for conditions of detention.[22] Also other positive rights are missing, notably a right of access to a lawyer[23] and a right not to be held incommunicado.

The absence of any right of privacy in this country means that for the purposes of art. 6, the right to a fair trial conducted by an independent court in any dispute concerning a *civil right* does not exist and thus the right to privacy is only protected to the extent of the provisions in art. 8 itself. This means that, for instance, a search of the home or the forceable taking of bodily samples by the police does not have to be authorised by an independent court-like body but merely has to be 'in accordance with the law'. Thus rights of due process in relation to privacy are not required by the Convention. This has meant that domestic telephone tapping[24] and security services tribunals[25] have been accepted by the

---

[21] Although this may be partly protected, see *Saunders* v *United Kingdom* (application 19187/91) (1994), European Commission of Human Rights.

[22] See, for example, the International Covenant on Civil and Political Rights, art. 10(1): 'All persons deprived of their liberty shall be treated with humanity and with respect for the inherent dignity of the human person'.

[23] The right to access to a lawyer has been litigated in Strasbourg but only as a consequential effect of the right to correspondence and right to access to courts. See, for instance, *Silver* v *United Kingdom* (1983) 5 EHRR 347 and *Golder* v *United Kingdom* (1975) 1 EHRR 524. These cases have not dealt with the right to see a solicitor on arrival at the police station as contained (in a less than perfect form) in s. 56 of the Police and Criminal Evidence Act 1984. In *Murray* v *United Kingdom* (Application 18731/91) (1994) the Commission has held that failure to allow access within a reasonable period and refusal to allow the lawyer to be present at police interviews breaches art. 6. This is not a right in itself but is dependent on the fact that the evidence (including 'evidence' inferred adversely from the suspect's silence) which led to the conviction may have resulted from the lawyer's absence.

[24] Interception of Communications Act 1985.

[25] Security Services Act 1989 and Intelligence Services Act 1994: see chapter 15 below.

Commission as providing sufficient protection.[26] Also absent from the Convention are any specific rights for children.[27]

Lastly it is important to realise that, while some additional rights are contained in the protocols to the Convention, most of these protocols have not been ratified by the United Kingdom and thus do not apply. Most of the attempts by Parliamentarians to incorporate the Convention into domestic law have been restricted to incorporating only the rights which have been ratified so that, in addition to the rights of those about to be expelled from the country mentioned above, other rights that are missing include: freedom from imprisonment for breach of contract,[28] freedom of movement and residence,[29] the right to appeal following conviction and the right of compensation for those wrongly convicted,[30] the prohibition on double jeopardy in criminal cases[31] and equality of rights between spouses.[32]

Gaps in the rights provided

Apart from wholesale omissions of important rights there are considerable gaps in the rights as provided by the Convention. I will choose a few to illustrate the problems.

---

[26] See respectively *Esbester* v *United Kingdom* (Application 18601/91) (1993), European Commission of Human Rights, and *Christie* v *United Kingdom* (1994) 78–A Decisions and Reports 119. See also J. Wadham, 'The Intelligence Services Act 1994' (1994) 57 MLR 916.

[27] Such as that contained in the International Covenant on Civil and Political Rights, art. 24:

(1) Every child shall have, without any discrimination as to race, colour, sex, language, religion, national or social origin, property or birth, the right to such measures of protection as are required by his status as a minor, on the part of his family, society and the State.

(2) Every child shall be registered immediately after birth and shall have a name.

(3) Every child has the right to acquire a nationality.

[28] Protocol 4, art. 1.

[29] Protocol 4, art. 2.

[30] Protocol 7, arts 2 and 3.

[31] Protocol 7, art. 4.

[32] Protocol 7, art. 5.

Whilst the right to life contained in art. 2 is protected by the condition that actions breaching the right need to be 'absolutely necessary', the limitations include allowing lethal force to be used:

>   (b)   in order to effect a lawful arrest or to prevent the escape of a person lawfully detained;
>   (c)   in action lawfully taken for the purpose of quelling a riot or insurrection.

It cannot be right to allow the State to kill merely to effect an arrest or to prevent escape or even in order to end a riot.[33]

Article 5(1)(e) allows the 'detention of persons for the prevention of the spreading of infectious diseases, of persons of unsound mind, alcoholics or drug addicts or vagrants'.

Surely no one drafting a Bill of Rights today could include a right to imprison vagrants and alcoholics, whatever differing views there may be of locking up those with infectious diseases?

The rights of privacy and the freedoms of religion, expression and assembly are all subject to similar limitations in the Convention which are all contained in the second part of the relevant article:

> ... except such as is in accordance with the law and is necessary in a democratic society in the interests of national security, public safety or the economic well-being of the country, for the prevention of disorder or crime, for the protection of health or morals, or for the protection of the rights and freedoms of others.[34]

Whilst significant numbers of cases against the United Kingdom in Strasbourg have succeeded because the interference with the right was not 'in accordance with the law' or the interference was not proportionate — not 'necessary in a democratic society' — few have succeeded because the purported aim of the restriction was outside of the range provided for in the second part of the article. There is not space here to deal with all of the difficulties that the expression 'national security'

---

[33] The Court has now in *McCann* v *United Kingdom* (27 September 1995), Series A, vol. 324, further restricted the ambit of this provision.

[34] This is from art. 8(2), privacy and family life.

creates for the courts[35] but it is arguable that the expression is too vague to be contained in a Bill of Rights.

Similarly the expression 'public safety' makes too wide an exception and Liberty has substituted 'imminent physical harm' in its Bill of Rights. Interestingly 'the economic well-being of the country' features only as a limitation in art. 8. Presumably this allows the Inland Revenue to pry! If this is its intention then it could be more accurately defined thus reducing the loopholes in other cases. It is difficult to oppose the provision of a prevention of crime clause although Liberty's Bill of Rights avoids this arguing that the 'protection of the rights and freedoms of others' is sufficient. For similar reasons exceptions based on the prevention of disorder or the protection of health or morals are not included because they are not only very vague but potentially unlimited in their effect and generally unacceptable as a limitation in themselves, particularly as limitations on the rights of privacy and the freedoms of religion, expression and assembly.

Article 12 of the Convention includes a right to marry and found a family but does not provide such a right for transsexuals.[36] It also of course only allows men and women to marry and makes no provision for partnerships between lesbians or between gay men.

Conclusion

One can certainly conclude from this brief analysis of the Convention that it is an inadequate basis for a Bill of Rights. A better foundation would be the International Covenant on Civil and Political Rights but better still would be a domestic Bill of Rights albeit based on such international treaties. My concern is that although the Convention should be incorporated into domestic law this first step should have been

---

[35] See L. Lustgarten and I. Leigh, *In from the Cold: National Security and Parliamentary Democracy* (Oxford: Clarendon Press, 1994). The courts have consistently refused to adjudicate in national security cases see *Council of Civil Service Unions* v *Minister for the Civil Service* [1985] AC 374 or the refusal of the court to intervene in a claim for public-interest immunity based on national security in a civil case *Balfour* v *Foreign and Commonwealth Office* [1994] 1 WLR 681.
[36] *Rees* v *UK* (1988) 9 EHRR 56 and *Cossey* v *UK* (1990) 13 EHRR 622.

taken at least 20 years ago[37] and that we now need to move beyond that position and rapidly into the second stage.

Enforcement

In the challenge to the ban imposed on broadcasts by members of Sinn Fein the House of Lords took the view that the European Convention on Human Rights did not have to be taken into account by the executive arm of the State when a wide-ranging discretion was being exercised.[38] This state of affairs could be overturned by statute and this would in fact be one of the effects of Lord Lester's Human Rights Bill.[39] It is possible to go further than this to use the statute incorporating the Convention[40] to overturn common law decisions that are in conflict with it. A further degree of strengthening could be developed using such a statute to ensure that subordinate legislation such as statutory instruments and orders in council were *ultra vires* to the extent that they conflict with the Convention. Finally the statute of incorporation could create new rights by, for instance, a tort of breach of statutory duty thus ensuring that the Convention was a source of law in itself. Similarly breach of the Convention (rather than just the failure to take it into account: see *R* v *Secretary of State for the Home Department ex parte Brind*) could in itself found a decision of unlawfulness in judicial review proceedings.

None of these options breach any implied constitutional axiom of the sovereignty of Parliament. Traditional constitutional wisdom would say that all such changes, particularly those that bind a future Parliament,

---

[37] In 1976 the International Covenant on Civil and Political Rights came into effect. More parochially Liberty first articulated its policy on the incorporation of the Convention into domestic law based on a publication by Liberty's sister organisation, the Cobden Trust, in 1976 of *Civil Liberties and a Bill of Rights* by Peter Wallington and Jeremy McBride.
[38] *R* v *Secretary of State for the Home Department, ex parte Brind* [1991] 1 AC 696.
[39] See above footnote 3.
[40] I am using the Convention as an example. It would be equally possible to have an alternative and I would say better basis for a Bill of Rights.

are impossible.[41] In fact the jurisprudence of the law of the European Union shows us that we can go further.[42] The courts are now obliged to strike down statute law which conflicts with the Treaty of Rome. A slightly less radical approach has been adopted by the Labour Party and is modelled on the procedure in the Canadian Charter of Rights and Freedoms. In Canada, whilst courts can overturn old and new legislation[41] which conflicts with the Charter, the procedure also allows the legislature to declare *expressly* in an Act of Parliament that a given provision operates notwithstanding the Charter. This 'notwithstanding clause' permits the Canadian Parliament to keep provisions on the statute book which the courts have overturned provided it is acknowledged that, in effect, they do not comply with the Charter. Unsurprisingly, it has rarely been used and when it has, it has been in the context of the tussle between Quebec and the Federal government.[44]

Liberty's proposals for enforcement go further than this but at the same time incorporate an important element of democratic control. The proposals involve dividing the rights in the Bill of Rights into two kinds. The basis is that described above — the 'notwithstanding clause' model. However, some rights would be 'judicially entrenched' on the lines of the American Bill of Rights. A distinction between two kinds of rights can be found in the European Convention on Human Rights itself. Article 15 asserts that those articles like the right to life,[45] freedom from torture, freedom from slavery, the restriction on the creation of retrospective criminal offences, freedom of conscience, freedom from

---

[41] 'That Parliaments have more than once intended and endeavoured to pass Acts which should tie the hands of their successors is certain, but the endeavour has always ended in failure' A. V. Dicey, *Introduction to the Study of the Law of the Constitution*, 10th ed. (London: Macmillan, 1964), p. 65. See by contrast A. W. Bradley, 'The sovereignty of Parliament — in perpetuity?' in J. Jowell and D. Oliver (eds), *The Changing Constitution*, 3rd ed. (Oxford: Clarendon Press, 1994), pp. 79–107.

[42] *R v Secretary of State for Transport, ex parte Factorame Ltd (No. 2)* (case C–213/89) [1991] 1 AC 603, ECJ.

[43] Ordinarily a 'chronologically superior' Act would take precedence in the case of conflict (*Vauxhall Estates Ltd v Liverpool Corporation* [1932] 1 KB 733; *Ellen Street Estates Ltd v Minister of Health* [1934] 1 KB 590).

[44] *Ford v Quebec (Attorney-General)* 54 DLR (4th) 577; see (1991) 13 Human Rights Quarterly 378.

[45] Under Liberty's proposals the rights in the Bill only apply to individuals from the moment of their birth thus avoiding the concern that rights under the Abortion Act 1967 could be questioned by the courts.

discrimination and the right to democratic participation cannot be subject to derogation except in times of war or other public emergencies. Liberty believes that the court should have the power to declare invalid other provisions of law incompatible with the terms of such articles and that Parliament could not use the 'notwithstanding procedure' to overturn such decisions. It may be that other rights, such as some of the detailed provisions currently contained in arts 5 and 6 of the European Convention, could also be included in this category.

The second category of rights would include all the remaining articles such as the right to privacy of freedom of expression, association or assembly. The rights in this second group are those which involve clear political conflict between different sets of rights. For instance, issues where the right to privacy clashes with the freedom of expression or information, or where the right to manifest one's beliefs conflicts with respect for, say, cultural diversity. In these cases it is suggested that where Acts of Parliament — rather than subsidiary legislation or administrative measures — are under review the final arbiter should not be the courts but should instead be Parliament, our elected representatives.

The division of rights into two sets and the binding category of the first group of rights is not intended by Liberty to imply that some rights are somehow more fundamental than others but rather that some are more clearly justiciable.

In drawing up its two categories of rights, Liberty is trying to bridge the gap between those who argue that judicial entrenchment of fundamental rights is the only means to enforce rights, and those who argue that such an approach involves an unacceptable transfer of political and policy decisions to unelected judges. We consider that there are rights whose meaning over time has become sufficiently clear and uncontroversial — such as freedom from slavery — that there is virtually no requirement to balance competing policy considerations and the jurisprudence in international human rights law is a sufficient guide for domestic judges in the application of these rights.

On the other hand, with the second set of rights there are certain issues which are likely to remain problematic. The balance between, say, protection from incitement to racial hatred and free speech is likely to remain the subject of debate and, in our view, this is how it should remain. To allow judges the ultimate say and not to allow Parliament any procedure whatsoever to overrule them on these issues is incorrect in our view. It is not so much the rights of politicians that we are concerned with here as the right of individuals and groups to lobby their elected representatives and to allow the political process to have the final say.

Scrutiny by a committee of Parliament

Liberty has also designed a new mechanism specifically to deal with this last category of rights.[46] A new committee of Parliament would be charged with the supervision of all human rights. The role of scrutinising legislation is usually the responsibility of the second chamber but unless and until the latter is democratically constituted we propose that it is a committee of both Houses. We would want to see the committee selected so that it was not dominated by any one political party — perhaps by the use of quotas. We particularly wish to avoid domination of the committee by the party which has formed the government, as is currently the case with select committees.

Liberty has also proposed that the committee would be assisted in its work by a new quango, a human rights commission, to monitor and promote human rights. This commission could assist the committee by submitting reports and expert advice providing some sort of balance against the resources available to the executive who are very likely to want to influence the committee in one particular direction.

The committee could also be given the task of considering new legislation and assessing its compliance with the Bill of Rights. Its role with regard to new laws would, however, be purely advisory.

Its most crucial role would be initiated if primary legislation (or a part of it) had been struck down by the courts for infringing one of the rights contained in the second category. Here the committee could review the legislation and decide whether it considered that it had followed the meaning, intention and spirit of the Bill of Rights. If so, Liberty proposes that it should have the power to certify that Parliament could subsequently re-enact the legislation without needing the 'notwithstanding clause' described above.

---

[46] See *A People's Charter: Liberty's Bill of Rights* (London: National Council for Civil Liberties, 1991) and F. Klug and J. Wadham, 'The "democratic" entrenchment of a Bill of Rights: Liberty's proposals' [1993] PL 579.

The committee would therefore have a role very like that of the Joint Committee on Statutory Instruments, which amongst other things, scrutinises all statutory instruments for compliance with the parent Act.[47]

There are a number of points to note here. First, the proposed committee cannot exercise its powers of review until *after* the courts have done so. Second, the committee is ultimately an advisory body — only Parliament can enact or repeal legislation. The consequence is to subject legislation affecting the rights within the Bill of Rights to scrutiny by the committee whilst at the same time leaving Parliament with the ultimate say.

The primary virtue of the model proposed is that it sets up a system of further checks and balances and does not give complete power to any one part of the constitutional structure. It does, of course, provide a further check on the executive even when it is acting through the medium of the Parliamentary process. It would create a hierarchy of laws giving primacy to the Bill of Rights over ordinary legislation.

The advantage of the democratic enforcement model is that it obviously allows for the introduction of a democratic element to have the final say in cases where there is a clash of rights. This not only avoids giving to the judiciary complete power to interpret the Bill of Rights but also allows democratic processes to have a role in shaping and developing fundamental rights.

One criticism of entrenched Bills of Rights is that they do not involve a procedure whereby Parliament can overturn court rulings to strengthen rights. This is particularly important in cases where rights collide and where the court supports the rights of one group against the rights of another. Liberty's procedure provides a democratic mechanism to deal with this which does not allow the executive, via the party whips, to have exclusive control over it.

It might be asked why Liberty did not go for full entrenchment given that such systems clearly guarantee rights. Apart from the issue of principle about whether all rights should be left for interpretation by judges alone, there is the practical issue of whether the judges, at least

---

[47] See E. C. S. Wade and A. W. Bradley, *Constitutional and Administrative Law*, 11th ed. (London: Longman, 1993), p. 633.

at present are equipped to deal with this increase in their responsibility.[48] The additional danger is that even if it were politically feasible at present, any Bill of Rights implemented in that way would be likely to be very weak since politicians would not wish to cede substantial power to the judges. The best chance of obtaining a Bill of Rights that is likely to give real rights is to provide a system that involves both a democratic and judicial role. In addition, of course, where Bills of Rights are fully entrenched there is always the danger that in difficult circumstances the judges will feel the need to bend the rules because they believe that the circumstances require it. This leads to a devaluation of both the judiciary and the Bill of Rights. There are many examples from the United States but one of the more obvious is the failure of the courts to uphold freedom of speech during the McCarthy era.[49]

Of course, even Liberty's proposals will give the courts significantly more power to control the executive and other public bodies and to strike down primary legislation. For this reason Liberty believes that reform of the selection, appointment and promotion of the judiciary must go hand in hand with these proposals.

Conclusion

The case for Labour to introduce a Bill of Rights is now overwhelming. It is time for the debate to move on to discussing the content and the enforcement process. They both raise very real issues and deserve further discussion and debate.

---

[48] See particularly J. A. G. Griffith, *The Politics of the Judiciary*, 4th ed. (London: Fontana Press, 1991) and K. D. Ewing and C. A. Gearty, *Freedom under Thatcher* (Oxford: Clarendon Press, 1990). Although perhaps there is now a new mood, see most recently *M v Home Office* [1994] 1 AC 377.

[49] *Freedom of Expression* (ACLU Briefing Paper No. 10) (American Civil Liberties Union, 1991).

11

Judicial Review

James Goudie QC, Chair, Society of Labour Lawyers

Judicial review is the process by which the High Court exercises a supervisory jurisdiction over the performance by public bodies of their functions.

There are three main grounds upon which administrative action is subject to judicial control.[1]

The first head of attack by judicial review is 'illegality'. In carrying out any particular function, a public body must direct itself correctly as to the law that governs its performance of that function and must act in accordance with that law. Whether it has done so or not, and whether matters which it has taken into account are relevant considerations or irrelevant ones, is generally a question of statutory interpretation. That, in the event of a dispute, is obviously a matter for judges to determine.

The second basis of challenge is 'irrationality'. The court will intervene if it regards a decision of an authority as so unreasonable that no reasonable authority applying its mind to the question to be decided could have arrived at it.[2] This entails a value judgment, but of a restricted kind.

The third head is 'procedural impropriety'. This covers both failure to observe express procedural rules and failure to act in a fair manner. In inquiring into this issue, the courts are exercising their responsibility

---

[1] *Council of Civil Service Unions* v *Minister for the Civil Service* [1985] AC 374.
[2] *Associated Provincial Picture Houses Ltd* v *Wednesbury Corporation* [1948] 1 KB 223.

to maintain the rule of law and restrain the abuse or excess of public power.

The development of judicial review is to be welcomed. A number of legislative reforms are, however, now called for, concerning matters both of substance and of procedure.

There should be an Administrative Justice Act, to codify and provide for the improvement of administrative justice in general and judicial review in particular.

Such an Act should specify to which bodies, and in respect of which of their activities, the Act will apply. This would clarify which bodies and activities will be subject to judicial review, and subject also to an important duty to give reasons for decisions, at least upon request being made. The abuse of private power should not be beyond the scope of judicial review. For example, a decision by a privatised utility to discontinue provision of a service to a disadvantaged section of the community should be open to challenge.

The Act should also clarify who can apply for judicial review, making clear that interest and pressure groups have sufficient standing.

One important exception from the reach of judicial review should be preserved. Parliament itself should remain sovereign and primary legislation should be incapable of being struck down, save in those circumstances where Parliament expressly cedes sovereignty, under the European Communities Act 1972, or under any Bill of Rights.

Moreover, due regard should be paid to the fact that local authorities consist of representatives elected by the public on a wide franchise for comparatively short periods on the basis of an election manifesto. Local authorities tend to be regarded at present as mere creatures of specific statutes. A varied mix of closely identified duties and powers are devolved to them. Beyond that in general they cannot go. They should be given a power of general competence. This will enable them to provide civic leadership and to act, innovate and integrate on behalf of their local communities. The power of general competence should be subject only to justified prohibitions, limitations, conditions and requirements.

An Administrative Justice Act should set out the (necessarily overlapping) grounds upon which judicial review may be granted, which would be along the following lines:

(a)   failure to perform a statutory duty;

(b)   failure to meet a legitimate expectation, whether of consultation or otherwise;

(c)   in the case of an elected body having a power of general competence, going beyond the area of competence;

(d)   in the case of an unelected body not having a power of general competence, acting in a way that is unauthorised by law;

(e)   acting contrary to an express statutory prohibition;

(f)   failing to satisfy or observe conditions or procedures required by law;

(g)   failing to take account of considerations which are specified by statute or are manifestly relevant;

(h)   taking account of considerations which are excluded by statute or are manifestly irrelevant;

(i)   error of law;

(j)   untenable conclusion of fact;

(k)   impermissible delegation;

(l)   breach of the principles of natural justice, i.e., failure to give a fair hearing or the presence of reasonably avoidable bias;

(m)   irrational exercise of discretion;

(n)   lack of proportionality, especially in cases affecting fundamental human rights;

(o)   unlawful fettering of discretion;

(p)   corrupt or improper purpose;

(q)   fraud, bad faith or abuse of power.

'Relevant considerations' will obviously include both the need for a public service to be provided and the cost of providing it. In striking a balance, however, there should be no undue loading against the former consideration. The so-called 'fiduciary duty' invented in the Poplar wages case and applied in the 'Fairs Fare' case should not be perpetuated.[3]

'Improper purposes' should not include setting out, in what is perceived to be the public interest, to achieve a laudable social objective by a lawful, even if ingenious, mechanism that seeks to order an authority's affairs so as to deploy the financial resources available to it

---

[3] *Roberts v Hopwood* [1925] AC 578; *Bromley London Borough Council v Greater London Council* [1983] 1 AC 768.

to the best advantage. 'Irrelevant considerations' should not include ethical considerations, at least in the case of an elected body having a power of general competence.[4]

An Administrative Justice Act should set out the remedies that the court may grant by way of relief on an application for judicial review and the circumstances in which relief might be refused. Remedies would be along the following lines:

(a)   a quashing order, for quashing unlawful acts;

(b)   a prohibiting order, for prohibiting unlawful acts;

(c)   a mandatory order for requiring performance of a public duty, including a duty to make a decision or determination or to hear and determine any case;

(d)   a declaratory order, including an advisory declaration;

(e)   an injunction, including an interim injunction;

(f)   damages, restitution and interest.

It is important that the courts should have jurisdiction to grant declarations when there is a serious issue of law to be determined as to the scope of the rights, powers or duties of a public body and the issue of law is relevant to the performance of the public body's function. The complexity of modern legislation makes such a jurisdiction highly advantageous. There are situations where there is real doubt about the legal position but where a public body will need to know the meaning of the law in deciding how to carry out its activities. In these instances, it is advantageous for a public body to have the matter resolved in advance, not to act on best advice as to the legal position and possibly subsequently find that its actions are unlawful. It is intolerable, and inconsistent with the constitutional role of the courts to determine matters of law, that legal views on a public body's powers, however wrong, and however damagingly restrictive, expressed by the Audit Commission or an individual accountant should be regarded as being beyond challenge in the courts.

Generally, on questions both of substantive law and of procedure, there should be a predisposition towards convergence between domestic law and EC law. In particular, the Law Commission should be invited

---

[4] See *R* v *Somerset County Council, ex parte Fewings* [1995] 1 WLR 1037.

to give consideration to whether, and, if so, in what circumstances and to what extent, compensation should be available where loss is suffered as a result of wrongful administrative acts or omissions.

In relation to procedure, a Labour government should lose no time in at least implementing the recent Law Commission Report No. 226, and enacting the draft Administration of Justice Bill annexed to it.

12

Freedom of Expression

Geoffrey Bindman, Solicitor, Visiting Professor, University College London

The right of the individual to speak and write freely — to communicate information and opinion without State interference — lies at the heart of a socialism which is democratic and civilised. This broad and fundamental right to freedom of expression embraces a concomitant right without which it is seriously undermined: the right of access to information of public concern. Alongside are other rights which sometimes seem to be in conflict: those which protect privacy and reputation. The task of the law is to provide a framework in which all these rights can be reconciled and safeguarded.

Unhappily, the random growth of the common law has failed to develop that framework. Nor has our domestic law kept in step with our international obligations. Rights to freedom of expression and to privacy are prescribed in the Universal Declaration of Human Rights, the International Covenant on Civil and Political Rights, and the European Convention on Human Rights — all of which are binding on the United Kingdom. Most European countries and the United States have constitutional safeguards for freedom of expression and for privacy. Our international obligations are not reflected in our domestic law.

The lack of a written constitution and of broad enforceable legal principles has often been presented paradoxically by British politicians as a source of pride. Increasingly, however, resistance to international norms is becoming untenable. The arrogant assumption that our legal system is inherently just no longer carries credibility, if it ever did.

Piecemeal development has produced a series of laws which give some protection to basic rights but without a coherent pattern. It is often said that any activity which is not prohibited is lawful. In the absence of specific restrictions deliberately imposed, therefore, it is argued that freedom of expression is automatically guaranteed.

In fact, however, a whole range of restraints on freedom of expression have been allowed to develop without thought to the consequences. Sometimes they can be justified on the ground that an important interest is protected. But does that interest outweigh the public interest in freedom of expression? In the past judges and legislators have failed to pose that vital question before sanctioning further limitations.

Since 1950 the right way to put the question has been clear. The United Kingdom then signed the European Convention on Human Rights, art. 10 of which says:

(1) Everyone has the right to freedom of expression. This right shall include freedom to hold opinions and to receive and impart information and ideas without interference by public authority and regardless of frontiers. This article shall not prevent States from requiring the licensing of broadcasting, television or cinema enterprises.

(2) The exercise of these freedoms, since it carries with it duties and responsibilities, may be subject to such formalities, conditions, restrictions or penalties as are prescribed by law and are necessary in a democratic society in the interests of national security, territorial integrity or public safety, for the prevention of disorder or crime, for the protection of health or morals, for the protection of the reputation or rights of others, for preventing the disclosure of information received in confidence, or for maintaining the authority and impartiality of the judiciary.

'Necessary' means that there must be a pressing social need for the exception from the general principle; any interference with either right must be proportionate to the satisfaction of the social need in question;

and the exception must be justified by reasons which are both 'relevant and sufficient'.[1]

No mechanism yet exists for bringing our domestic law into line with these guiding principles. That will be a task for the new government, which is already committed to incorporating the European Convention into domestic law. Incorporation alone will not be sufficient, however. It will be necessary to examine all the areas of law in which freedom of expression is curtailed in order to ensure that they are brought into line with the standards laid down in art. 10. This chapter does not claim to perform this task. Rather, it concentrates on the two main areas in which restrictions on freedom of expression are commonly thought to be justified: the protection of reputation and the protection of privacy.

Defamation

Protection of reputation is a limitation on freedom of expression recognised by art. 10, but the law of defamation (embracing libel and slander), which exists for this purpose, is a mess. Its major characteristics have remained unchanged since the aftermath of the French Revolution, when, in both its civil and criminal versions, it was the means used by those in power to suppress the propagation of democratic ideas. Tom Paine was an early victim. Libel law is still frequently used to suppress publication of information which the public ought to know. The late Robert Maxwell made effective use of it to advance his fraudulent schemes.

Liability for defamation is absolute. It makes no difference that those involved in communicating libellous statements have done so honestly believing them to be true, or even that they do not know what they are communicating. Hence the *printers* and *distributors* of the *New Statesman* paid damages and legal costs to John Major and Clare Latimer for their 'publication' of an article in the magazine (which had to reimburse them) although the magazine itself continued to deny liability.

Leaving aside the unusual cases where special privileges arise, a defendant in a libel action can only succeed by proving that the published facts are true (a presumption of guilt) or by persuading the

---

[1] *Observer and Guardian* v *United Kingdom* (1992) 14 EHRR 153.

court that what is published is fair comment based on true facts and on a matter of public interest. Nor does the plaintiff have to prove any loss. Good reputation is presumed and the defendant is not allowed to call evidence to the contrary. A jury trial, which either party may choose, adds to cost and uncertainty. The jury must answer abstruse and ill-defined questions with minimal guidance.

Ironically, the imbalance in favour of plaintiffs is mitigated by the exclusion of defamation from the legal aid scheme. But this compounds the injustice of a system in which the cost of litigation, and often the result, is to a large extent dictated by the wealthier party. Only the rich or the exceptionally confident can risk suing for libel or defending a libel action. It is true that there have been some recent improvements, fuelled by public disquiet. In December 1992 the government announced that a number of technical changes would be introduced to speed up and simplify cases. These changes were not implemented until September 1994. They make the parties to a libel action put their claims more clearly and fully on paper at an earlier stage, thus promoting speedier settlements and saving costs. But the most important reform promised in 1992 was omitted: a proposal by Lord Hoffmann for a simplified procedure without a jury, in which the judge could award up to £5,000 damages and order publication of a correction and apology.

In July 1995 the Lord Chancellor issued a consultation paper annexing a draft Bill to amend the law of defamation.[2] A proposal similar to Lord Hoffmann's is included, with the maximum damages figure raised to £10,000. However, the simplified procedure would only be available in very clear cases (which even under present rules are usually compromised at an early stage), and a defendant able to put forward an arguable defence would still be entitled to a full-scale jury trial. Nevertheless, there are wealthy media organisations which reject obviously valid but modest libel claims because they judge that the victim cannot afford the financial risk of a trial. The summary procedure will alleviate that problem.

Other proposed reforms would remove obvious anomalies and could speed up the legal process. The defence of 'innocent dissemination' would be extended. Printers, distributors and sellers of publications

---

[2] 'Reforming Defamation Law and Procedure — Consultation on Draft Bill' (Lord Chancellor's Department, July 1995).

containing defamatory statements could find it easier to escape liability. (If the change had been made before 1993, John Major and Clare Latimer could have been denied their handsome payouts from the distributors of the New Statesman.) But, as proposed, those claiming to escape liability, rather than the plaintiff, would still have the burden of proving that they had no reason to suspect their involvement in a defamatory publication.

Another recommendation is to shorten the limitation period, within which an action must be started after the defamatory publication, from three years to one year. This would cut out some stale cases and put pressure on complainants to act promptly. The impact would be marginal, however, because the vast majority of current cases are already started well within a year.

Another current anomaly is the inadmissibility of evidence attacking the plaintiff's reputation (the rule in *Scott* v *Sampson*). This has long been criticised and has led to unmerited awards. Under the new proposals the defendant would be entitled to rely on evidence diminishing the plaintiff's reputation.

These proposals, if implemented, will shift the balance of defamation law in the right direction: extending freedom of expression and at the same time helping the plaintiff with limited resources to pursue a case if it is a strong one.

Yet they fall far short of the fundamental re-appraisal which is needed, and they will raise new areas of dispute which could lead to more litigation. The only satisfactory way forward is to scrap the present law of defamation and start afresh.

Privacy

The most important area in which limits on freedom of expression can be justified — and in which the current law is widely criticised — is privacy. Like freedom of expression itself, privacy is explicitly protected by the European Human Rights Convention.

Article 8(1) states: 'Everyone has the right to respect for his private and family life, his home and his correspondence'. This general principle is subject to such exceptions as the law of each member State may decide *but* — as in art. 10 — exceptions will be valid only if they are prescribed by law and are 'necessary in a democratic society'. In short, exceptions will be strictly limited. The test is the same as under art. 10.

There is no general law in the United Kingdom which protects privacy. Nevertheless, there are several discrete laws which protect privacy in many situations.

For example, entering another person's house or land without permission, or remaining after permission has been withdrawn, is trespass, a tort for which an action for damages can be brought.

Under the controversial Criminal Justice and Public Order Act 1994, trespass can be a crime when allied to intimidation or obstruction.[3] Other intrusions on occupation of premises, such as noise disturbance, may likewise be the tort of nuisance.

Recently, the courts have shown an inclination to extend the scope of nuisance to cover cases where no property right is involved. In 1993 the Court of Appeal granted an injunction to stop someone being pestered with telephone calls.[4] She was not the occupier of the house to which the calls were being made — it belonged to her mother — but the court sensibly ruled that it would be ridiculous to deprive her of a remedy which the law would have given to the occupier without question.

Furthermore, harassment resulting from the use of threatening, abusive or insulting words or behaviour can now be a criminal offence under the same 1994 Act.[5] Probably a civil action could also be brought for a breach or threatened breach of this section.

Other legal remedies are available to protect the disclosure of confidential information. A civil action can be brought to prevent or (if it is too late to stop it) recover damages for breach of confidence. This type of action is more common and more highly developed when the object is to protect commercial confidentiality, but it has been applied to other cases, for example, to protect the disclosure of hospital records to the detriment of the patient.[6]

The publication of *false* information about a person may also, of course, justify an action for defamation or malicious falsehood.

These various laws very nearly add up to sufficient protection of privacy to comply with the European Human Rights Convention. There

---

[3] Section 68.
[4] *Khorasandjian* v *Bush* [1993] QB 727.
[5] Section 154.
[6] *X* v *Y* [1988] 2 All ER 648.

144

are loopholes — the publication of truthful and non-confidential information is lawful, however personal and embarrassing, but should the protection of such information override freedom of expression?

There is a good case for rationalising the existing law, but governments have shrunk from systematic reform. The main reason is the tension between the right to privacy and the right to freedom of expression. Article 8 must be reconciled with Article 10.

Understandably, the media have resisted blanket attempts to curtail their freedom to publish what they think fit, whether in the name of privacy or protection of reputation. The media have a vital, virtually constitutional, role ('the Fourth Estate') in discovering and publishing information for the benefit of the public. That vital role as the watchdog of the public has received judicial recognition in the English courts, as well as in the European Court of Human Rights.[7] Any restriction on their freedom must be justified to the hilt. But the Convention does not give freedom of expression precedence over privacy.

In the last few years a number of reports have attempted to grapple with the problem of reconciling the two rights. They have failed to tackle the problem as a whole; in most cases they have been commissioned hastily in response to revelations which have hit the headlines — often involving the royal family.

Thus the Calcutt Committee, appointed to consider what measures were needed to give further protection to individual privacy from the activities of the press, began its report in June 1990 with the following explanation:

> During the two years or so before our appointment, there were a number of striking instances in which sections of the press had been severely criticised for intruding upon accident victims and other victims in hospital, for using stolen private correspondence or photographs and for publishing scurrilous (and sometimes false) details of individuals' private lives. The climax was a one-million pound out-of-court libel settlement following stories in the *Sun* about Elton John's private life.

---

[7] *R* v *Felixstowe Justices, ex parte Leigh* [1987] QB 582; *Holy Monasteries* v *Greece* (1994) 20 EHRR 1.

Most if not all these examples involved a breach of existing law. The Elton John case was a libel claim and outside the committee's brief. Nor can the hugely wealthy pop star be seriously presented as an inadequately protected victim.

The Calcutt Committee recommended a new Press Complaints Commission, to provide a more powerful form of voluntary self-regulation than the much-criticised Press Council. It thought that a new tort remedy for infringement of privacy was viable and proposed a range of new criminal offences to prohibit the more blatant forms of physical intrusion not already criminal. The latter included placing surveillance devices on private property with a view to obtaining personal information, and photographing or recording a person on private property. The criminal offences were to be subject to a broad public-interest defence and prosecutions could only be initiated with the consent of the Director of Public Prosecutions. However, implementation of these changes, and the appointment of a statutory press tribunal, should only occur if the PCC proved ineffective.

The PCC duly came into being, and two years later the government asked Sir David Calcutt personally to review its effectiveness. He reported in January 1993 that he was not satisfied: he did not consider it an effective regulator; it did not command the confidence of the press or the public; it did not hold a fair balance between press and individual; nor was it truly independent.

It followed that the Calcutt Committee recommendations should — in Calcutt's opinion — now be implemented, and the introduction of a civil remedy seriously considered.

Two months later the National Heritage Select Committee of the House of Commons published its recommendations. It preferred strengthened voluntary regulation to a statutory tribunal, adding an 'ombudsman' to a more powerful PCC. However, its conclusions coincided with those of Calcutt in accepting the argument for new crimes aimed at invasive use of technology. It went further by imaginatively suggesting the resurrection of the Conspiracy and Protection of Property Act 1875 — originally a weapon against picketing trade unionists and long fallen into disuse — in order to criminalise doorstepping reporters.

More progressively, and unlike Calcutt, it tried to relate its proposals to the broad and fundamental right of freedom of expression. Any greater protection of privacy should be accompanied by freedom of information legislation. Nor should any restrictions be directed exclusively against the media.

In July 1993, the Lord Chancellor published a review of the current law in a consultation paper, *Infringement of Privacy*. Though presented as a consultation document it leaned heavily in favour of creating a new tort remedy against infringements. For this purpose privacy of a person would be defined to include 'matters appertaining to his health, personal communications, and family and personal relationships, and a right to be free from harassment and molestation'. Defences to a legal action would be 'consent, lawful authority, absolute or qualified privilege'. The remedies available would be an award of damages and an injunction to restrain violation or its repetition.

Perhaps unsurprisingly, in the light of his wider cost-cutting mission, the Lord Chancellor's paper suggested that legal aid might not be appropriate. But there is no rational basis for treating the new remedy differently from the civil remedies described earlier, all of which qualify for legal aid. The parallel relied on is the exclusion of defamation actions from the legal aid scheme. But this anomaly, which equally lacks justification, has been repeatedly criticised, not least by the Lord Chancellor's own Advisory Committee on Legal Aid and a working party in his own department which published a thorough study of the question as long ago as 1975. The recommendation to extend legal aid to defamation cases was repeated by the Royal Commission on Legal Services in 1979 but, in an increasingly cold climate for legal aid, has never been implemented.

To introduce a civil action for infringement of privacy without access to legal aid would not merely add another anomaly to the denial of legal aid for defamation. It would effectively restrict the remedy to those who are least likely to deserve or need it, the politicians and public figures with the means to litigate at their own expense. A defence of public interest would no doubt be available against such persons, but the scope of such a defence is uncertain and there is a serious danger that the risk of failure would deter the publication of genuinely important information.

Those who court the media ought fairly to accept the rough of notoriety with the smooth. Just as in the United States — and increasingly in other common law countries such as Canada and India — the privacy and reputation of public figures, as distinct from those in whose activities no legitimate public interest can be justified, are legally

147

protected only against reckless or malicious attacks. It is important that in Britain any legal reform should recognise a similar distinction. Moreover, it is not a necessary restriction on the right of free expression to require the media to prove in each instance a public interest in publishing information about a public figure, especially a government official or politician. Because the burden of proof rests with the defendant who seeks to exercise freedom of expression, the public interest defence itself detracts from that freedom.

In summary, while there is a strong case for re-conceptualising the law to safeguard both freedom of expression and privacy, in line with the European Convention on Human Rights, the need for any significantly broader legal protection for privacy does not seem a pressing one. Decent and professional behaviour by those who work in the media should obviously be insisted upon. The Press Complaints Commission on which the media organisations themselves are heavily represented has acquired wider powers (including its own ombudsman) and — no doubt under threat of legislation — is being treated with greater respect by the tabloid newspapers who have been most criticised. While the statutory guidelines under the Broadcasting Act 1990 and increased vigilance by the PCC do not guarantee good behaviour, the heavy-handed intervention of the law is not a solution either.

After the plethora of official reports and enquiries the government itself now seems to have accepted the view that no new legal protection for privacy is needed. In July 1995, it produced a belated response to the National Heritage Select Committee's report of March 1993.[8] At the same time it commented on the Lord Chancellor's consultation on a tort of infringement of privacy.

While supporting the strengthening of the role of the Press Complaints Commission it rejected the proposal for a statutory Press Ombudsman. It also rejected the new criminal offences proposed by Calcutt and the Select Committee on the ground that:

> they would either prevent responsible journalism or — in anxiety to protect the interests of the responsible journalist — create defences that were so wide as to render the offences meaningless.[9]

---

[8] 'Privacy and Media Intrusion — The Government's Response' (HMSO, Cm. 2918, July 1995).
[9] *Op. cit.* p. 13.

The proposal for a new civil action for invasion of privacy was also rejected, apparently because there was no consensus in its favour from those who responded to the Lord Chancellor's consultation paper. The government was clearly unwilling to contemplate enlarging the legal aid budget to accommodate it. Without legal aid it would benefit only the rich.

Though right to reject arguments for new legal controls on the Press, the government's response reflects indecision and fear of upsetting its supporters rather than a principled desire to reconcile the right of privacy with the right to freedom of expression. The task of delivering a coherent legal framework consistent with international human rights obligations in this field is plainly beyond the capacity of a Tory government.

Freedom of information

The National Heritage Select Committee was right to link its recommendations on the protection of privacy to the need for greater access to government-held information, and information of public concern held by other authorities. Mark Fisher MP introduced a Right to Know Bill in February 1993 which would have given the right to any member of the public to see any records held by any public authority. To help applicants authorities would have had to provide indexes showing what records they hold. Documents containing personal information would have been made available free of charge apart from photocopying costs. Some categories of information would inevitably have been exempt from disclosure, on grounds such as national security, personal privacy or law enforcement, but a claim to exemption could have been challenged before an independent commissioner and a tribunal having power to overrule the authority.

The Tory government rejected this reasonable and long overdue measure, which would have given the people of Britain similar access to information collected in their name as is given to the people of the United States and other democratic countries. Instead it issued a White Paper promising concessions substantially weaker than the rights proposed by Mark Fisher. A right to see personal files was offered, and access to information about health and safety, to be modelled on the right to environmental information granted under pressure from

Brussels. The Code of Practice issued in April 1994 to give effect to the White Paper purports to give a right to information but it does not do so. A Code of Practice cannot confer rights because it has no legal force and there is no effective sanction for its breach. The Code of Practice on Access to Government information provides for release of factual information on payment of a standard fee (£10 for each piece of information) but it is a fundamental weakness that only *information* can be required — not a copy of an actual document. The public authority itself controls the form in which the information is disclosed, allowing it a freedom to paraphrase or interpret the original material in ways which may create a wholly misleading or distorted impression.

Furthermore, the only means of challenging a refusal to disclose information is a complaint to the Ombudsman, who cannot carry out a proper investigation without the cooperation of the government or the relevant department. In the one case up to March 1995 in which the Ombudsman attempted to investigate a complaint (against the Lord Chancellor's Department) the Department blocked it by refusing to let the Ombudsman see the report which the complainant was seeking to have disclosed.

The point has already been made that access to information is an integral element in the democratic right to freedom of expression. It is especially important to facilitate the essential role of the press as the public's watchdog, a role which it cannot perform effectively if its power to gather and disseminate information is arbitrarily curtailed.

There is, of course, an important countervailing need to protect those who choose to keep out of the public arena and whose activities are not a matter of public interest. But the difficult task of drawing a line round such people should not be allowed to undermine the essential value of freedom of expression. That is why a new comprehensive code implementing the principles in the Convention, embracing freedom of expression and freedom of information, and coupled with the necessary safeguards for privacy and reputation, is the best way forward. What we certainly do not need is more of the piecemeal tinkering which has typified recent proposals from government sources.

Such a statutory code could regulate all the other restrictions on freedom of expression embodied in current law. Obscenity and blasphemy rarely give rise to prosecutions and it cannot be claimed that the reform of the law on these topics is a high priority. Nevertheless the law in these as in all matters involving freedom of expression needs to be brought within the conceptual framework imposed by the European Convention. Another restraint which sometimes arouses controversy is incitement to racial hatred. The provisions of the Public Order Act 1986 and of the Criminal Justice and Public Order Act 1994 which deal with this subject are open to criticism more for being too weak than for infringing freedom of expression. Problems arise over national security, official secrets, and the use of confidential information in commercial and other contexts. These also need to be reviewed against the same background of principle.

Creating a rational and workable framework, in which freedom of expression can be fully protected while at the same time all competing interests are duly acknowledged, is a complex and challenging task which the next Labour government must — in contrast with the vacillations of the Tories — tackle with decisiveness and vigour.

13

Discrimination Law: Towards a Principle of Equality

Rabinder Singh

Introduction

When *Law Reform Now* was published over 30 years ago, it contained no chapter on discrimination law. There was no such concept in the common law, although a few haphazard steps had been taken in that direction through other means: see, e.g., *Constantine* v *Imperial Hotels Ltd* [1944] KB 693. That is not to say that discrimination was not a problem at that time. Racial prejudice was openly expressed and practised. Women were paid much less than men for the same job. Homosexual acts between consenting adults in private were still offences under the criminal law. But change was on its way and those who were committed to equality in society found that their cause was an international one, as the civil rights movement and the women's liberation movement grew stronger in the 1960s and 1970s.

The campaigns against discrimination, in particular racial and sex discrimination, bore fruit when the Labour Party was in power in the 1960s and 1970s. The Labour Party can rightly be proud of its initiatives in enacting legislation in those fields. The Race Relations Act 1976 (which followed earlier, more diluted legislation in 1965 and 1968) together with the Equal Pay Act 1970 and the Sex Discrimination Act 1975 remain the foundation of discrimination law in this country. The Conservatives have not amended the legislation in substance, except in response to pressures emanating from the European Court of Justice, which led, for example, to the Equal Pay (Amendment) Regulations 1983 (SI 1983/1794), which provide for equal pay for work of equal value.

The British legislation built upon the experience of the US Civil Rights Act 1964. In particular it introduced the two concepts of direct discrimination and indirect discrimination into this country's law, although those phrases are not used in the legislation itself.

The Labour Party cannot, however, afford to be complacent. There have been episodes in its own history when it has failed to live up to its own ideals of equality. For instance, the Commonwealth Immigrants Act 1968 was condemned by the European Commission of Human Rights as being expressly motivated by a racist purpose: see *East African Asian Cases* (1981) 3 EHRR 76. The Commission reached that conclusion after referring to what was said in Parliament at the time that the Act was passed.

Towards a principle of equality

The task now is to look forward. It is to devise practical reforms that are both true to the enduring values of the Party and attainable. The theme of this chapter is that the long-term project should be to move from the first stage of discrimination law, whereby specific acts done in specific circumstances are prohibited, to a general principle of equality in our society. There are general statements of equality or its correlative, a general principle of non-discrimination, to be found in various international treaties and declarations: see, e.g., art. 7 of the Universal Declaration of Human Rights and art. 14 of the European Convention on Human Rights. Article 26 of the International Covenant on Civil and Political Rights, which the United Kingdom has ratified but not enacted into domestic law, could provide the model for a general statement of the principle of equality. It provides that:

All persons are equal before the law and are entitled without any discrimination to the equal protection of the law. In this respect, the law shall prohibit any discrimination and guarantee to all persons equal and effective protection against discrimination *on any ground such as* race, colour, sex, language, religion, political or other

153

opinion, national or social origin, property, birth *or other status*. (Emphasis added.)

The Labour Party is nothing if it is not about equality. The principle of equality, though it could be debated at length, embraces at least the core idea that human beings are entitled to be judged on their merits and not by reference to some criterion which has no impact on their merits. As it is put in the jurisprudence of various jurisdictions overseas, similar situations should be treated in the same way and dissimilar situations should not be dealt with in the same way.

The principle of equality is not simply moral and fair, though it is both of those things and for that reason alone should commend itself to a radical party. It is also efficient. Whenever a decision is made that is based on irrelevant characteristics, such as a person's sex or ethnic origin, the market place is impeded from functioning as efficiently as it would if the decision were based on purely rational considerations. Labour can, therefore, proudly march forward in the knowledge that equality is both fair and efficient.

But to state a political ideal is one thing. To translate it into action through law is another. And lawyers should be humble in this, as in other contexts. Radical change in society is not necessarily going to come about through the law. But, at the same time, there are practical reforms that could help on the way. Again, in tune with the themes of New Labour, they are reforms which are attainable and practical.

The next Labour government should try to bridge the gap between what has been achieved so far, in the form of laws prohibiting discrimination in certain circumstances, and a general principle of equality through a programme of both short-term and long-term reforms. The precise contents of such reforms could again be debated at length. The government should listen to the Commission for Racial Equality and the Equal Opportunities Commission, for their expertise and experience in these fields are second to none. Too often they have spoken in vain about the need to improve the existing legislation and the means for its enforcement. In what follows I set out a personal 10-point programme for action: five reforms could be implemented in the short term, the other five in the long term. At least the first five should be part of what can realistically be achieved in one Parliament. The others may have to wait longer.

Short-term reforms

First, the powers of the EOC and CRE should be extended. At the moment they have limited abilities to take action themselves. They may, for example, issue non-discrimination notices and they may have standing to bring judicial review proceedings. But they need to be given the right to bring actions in their own names where, for example, they have evidence of systematic discrimination in areas of social life. One of the important areas in which the discrimination legislation has been regularly invoked is the field of employment. But there is a tendency among lawyers to regard discrimination law as a part of employment law only. In fact there are other important areas of social life, such as housing, education, and the provision of services such as insurance, where practices have gone unquestioned without having the sunshine of the law shed upon them. It is in such fields, as well as in the employment field, that the EOC and the CRE could use their expertise and resources to full advantage by bringing actions in their own right.

Traditionally discrimination law has tried to remedy social injustice which affects groups through a legal system that requires individual victims to complain of particular acts of discrimination. Even the concept of indirect discrimination has gone only part of the way in squaring this circle, because it still requires individuals with standing to complain of a particular condition or requirement applied to them. The EOC and CRE could bring actions to tackle wholesale discriminatory practices and so benefit many people at one go: they could help to bring about the long-term goal of discrimination law, which is not just to remedy injustice done to individuals, but to achieve equality of opportunity for all, including those that may have not yet even reached the stage of applying for a job.

Secondly, the burden of proof in discrimination cases should be shifted to respondents/defendants where the applicant/plaintiff has shown a prima facie case of less favourable treatment (the current definition of direct discrimination). It is notoriously difficult to prove that an act was done on the ground of a person's sex or race. It is easier for a respondent or defendant to prove that it was not. If there is insufficient evidence, objectively considered, to justify the inference that the less favourable treatment was not meted out on the discriminatory ground in question, the case should succeed. So long as the applicant or plaintiff bears the legal burden of proof, and in spite of some mitigation of the problem by the tribunals and courts, there is a risk that injustice will go unremedied even though an employer (for example) could not show that the refusal to employ someone was not based on that person's sex or race.

Thirdly, the training of tribunal members and circuit judges in discrimination matters should be improved. To some extent improvements have already taken place, especially in the tribunals. But there remains a need for specialists to be appointed and used regularly so that a corps of experts in discrimination law can be established. This might in due course develop into a human rights tribunal (a long-term reform which is suggested below).

Fourthly, the aim should be to provide comprehensive legal services for those who claim to have suffered discrimination. At present it is possible to obtain limited help from the EOC or CRE. But they understandably tend to back the cases that raise some general point of importance: this is not necessarily of great comfort to the individual victim of injustice. There is also some limited assistance available from law centres and the Free Representation Unit. But an incomplete system of representation is unacceptable in such an important area of social life. The CRE has called for some time for legal aid to be extended to discrimination cases: see its *Second Review of the Race Relations Act 1976* (1991). But, given the concerns that New Labour has about public expenditure generally and the size of the legal aid budget in particular, other means such as a community legal service may have to be used if one is serious about achieving realistic reform.

Fifthly, the law should permit awards of exemplary damages to be made in suitable discrimination cases. At the moment, quite apart from the general attitude of English courts that punishment is an anomalous function of civil law, whose primary purpose is compensation, it is in law impossible to award exemplary damages in racial discrimination cases: see *Deane* v *Ealing London Borough Council* [1993] ICR 329. This has now been accepted as being true also in the context of sex discrimination law, although the issue of whether claims made directly under the Equal Treatment Directive (Directive 76/207/EEC) may include claims for exemplary damages has yet to be resolved beyond the level of the Employment Appeal Tribunal: see *Ministry of Defence* v *Meredith* [1995] IRLR 539. The current state of the law fails to recognise that, if the law is to make a serious impact on the disparity of treatment that is evident between groups in society, it must take all effective measures to do so. The experience of countries like the USA and common sense suggest that, when an award of exemplary damages is made, it tends to concentrate the mind and is likely to have a greater deterrent effect than merely compensating the particular victim. In an extreme case, a well-qualified applicant who has been refused a job on discriminatory grounds may have suffered little or no financial loss because another job can be obtained elsewhere, yet the case may reveal the most heinous discrimination which, if uncorrected, will prejudice others in the future.

Long-term reforms

In the long term there should be a twin-track strategy. First, there should be created a constitutional right to equality: this should be part of Labour's Bill of Rights. In the short term the Party is committed to enacting the European Convention on Human Rights into domestic law. However, laudable as that policy is, it will not help in the context of discrimination. This is because art. 14 of the Convention is not a free-standing provision. The article only operates in conjunction with some other right in the Convention. As mentioned above, a provision such as art. 26 of the International Covenant on Civil and Political Rights would be a more apt model.

Secondly, there should be created a statutory right to equality, which would prohibit all kinds of arbitrary discrimination, e.g., on grounds of sexual orientation, religion, disability or any other status. There should be a general Civil Rights Act for this country, which would bind private entities and individuals, in tandem with the constitutional right to equality which is likely, on the experience of other jurisdictions, to bind only the State.

Thirdly, there should be established a human rights commission to implement the above equality rights. This could be an umbrella organisation that would embrace the CRE and the EOC, or it could be a separate organisation that would deal with types of discrimination, such as that against gay people, not already covered by other organisations. Its particular virtue would be that it could evolve the concept of equality. As social norms change, it could through test cases

157

bring the law of equality to bear upon new kinds of discrimination, for example, on the ground of age or the ground that someone has HIV.

Fourthly, there should be established a human rights tribunal to deal with all equality cases, not just those dealing with employment matters. The specialist corps of judges and tribunal members could be entrusted with cases from all fields, such as education and housing as well as employment, and all types of discrimination. Its exact composition and status can be debated in due course but it should probably have High Court judges or the equivalent on it, as well as lay members, and be similar to the Employment Appeal Tribunal.

Finally, perhaps most importantly, this country should take the initiative in Europe, both in the European Union and in the Council of Europe, in matters of equality. It should work in partnership with others to enact European legislation on equality which goes beyond issues of sex discrimination (see art. 119 of the EC Treaty and the various equal treatment Directives) or a narrow class of discrimination on the ground of nationality (see, e.g., art. 48 of the EC Treaty). This country, in part thanks to the efforts of past Labour governments, has more progressive laws against racial discrimination than most European countries. The Labour Party in power should build on that record to promote the cause of equality throughout Europe.

Conclusions

The next Labour government should adopt a 10-point programme of short-term and long-term reforms which should assist in the task of moving this country's law from a set of particular prohibitions of discrimination to a general principle of equality. Through that process it will help to achieve fairness and efficiency in society.

14

Immigration Law

Keith Vaz MP and Maria Fernandes

Current immigration policy claims to be 'firm but fair'. The reality is that it is racist, sexist and steeped in unfairness. Despite the emphasis on family values the rules separate husband from wife; despite claims by the government to be champions of democracy, detention is routinely used as a means of deterring applications by asylum seekers; despite talk about the Citizens Charter and promises to reduce delays and introduce more openness, administrative delays running into years at British missions in India, Pakistan and Bangladesh are commonplace as a means of maintaining quotas. And as for 'openness' the Home Office have a body of rules which are unpublished and therefore not open knowledge to those who do not practise immigration law, and because they are concessions are deliberately kept outside the scrutiny of the courts and tribunals. Furthermore, secret instructions given to officials on how to interpret the rules are not always consistent with the rules themselves. Over the past 14 years, the independent review of the decision-making process has gradually been eroded leaving the immigration authorities less and less accountable for their actions. It is against this background that reform should be approached. This chapter will look at a number of areas which require immediate reform. It has to be said at the outset that there has to be a major shift in the way in which immigration is perceived in order to introduce policy changes. The policy has to be positive without losing the element of control. A responsible government must ensure that immigrants are not used as scapegoats.

Visitors

Independent review of decisions

Since the right of appeal for visitors refused entry was removed in 1993 there is no effective means of challenging decisions of entry clearance officers abroad. While the appeal system existed around 40 per cent were successful. (It has to be remembered that many did not exercise a right of appeal because the event that they were coming to attend, for example a wedding, had passed.) The percentage of successful appeals suggests that there was a serious flaw in the decision-making process. In these circumstances rights of appeal should never have been removed and should be restored. In any event, when MPs intervene in such cases they should be provided with a detailed explanatory statement, rather like that prepared for appeal hearings, instead of the cursory reasons currently provided. As to the government's concession of an independent monitor to act as a check on the decision-making process, although it is useful as a check on the powers of immigration officers as a whole, it is totally inadequate as a remedy. The monitor (who incidentally is appointed and paid by the government) does not investigate individual claims or reverse decisions. Furthermore he or she is largely provided with one version of events, that of the officer who refused the application.

Family visits

To promote good race relations it is important to recognise that many persons from the ethnic minorities have parents and grandparents who are settled abroad but who would like to visit their family. Rather than this being viewed as a reason for refusing entry there should be specific recognition of the right of such family members to visit and they should be allowed longer periods of stay than ordinary visitors.

Family reunion

A right to family life is enshrined in international law. Any State which denies, divides or otherwise interferes with the family cannot claim to be democratic.

Primary purpose

This rule is by far the most outrageous and blatant example of a government seeking at any cost to restrict the entry of immigrants from non-white Commonwealth countries. It is a classic case of the State interfering and discouraging the continuity of the cultural traditions of communities that arrange marriages. There is no equivalent rule in any European country or indeed in any of the developed countries. The applicant must prove a negative fact, that the 'primary purpose' or main motive of the marriage is *not* to gain admission to the UK. It is left to an officer abroad to decide what the main motive of a perfectly genuine marriage is. Therefore the results are totally inconsistent. The rule in effect restricts the right of a person to choose their partner. How can a government possibly claim to promote race relations whilst this rule continues to blight the lives of so many? It is morally indefensible and has no place in a civilised society. It should be abolished immediately.

It is also questionable whether the current system of granting a probationary period of 12 months is necessary. Once it is accepted that a marriage is genuine there should be no need for the probationary period. There would be an outcry if a condition such as this was placed on the public at large in other areas. The probationary year is used by the unscrupulous few to exert control over the foreign spouse (usually a woman) who may risk life and limb to remain in a marriage which is violent rather than face returning to a society which would regard her as an outcast. Once a marriage is accepted as genuine that should be the end of the matter.

Same-sex relationships

The right to family life should not be confined merely to heterosexual couples. At present couples who cohabit can qualify for entry under a well-known policy providing they can prove that they are involved in a stable relationship. This policy does not extend to same-sex relationships. There is no reason for distinguishing the unmarried couple from the same-sex couple. The immigration rules should make specific provision for both. It is discriminatory to do otherwise.

161

Detention

The right to liberty is a fundamental right under national as well as international law. Immigration detention is permitted by international standards for some reasons, for example, to stop illegal entry, to establish the identity of asylum seekers or for reasons of national security. Over the past few years the use of detention has increased significantly. There is evidence to suggest that it is being used as a means of deterring asylum seekers from applying to remain here. The majority of those detained are not convicted of any crime. They are detained under administrative powers and have no right to apply for bail. There are no time limits on how long they can be detained and there is no independent body to scrutinise the use of detention. The law permits the authorities to lock them up and throw away the key. The policy and practice of immigration detention should undergo a complete and thorough review. Detention should only be used as a last resort and only where there is a risk that the person will abscond. Any decision should be accompanied by written reasons for the decision in a language understood by the individual. Decisions to detain must automatically be subject to independent and regular review. All detainees should have a right to apply for bail. There is a case for having a set of rules rather like the PACE rules in criminal law.

Asylum

The UK fails dismally in this area. It does not comply with the obligations laid down by the UN Convention and Protocol (of which we are signatories) but merely pays lip-service to them. In addition to concerns about the use of detention to deter asylum seekers from applying for asylum, there is a need to improve the asylum seeker's access to the appeal system. Furthermore the extreme speed of the process militates against a case being properly prepared by the appellant or the appellant's advisers. There is also need to consider extending legal aid to advisers to bring appeals as the current advice centres are overstretched. This will ensure that asylum seekers are granted a fair opportunity to present their case before tribunals.

In November 1995 a number of new measures were announced. Firstly the Social Security Secretary has announced that state benefit is to be denied to two categories of people:

(a)   Those seeking asylum in this country after having passed through a port of entry. Around 70 per cent of applications for asylum are made after entry usually within a week of arrival. Most asylum seekers do not make applications at ports of entry for many reasons. Many do not speak the language, are mistrustful of those in authority and many are still traumatised by the torture they may have suffered abroad.

(b)   Those whose applications are refused by the Home Office. They have a right of appeal. Giving them a legal right whilst removing their right to economic support makes the exercise of the right superficial.

Secondly, the Secretary of State for the Environment is to restrict housing entitlement broadly in line with the benefit restrictions.

Thirdly, the Home Secretary is to introduce a Bill on asylum and immigration to, he claims, curb the rising tread of bogus asylum applications. There is a presumption that the rise in applications is due to bogus applications rather than a reflection of world upheavals. The Bill proposes that:

(a)   There is to be a 'white' list of countries which do not give rise to a serious risk of persecution. Although assurances have been given that Nigeria is not to be on the list, only one application for asylum has succeeded from this country. There is a danger that where there are vast numbers of applications from a particular country it can be added to the 'white list'.

(b)   Appeals against return to safe third countries will only be exercisable after removal. Therefore applicants arguing that a country is not a safe country will nevertheless be removed there.

(c)   The accelerated appeal procedure, a much criticised procedure, is to be extended to a wider category of cases.

(d)   Employer sanctions are to be introduced. There are serious concerns that employers will not employ ethnic minorities for fear of falling foul of the law.

The Asylum and Immigration Act 1993 was passed to address the same issues. It is surprising that it is necessary to introduce another Bill so soon and it can only be concluded from this that the government is playing the race card. It is worth bearing in mind the words of Andrew Lansley, then the Conservative Director of Research:

Immigration, an issue we raised successfully in 1992 and again in the 1994 election, played particularly well in the tabloids and has more potential to hurt. (*The Observer*, 3 September 1994.)

What is equally worrying is that the government is trying to save money wherever possible and is selecting the most vulnerable group with total disregard for human rights.

Unpublished rules

Alongside published rules there is a body of unpublished rules which, although they are well-known, have not been incorporated into the rules. This means that there is no right of appeal against refusal. There is no reason why there should be this two-tier system.

Of particular concern is the special voucher system for British overseas citizens. Apart from the fact that applicants are left waiting for years to be granted entry, the whole system is kept outside the rules. Why?

Europe

It is worrying that immigration policy is discussed and agreed in secret by groups of ministers. It is essential for discussions of this nature to be in the public domain.

The rights of free movement should be extended to non-European Union citizens who are legally resident in the European Union.

Rights of MPs to intervene

With the loss of rights of appeal in many areas the role of the MP is crucial as an independent form of redress. It is essential that MPs are given a right to intervene and delay the departure of passengers in specific types of cases particularly where they involve families or asylum seekers. Furthermore any representations by them should automatically be dealt with by a specialist group which is part of the minister's team rather than by the Home Office.

Procedural changes

Complaints procedure

There is widespread distrust of the complaints procedure, particularly in British missions abroad, as it is regarded as a purely internal matter. It is necessary to have a system which is totally independent or at the very least has some independent participation. The independent element could be drawn from a recognised body such as the Commission for Racial Equality or the Immigration Advisory Service. It should have overall jurisdiction over the entry clearance officers abroad, the immigration service and the Home Office staff.

The use of force

Recent cases have highlighted the need for adequate safeguards to prevent excessive use of force. Officers should undergo proper training. There is a case for introducing a published set of guidelines which must be observed with failure to do so becoming a disciplinary offence. The Joy Gardner case left the black community and campaign organisations outraged at the circumstances of the attempted removal and its aftermath. The use of force can never be justified.

A note on nationality laws

Unlike any country in the world British law divides its own citizens into categories granting first, second and third-class status according to the colour of their skin. This situation has existed for far too long. There is an urgent need to examine the whole basis for this classification.

A number of trends emerge from the current system. The rules continue to be drafted and administered along racist lines. Second-class treatment is constantly meted out to the non-white community. Those fleeing persecution are granted lesser rights than those accused of criminal activities. The right of independent review and of accountability have been eroded. Immigration policy is less about an objective assessment of the country's needs and more about playing on the public's fears. How can we begin to successfully tackle the issue of race relations when we continue to maintain a racist immigration policy?

15

Official Secrecy

Michael Supperstone QC

Freedom of information

'Secrecy', said Richard Crossman, 'is the British disease'. Little has changed. Ours remains an excessively secret State. Countries throughout Europe, North America and Australasia have enacted freedom of information legislation creating a general public right of access to information, subject to specifically stated exemptions. We too should do so and give effect to Madison's vision of representative government:

> Knowledge will forever govern ignorance. And the people who mean to be their own governors must arm themelves with the power knowledge gives. A popular government without popular information or means of acquiring it is but a prologue to a farce or a tragedy, or perhaps both.

Access to official information should only be denied if:

(a)   the information falls within a specific category of information, such as information relating to national security, and

(b)   the nature of the information is likely to result in identifiable harm.

Any decision restricting disclosure should be reviewable in the spirit of Justice Stewart's injunction to the United States government in the

Pentagon Papers case (*New York Times Co.* v *United States* (1971) 403 US 713 at p. 729):

I should suppose, in short, that the hallmark of a truly effective internal security system would be the maximum possible disclosure, recognising that secrecy can best be preserved only when credibility is truly maintained.

The present position in Britain, which is governed by the Public Records Act 1958 as amended by the Public Records Act 1967, is unacceptable. There is a need to provide a legal right of appeal against over-secretive bureaucratic decisions to close files to public inspection for unreasonable periods. A British student of government will often learn more from a short stay in Washington about the UK administrative process than can be learnt from a lifetime in this country. This is because many of the documents withheld from the public in the UK are sent, under bilateral arrangements, to other countries, where they become immediately open to inspection.

Official Secrets Act 1989

A new framework for national security and official secrecy needs to be created. The Official Secrets Act 1989 repealed the 'catch-all' provisions of s. 2 of the Official Secrets Act 1911. The stated purpose of the 1989 Act was to reduce the amount of information protected by criminal sanctions to areas where disclosure would be harmful to the public interest. However, it was no liberalising measure. One Act, which was becoming substantially inoperable in practice, has been replaced by another capable of being repressive in practice. The new Act narrows the absurd breadth of the discredited s. 2, but 'in the armoury of criminal sanctions, it replaces a blunderbuss with an Armalite rifle'.[1] Doubtless influenced by the *Spycatcher* affair, the Act imposes a lifelong duty of confidentiality upon all members and former members of the Security Service. It is an offence for a member of the Security Service to disclose confidential information, even if it causes no harm.

---

[1] *Freedom, the Individual and the Law* (7th ed., 1993), p. 141.

In the course of the Parliamentary debates on the new law most attention was directed to the need for a public interest defence. It was argued that such a defence should be available to an individual charged with an offence under the Act if the accused can demonstrate that all avenues for prevention of serious misconduct were exhausted before the unauthorised disclosure was made. However, the government rejected an amendment which would have allowed officials to reveal serious misconduct involving crime, fraud or other gross impropriety, even where the benefit of revelation plainly outweighed any damage which might be caused by it. The Act excludes any public interest defence by focusing on the disclosure of information rather than the reasons for disclosing it. In the categories where information is classified as secret for the purposes of the Act, 'whistle-blowers' are not able to defend their actions on the grounds of public interest.

The absence of a public interest defence contributes to a climate of caution and inhibits legitimate discussion for fear of breaching the Act. It applies not only to civil servants disclosing unauthorised material, but also to journalists and editors, who are at risk if they publish information, however true, which they have reasonable cause to believe has been disclosed without official approval, provided that the truth can be shown to be damaging. English law does not reflect the balance that a modern democratic society requires between the public interest to receive, and the State interest to withhold, information. It fails to recognise the public interest to know of abuses by government of its powers.

Security Services Act 1989

The Security Services Act 1989 places the Security Service (MI5) on a statutory footing, but gives it very wide statutory functions and fails to constrain the service with any meaningful system of accountability. Rather than leading to the liberalisation of the security system, it gives considerable statutory powers to the executive without any effective method of scrutiny and accountability. The government refused to accept an amendment based on the Canadian legislation, which would have excluded from the lawful surveillance of the Security Service those engaged in 'lawful advocacy, protest or dissent'.

Criticisms of the Security Services Act 1989 include the following:

(a)   The broad definition of the functions of the service reflected in s. 1(2) which include 'the protection of national security . . . from actions intended to overthrow or undermine Parliamentary democracy by political, industrial or violent means'.

(b)   Lack of clarity in the arrangements for ministerial responsibility and control. The Act fails to acknowledge the central place of the Prime Minister in the security and intelligence scheme, and leaves unclear the extent to which the Director-General may be given direct orders and the extent to which, conversely, ministers should be consulted by the Director-General.

(c)   Absence of Parliamentary oversight.

(d)   The inadequacy of the complaints mechanism. Particular difficulties include how a person would know whether he is being bugged, burgled or investigated.

Intelligence Services Act 1994

The aspect of the Security Services Act 1989 which attracted most criticism was the absence of any form of Parliamentary oversight. To a certain extent that omission has been corrected by the Intelligence Service Act 1994. What is welcome in the 1994 Act is that for the first time a committee has been set up to oversee the expenditure, administration and policy of the Security Service (MI5), the Intelligence Service (MI6) and GCHQ. However, the Intelligence and Security Committee established by s. 10 of the Act is not a select committee or a Parliamentary committee, although it is made up of members of Parliament. It is not, therefore, governed by the normal rules that apply to select committees. Under the Act the Committee does not have the power to call witnesses or demand documents to be brought before it. By para. 3(1)(b)(ii) of sch. 3 to the Act information sought by the Committee may be denied 'because the Secretary of State has determined that it should not be disclosed'. That is a sweeping power. These are serious weaknesses for a Committee that is expected to provide oversight of the security services. The services should be subject to proper Parliamentary oversight and scrutiny. The Committee must be given real powers which are capable of being exercised effectively. Moreover independent Parliamentary oversight would provide reassurance that the security services are not targeting trade unionists and civil liberties groups as 'subversive'. As former Home Secretary Roy Jenkins said:

> I am convinced now that an organisation of people who live in the world of espionage and counter-espionage is entirely unfitted to judge between what is subversive and what is legitimate dissent.

There is no evidence that national security in the United States, Australia or Canada has been damaged by democratic controls over forces whose methods of operation and selection of targets can vitally affect the liberty of the subject. There can be no doubt that the operational activities of MI5, MI6 and GCHQ require secrecy. There can be no objection to the gathering of information about individuals or organisations which use violence, so long as there are clearly defined limits on the use to which such information is put. If the trust of the public in our intelligence services system is to be restored and maintained the 1994 Act should be strengthened in several areas:

(a) Clear principles should be provided for the operation of the security services. Clear standards should be set below which the services are not expected to fall.

(b) Before a Parliamentary committee can conduct effective oversight, a framework in which it can operate must be created.

(c) A charter for the security services should be established. The charter should contain comprehensive treatment of the functions, powers and duties of the security services. It should not attempt to dictate day-to-day operations, rather it should provide an organisational and institutional structure to facilitate the proper and effective conduct of intelligence activities. Clear guidelines should be laid down as to persons who can be investigated for intelligence gathering purposes, the standards that should be met before an investigation can be instituted, the restrictions that there should be on the scope of an investigation and the investigative techniques that may be used.

(d) The role of the security services should be limited to real threats to national security by unlawful or violent actions which are intended to destroy or undermine our constitutionally established government. Lawful political or trade union activity should be specifically excluded from their remit.

To this end the Security Services Act 1989 and the Intelligence Services Act 1994 should be repealed. They should be replaced by a single statute which contains a comprehensive statement of the functions, powers and duties of each service and which brings all the services under Parliamentary control with a proper system of accountability and review. To command consensus in the 21st century, respect for democratic rights should be given a proper place in the charter of the security services.

Interception of Communications Act 1985

The Interception of Communications Act 1985 needs to be revised to better protect the citizen from improper telephone tapping and similar intrusions against privacy. The most significant feature of the 1985 Act is the reluctance on the part of the executive to subject the process of intercepting communications to any satisfactory scrutiny or control.

On the one hand the interception of communications constitutes a major invasion of privacy, while on the other it is an important weapon available to the police and to the security services, whose business it is to maintain law and order and protect national security. Although it may be necessary to tolerate the practice, it should be conducted only in exceptional and highly controlled circumstances under which there is adequate scrutiny and review by institutions independent of the executive branch of government.

Section 2 of the 1985 Act authorises warrants to be issued by the Home Secretary for the purposes of interception and provides that a warrant should not be issued unless the Home Secretary considers that it is necessary, *inter alia*, in the interests of national security. At the time of the passage of the Bill, Labour contended that the words 'in the interests of national security' were too vague and too wide and conferred too much discretion on the Home Secretary and the security services. The term 'national security' is not defined in the Act and the government refused to accept an amendment which would have restricted the power to issue warrants on national security grounds for reasons connected with subversion, terrorism or espionage. 'National security' has, as former United States Attorney-General Griffin Bell commented, become a 'talismanic phrase' which has been used 'to ward off any questions about the legitimacy of any governmental conduct to which the phrase was applied'.

The time has surely come when legislation should provide for a system of judicial, rather than ministerial, warrants before surveillance devices are deployed. In *United States* v *United States District Court* (1972) 407 US 297 the government of the United States submitted that the courts as a practical matter would have neither the knowledge nor the techniques necessary to determine whether there was probable cause to believe that surveillance was necessary to protect the national security. These security problems, the government argued, involved a large number of complex and subtle factors beyond the competence of the court to evaluate. In rejecting this argument, Justice Powell, delivering the opinion of a unanimous Supreme Court said (at p. 320):

> We cannot accept the government's argument that internal security matters are too subtle and complex for judicial evaluation. . . . There is no reason to believe that federal judges will be insensitive to or uncomprehending of the issues involved in domestic security cases. . . . If the threat is too subtle or complex for our senior law enforcement officers to convey its significance to a court, one may question whether there is probable cause for surveillance.

The Supreme Court thus refused to relinquish the power to balance government interests, however urgent, against the fundamental rights of citizens.

The 1985 Act provides for the appointment by the Prime Minister of a tribunal with very limited powers to regulate the way in which ministers use the very extensive powers given to them under the Act. The tribunal has no power to determine whether unauthorised interceptions are taking place. Moreover, the Act contains an exclusion clause to prevent review of the decisions of the tribunal so that its decisions 'shall not be subject to appeal or liable to be questioned in any court'. The Act also creates the office of Commissioner. The arrangements for review of the procedures under the Act given to the Commissioner were strongly condemned by Labour which argued that the monitoring should be undertaken by a select committee of the House of Commons which would oversee the work of any person responsible for, or making use of, interception of communications. At the very least there should be a select committee confining itself to the Commissioner's report so that in turn it would report and give some reality to Parliamentary accountability.

Proposals for reform

A new framework for official secrecy requires that:

(a) A general public right of access to official information be created. The Public Records Act 1958, as amended by the Public Records Act 1967, should be replaced with a Freedom of Information Act creating such a right, subject to limited exemptions.

(b) The Official Secrets Act 1989, s. 2, should be reformed by creating a public interest defence.

(c) The Security Services Act 1989 and the Intelligence Services Act 1994 should be repealed and replaced by a single statute establishing a charter for the security services and bringing them under an effective system of accountability and review by a select committee of Parliament.

(d) The Interception of Communications Act 1985 should be revised to give better protection to the citizen from improper telephone tapping and similar intrusion into privacy. Judges, not ministers, should issue warrants permitting interception of communications.

16

Family Law

Maggie Rae, Solicitor and Wendy Mantle, Solicitor and Mediator

Introduction

There have been many substantial changes in the legal framework of family law since Labour was last in power. Many of these have been carried through with Labour Party support. The Children Act 1989 not only received the support of the Labour Party in its passage through Parliament but was in no small measure based on the *2nd Report from the Social Services Committee* (Session 1983–84) chaired by the Labour MP Renee Short.

Family law brings more people into contact with legal services and the courts than any other branch of law. Quite apart from other family disputes, one in three marriages ends in divorce. Divorce inevitably involves the law. It is an area where the requirements of strict legality can be less important than sensitivity and common sense. A range of services is more appropriate to deal with family problems than a service simply composed of lawyers.

Generally, and like other parts of the legal service, the way the legal service operates tends to be disempowering. Rather than encouraging people to take responsibility for their own lives it tends to impose solutions and encourage the use of professional services in arriving at them. This is true of the services provided by lawyers and the courts.

In recent years society has moved away from rigid forms of imposed dispute resolution towards more flexible systems in which those directly involved can play a greater part at less cost. Reform should have this general aim as a backdrop. This should not be at the expense of quality. There is a real need for quality services. These should be provided by a range of people with training and expertise, for example, counsellors, mediators, psychotherapists, advice workers and lawyers.

There has been much criticism of the expertise of lawyers. Some of this is well founded. Too many family lawyers lack the specialist training needed to provide a cost-effective and professional service. The Children's Panel established by the Law Society shows what can be done. Here solicitors undertake some further training and an interview as part of a process to join the Panel. Once on the Panel, they can represent children in public law cases. Their membership of the Panel is reviewed at regular intervals.

A similar system of specialist qualifications should be available for family lawyers as a whole. There are several ways in which this could be accomplished. For example, a panel system similar to the Children's Panel could be established, or alternatively some kind of diploma. The need for specialist training is acute. Approximately 20,000 solicitors each year do some divorce work but only 3,500 are members of the Solicitors Family Law Association. This suggests that family law is still regarded as a subject which any lawyer can do. That is patently not so. The efficient practice of family law requires specialist skills. The problem is likely to get worse now that family law is not a compulsory subject in the solicitors' final exams.

Quality should also be a requirement for publicly funded assistance through the legal aid scheme. Quality requirements should pertain for all others involved in the family law arena. One criticism of the Conservative government has been that it has failed to take on board the proper training and supervision of guardians *ad litem*. This should be remedied. Guardians *ad litem* should be nationally funded, trained and organised. Mediation and counselling services too should meet quality standards before receiving public funding.

Most importantly, people should be given enough information to enable them to make informed choices about the services and the providers on offer.

Divorce

In November 1995 the government published a Family Law Bill proposing a system of no-fault divorce available after a period of a year's separation. This period, described as being for reflection, will enable the parties to reconsider whether or not their marriage is at an end and, if it is, to try to reach mediated solutions to outstanding issues.

The principle of 'no-fault divorce' is to be welcomed. Courts are not the place to adjudicate on the rights and wrongs of individual marriages. Such an exercise serves only to increase bitterness. As published, however, the Bill contains some worrying features. There is no power to abridge the one-year period, say in the case of someone who is terminally ill and wishes to marry his partner so that she can receive a widow's pension. People are to be required to attend an information session before the period of separation can begin. The period of separation must start with a statement of marital breakdown. Both these measures are likely to exacerbate ill-feeling. There is also concern that legal aid to enable parties to get independent advice from their own solicitors may be conditional upon attendance at mediation first.

If the Bill fails, Labour should look again at the introduction of no-fault divorce. The present system is widely misused. Divorces based on the 'fault facts' of unreasonable behaviour and adultery are routinely employed simply as a way to obtain a quick divorce. This is not a good example and does nothing to enhance the institution of marriage.

The government has suggested that people wishing to start the legal separation process must first attend an information session, where they would be told about the process and the range of services on offer. Attendance at a meeting with other people in a similar situation is not on the face of it attractive or necessary. It is likely to cause embarrassment. In an era when information has never been easier to produce, it must be possible for people to learn about separation and divorce without attending a meeting such as that proposed, for example through videos or telephone help lines to name just two. The government has rejected the idea of a new agency to help families.

However, some form of advice centre will be needed, such as an agency to which people can go for help with all kinds of family problems. A first-stop shop should be considered. This could be based around the Citizens' Advice Bureaux or a separate organisation. It should be staffed by people (probably lawyers) who have been trained as family advisers. They would have a working knowledge of the legal consequences of family breakdown, would be able to direct people where necessary to lawyers, mediators and counsellors etc. They could also give people assistance in compiling the documentation necessary to go to lawyers or mediators. For example, much of the cost of ancillary relief cases is taken up by lawyers putting together the financial documentation required. A lot of this work can be done by people themselves although they may need some assistance in doing so.

The first-stop shop should be independent and properly resourced. Some of its services could be free and others could be means-tested. For example, the provision of general information, such as giving the names of mediators, falls into a category where advice ought to be free. Providing assistance in the compilation of financial information to save lawyers and mediators time and costs could be means-tested.

Reordering the family assets on divorce (ancillary relief)

This is an area where the service provided by lawyers and courts is widely regarded as both inadequate and expensive. The world has changed since 1973, when the major legislation was passed governing ancillary relief. Many more people now own their own homes, have pension schemes and a variety of other assets, such as privatisation shares, TESSAs and PEPs, often held in very small amounts. Procedure has not moved to keep pace with this change.

The service offered by the courts needs to be radically restructured. In the first place, there is a clear need for ancillary relief cases to be heard by judges who have had specialised training in family finance, tax, benefits and pensions. This is the case in the Principal Registry in London where the district judges are experienced family law specialists.

The Lord Chancellor's Department is presently looking at restructuring the court system and making the court a more proactive organisation. This is sensible and highlights the need for a specialised judiciary.

Solicitors are obliged to prepare documentation in ancillary relief cases according to a court direction requiring a sworn document or affidavit setting out the salient facts of the financial history of the marriage, the income and outgoings of the person swearing the affidavit, and his or her assets and debts. The preparation of a schedule of financial information and supporting documentation to verify it could be done with the assistance of a first-stop shop. The financial position of the parties can be set out in schedules rather than lengthy affidavits which often have no structure and do not contain all the relevant material. The values of significant assets, liabilities, income or outgoings can be listed in summary form. This is now often produced by lawyers prior to trial. It could, however, form the basis of the discovery process. That is not to say there will not be occasions when statements will be necessary, for example, where there is a dispute over the ownership or acquisition of an asset, or an explanation is needed say of illness affecting earning capacity.

If a form or a schedule is used, then this would make it easier for people to compile the information themselves with the assistance where necessary of the first-stop shop. There should be one form of disclosure which can be used by both mediators and the courts.

At present the exchange of sworn documents is followed by questionnaires to fill gaps in the financial information which has been provided. Lawyers face, on the one hand, problems of inadequate disclosure and, on the other hand, the need to avoid asking unnecessarily trivial questions. These problems may be simplified by ensuring that the information provided about divorce contains clear warnings about the necessity to make full disclosure and perhaps the imposition of harsh costs penalties for those who do not comply. This should enable family lawyers to concentrate on identifying the financial questions which the courts will have to determine if mediation or negotiation fail to produce agreement.

The court service often lets people down. Court buildings themselves are rarely designed for the convenience of those participating. Simple things like tables, chairs, areas where people can write notes, facilities for tea and coffee are simply not provided. All too often the court culture gives the impression that it is bestowing favours on the parties, rather than providing a service for which the public pays.

The judges have often not read the papers before the case. Like lawyers, they often have no training in financial matters.

Just as barristers are required to read the papers before going into court, so should judges. This process will be facilitated if the paperwork is reorganised.

A discretion-based system?

The reordering of financial assets on divorce in England and Wales is based on the exercise of discretion. This discretion is circumscribed by the Matrimonial Causes Act 1973, s. 25, which lists a number of factors which have to be taken into account, including and prioritising the needs of any children. The discretion-based system has great virtues. Foremost is its flexibility: it can take account of the particular needs of the individuals concerned. It has drawbacks too. It leaves people with very little guidance. Lawyers cannot predict outcomes with anything approaching certainty. It can be very confusing for participants. Wide variations occur in practice. It is likely that it leads to higher legal costs. Although there are 118 courts in England and Wales which have jurisdiction to deal with divorce and its consequences, there is no database of decided cases.

There seems little enthusiasm, from lawyers at least, for a move towards a system based on community of property or a more rigid division of property on divorce.

But people are becoming more proactive in relation to divorce. They are less inclined to accept the nostrums of their legal advisers. The way in which discretion operates needs to be looked at to see if it does meet peoples' needs or whether the criticisms outlined above are of such an order as to make a different system desirable.

Mediation

Access to mediation as a civilised method of dispute resolution is arguably a more important priority for family law than other areas of dispute because the parties involved if they have children inevitably have continuing contact with each other.

It is not yet clear what principles will inform the system of mediation the government will introduce for couples to use prior to divorce. It is likely that it will be based on one or other of the several models provided by the principal mediation organisations, Family Mediators Association (FMA) and NAFMACS (formerly National Family of Mediation). These organisations share a Code of Practice which they themselves administer and they have recently agreed a merger of their two organisations under the title of UK College of Family Mediators. Each has a supervision and accreditation system.

A national system will not attract public confidence as an alternative and additional avenue to the court system unless it is underpinned by three clear principles:

(a)   It should be voluntary: it is inappropriate where one party or a child of one party has been the subject of violence or when one party feels at a disadvantage as a result of the imbalance between them.

(b)   Each party should have access to independent legal advice: this means that where one party is poor and the other is rich the poor party should have legal aid to obtain that advice.

(c)   Mediators must have professional indemnity insurance equivalent to that which solicitors are now obliged to obtain. If the wife of a long marriage negotiates a settlement based on an offer made at mediation by her husband where the mediators have given insufficient weight to the widow's pension the wife will forego by divorce, she must have available to her the same remedy as she would against a solicitor who had failed to give her proper advice. The fact that she does not choose to obtain independent legal advice or, more importantly cannot afford it, should not affect the mediator's potential liability.

The following are compelling arguments for the State to provide a nation-wide mediation system and support to enable people to seek mediation:

(a)   An alternative system is likely to reduce the demands on the court system now severely stretched by the numbers of litigants in person who are no longer eligible for legal aid and whose use of the system takes up so much court time.

(b)   A properly administered system will save the time and costs of two sets of lawyers in the laborious process of financial disclosure, while the availability of experienced counsellors may improve still further the prospects for settlement of disputed issues concerning children in the way which court conciliation officers have already reduced them.

(c)   Because mediation is designed to help couples make their own decisions with professional help it is likely, if properly administered, to inspire the public confidence which to some extent the court system now lacks.

Pensions

The Matrimonial Causes Act 1973 listed as one of the matters for the courts to consider 'the value to each of the parties to the marriage of any benefit (for example, a pension) which by reason of the dissolution or annulment of the marriage that party will lose the chance of acquiring'. The 1973 Act also obliged the court to consider the appropriateness of exercising its powers so that the 'financial obligations of each party towards the other will be terminated as soon after the grant of the decree as the court consider just and reasonable'.

The Pensions Management Institute in its 1993 report and the Pension Law Review Committee chaired by Professor Goode in its subsequent report 'Pension Law Reform' recommended that the law be reformed by providing a system of pension splitting on divorce.

Amendments to the government's Pensions Bill 1995 to give effect to these recommendations were not accepted by the government. However, some changes have been made in the Act. First, the court is now under a duty to consider the pension position of spouses when it is considering financial matters. Secondly, in certain cases the court will have power to provide for part of a husband's future pension entitlement to be paid to a former wife. Regulations to give effect to the changes will be published in 1996. It would be premature to anticipate how they will affect divorce although it seems certain that the number of clean break cases will continue to reduce and that the changes will provide a fertile ground for litigation.

Pension splitting is often the only way to achieve justice between the parties. Labour should support attempts to introduce it.

Child Support Act 1991

The Child Support Act 1991 has attracted as much criticism as the ill-considered poll tax. It was introduced by the Conservative government without any of the safeguards and none of the flexibility which would have made it palatable to the public. The Act's ostensible purpose was to recover maintenance from separated parents who were paying no or insufficient maintenance in order that children would be better off. The reforms introduced over the last two years have reduced the burden on the worst-off and the better-off absent parents but the administration of the system by the Child Support Agency leaves many of the badly off unable to pay for appeals through the administrative system.

The State has a legitimate interest in recovering income support it pays out to separated families and in ascertaining how much money a particular parent should pay for the support of his or her child but the recent report showing a fivefold increase in unpaid child maintenance from £95 million to £525 million between March 1994 and March 1995 does not inspire any confidence that the performance of the Child Support Agency has improved after the poor record of its first year of performance.

The introduction in the Child Support Act 1995 of directions permitting departure from the formula system will introduce some much needed flexibility into the scheme but has further enlarged the discretion available to child support officers and probably widened the possibilities for challenge of the system through the courts by applications for decisions of the agency to be judicially reviewed. The way in which the legislation is framed seems on the face of it to favour absent parents rather than those looking after children. Care needs to be taken to ensure that the formula and the discretion get the balance between these two groups right.

A Labour government should give priority to ensuring that the Agency is staffed by experienced civil servants and consideration should be given to making the agency an arm of the Inland Revenue an organisation with experience of collecting money. Such a system would be more likely to be seen to have authority and gain the acceptance of the public.

Cohabitees

Many couples now cohabit. The breakdown of these relationships is as devastating for those involved as the breakdown of a marriage. The range of financial remedies available is, however, much more limited. That does not mean that cohabitees should be excluded from many of the family services provided. The Law Commission is presently looking into the law governing cohabitation and the Solicitors' Family Law Association has established a working group to consider this subject too. A Labour government should give careful consideration to reforming the law in this area, whilst recognising that it poses difficult moral questions.

There is no reason why a first-stop shop, as outlined above, should not give assistance to cohabitees.

Domestic violence

The Family Homes and Domestic Violence Bill 1995 failed to pass into law because of the actions of a small number of misinformed right-wing

Conservative MPs. It was a good Bill and has, at the time of writing, been reintroduced as part of the Family Law Bill. If this attempt to enact it fails, a Labour Government should give a commitment to reintroduce it. The Bill is a good one and the improvements it makes to the present law are much needed.

Children Act 1989

Private law

The Children Act 1989 has been an almost unqualified success. The terminology that the Act introduced (doing away with words such as 'custody' and 'access') has greatly improved matters. Its simplified procedures are also helpful. The form-based application means that people are much more able to use the process without the assistance of lawyers. The special training that judges and magistrates receive also helps.

The need now is for more and better conciliation services. Many parts of the country have worked hard to provide these. Their effectiveness needs to be assessed, particularly where they are linked to court proceedings. In-court conciliation services can be demeaning for those who participate. There is a temptation to evaluate success by the number of cases that are resolved. That is not a particularly effective test if solutions have been arrived at by banging heads together in a way which leaves families damaged and resentful.

Public law

The number of public law cases involving children has dropped. The cases themselves cost more. This is probably inevitable if we are to ensure that everyone is properly represented. Efforts to improve the procedure by ensuring the court is more proactive seem sensible.

The organisation of the guardian *ad litem* service is, however, patchy and the service is underfunded. Guardians *ad litem* work for low rates without any effective supervision. They do a difficult job in isolation. There is a clear need for a nationally organised service.

Adoption

The proposals contained in the adoption law consultation document published in October 1992 should be acted upon. These would take away some of the present difficulties. In particular, the present ground for dispensing with a parent's consent to the adoption of his or her child would be simplified so that the consent could only be dispensed with on the basis that a parent could not be found, is incapable of giving argeement or that the court is satisfied that the advantages to the child of being adopted are so significantly greater than the advantages to the child of any alternative as to justify overriding the wishes of the parent or guardian.

A child over 12 years would have to consent to his or her adoption unless incapable of giving agreement.

A new and more logical system of dealing with step-parent applications is needed. The consultation document envisages a new type of adoption order covering these situations.

Inter-country adoption continues to be a problem. It is a controversial area. Many object to it in principle. Others feel quite the reverse. It is, however, here and here to stay. At present it operates outside the normal arrangements for vetting and approving prospective adopters and arranging for the placement of children. Whilst many prospective adopters follow the arrangements laid down by the Department of Health and the Immigration and Nationality Department, many do not. It is still possible for people to bring children into this country for adoption without the knowledge of the Department of Health and without the approval of the Immigration and Nationality Department.

There are still disturbing reports of children being obtained for adoption fraudulently overseas and being adopted by people who are unsuitable.

The effective way to address this problem is to implement the procedures in the Hague Convention which would permit inter-country adoption to take place where it is in the interests of a particular child but would contain safeguards designed to protect the welfare of the child and eliminate corrupt practices.

The government has suggested that the discretionary arrangements for the admission of children to the United Kingdom should be changed and dealt with in adoption legislation. This would prevent entry clearance continuing as the vehicle for entry into the United Kingdom. Once this has been achieved, then the consultation paper recommends that it should be made a criminal offence to bring a child to the United Kingdom for adoption without having obtained authorisation to proceed from the relevant authority.

The recommendations are sound but much work will be needed to bring them into operation.

International child abduction

This is another growing problem. The Hague Convention, implemented by the United Kingdom in the Child Abduction and Custody Act 1985, has proved to be a modest success. There are, however, two difficulties.

The first is that not enough countries are signatories, although the number keeps on rising. A Labour government should lobby for more States to sign.

The second difficulty is that not all signatory States operate the Convention in the same way. This was only to be expected but needs to be kept under review. Consistency of practice is important to public acceptance. Governments can and should play a part in assisting this process. International child abduction is a growing problem which can only be dealt with successfully by international co-operation.

17

Personal Injury Law

Andrew Dismore and Fraser Whitehead

Support for the fundamental right of an individual not to suffer avoidable personal injury as a result of the actions of others is an absolute requirement of any society seeking fairly to define the relationship between its citizens.

In the UK this principle is so subjugated to argument about its effective implementation that the principle itself is being overlooked and as a result seriously undermined. This is operating to the detriment not only of the injured but to society as a whole. The positive reassertion of the right must be at the heart of any proposals to improve processes for the resolution of disputes about culpability and redress for injury.

This is reinforced by the underlying economic facts. The most recent information available suggests that the cost of injury to the population of the UK in 1990 was a staggering £4.5 billion from *just* road accidents. From such a sum significant reduction not only must be possible but is essential. And that figure takes no account of the incalculable cost in terms of human suffering.

The most effective assertion of the right is through a process targeted at injury prevention. The ultimate objective of the law and legal process should be to encourage accident prevention.

Regulatory law in itself is not the answer as its policing is expensive, though more effective enforcement than under the present regime would assist. Instead the underlying economic reality must be addressed. Our current compensation system is simply ineffective.

Injury and its compensation are dominated by an insurance industry which is based on the commercial exploitation of the myth that the costs of injury prevention can be greater than the consequence of injury materialising so that it is cheaper to insure than prevent. This equation is perversely supported by the association between the cost of insurance and the value of compensation awards. The increasing cost of premiums coupled with increasing unhappiness at the level of personal injury damages illustrates that the current approach is completely flawed.

The premise that underlines the proposals set out below is that in balancing the various interests, the right of British citizens not to be needlessly injured should be clearly dominant. We believe that if the right is more effectively affirmed through the enforcement of private rights then there will be a significant shift to prevention at no direct cost to the State and to the benefit of all.

Liability for accidents

The present system requires the injured party to prove fault against the injurer and it is from there that many of the problems of the cost-benefit analysis arise. This is because the insurer has a significant interest not in the application of legal principles but of its own commercial objectives in the determination of the key legal issues. The result is that the industry spends huge resources in the avoidance of compensation. There is little if any focus on prevention as the alternative commercial balance. The opportunity to concentrate on prevention cannot be realised without bold initiative in this area. There is also the inherent unfairness of pitching David against Goliath, the individual victim against the massive bulk of the experienced and resourced insurer.

Strict liability

This is not novel, indeed outside the United Kingdom it is increasingly widespread. If there were strict liability, subject to proof of causation, for accidental injury, much of the cost or delay associated with the present procedure would evaporate. Indeed, what would be lost when it is widely recognised that most claims are justified and are successful, eventually, under the current tort system? There would be additional cost to insurers but the argument that the cake is round and that strict liability would mean a reduction in damages for those currently successful in order to benefit those currently without remedy is baseless. There is no reason why damages should be reduced other than under a capped system operated by the State, which we do not propose. Our belief is that any temporary increase in premiums would be balanced in the longer term by the economic consequence of the benefit of investment in prevention, namely lower premiums.

Strict liability could be introduced progressively, initially for road accident claims. Such a proposal was put forward by Lord Mackay in 1993, but dropped under pressure not from road users or victims, but from the insurance industry. Yet both France and Spain operate what is virtually strict liability for road accident victims. The suggestion could reduce accidents if premium levels were properly used to deter poor driving, rather than cut to secure market share.

Strict liability can and must be imposed in the workplace. Despite the best endeavours of the European Commission, the UK drifts steadily away from strict liability at a time when many other jurisdictions embrace it. The entitlements conferred on many workers by the Factories Act and its Regulations have been replaced by a series of Regulations based on reasonable practicability in defiance of the higher standard imposed under the related European health and safety Directives. This unnecessary erosion of long-established rights for short-term corporate benefit must stop, and the process of strict liability in the workplace must be reaffirmed and extended. It is a strange comparison of values that our law currently imposes strict liability on the owner of a dangerous dog but not on the owner of a dangerous machine. There is nothing new in strict liability — it exists in limited form in some industrial sectors, for example in our nuclear industry. But we must grasp the message and quickly. European law, through legislation such as the Product Liability Directive and the proposed Service Provider Directive, puts the emphasis on strict liability, because the European Union clearly understands the need for prevention at source. The extension of strict liability into the field of personal injury is not the introduction of a new concept, it is the erosion of an anomaly.

Reversal of the burden of proof

Pending the progressive extension of strict liability, a simple but highly effective interim measure would be to reverse the burden of proof from the plaintiff to the defendant, so that the presumption would be in favour of the victim, not in favour of the insurer. This can be achieved at no cost to the State, but would have significant impact on the economics of litigation to the advantage of the victim and to the cause of accident prevention.

Once insurers are faced with the burden of proving that the facts alleged do not amount to negligence or breach of duty, they will have to take a far more realistic approach to the resolution of disputes. The opportunity to grind the plaintiff down through the abuse of a dominant commercial position would reduce significantly.

More effective use of inquests and inquiries

We need to give close attention to better use of inquests and inquiries. In any significant incident or catastrophe, there is inevitably an inquest or inquiry when evidence is gathered at an early stage, through independent and resourced means, external to the parties and the adversarial system. Yet inquiries and inquests are either prohibited from proceeding to deal with issues of culpability, or their findings are subject to much later analysis and challenge within the adversarial framework. And the precedence which is given to inquests and inquiries in procedural terms means that they contribute to delay, whereas if properly used they could reduce it significantly. Inquests and similar tribunals should be given the power to make binding determinations of issues of fact and culpability, and the parties who appear before them should have access to the same resources as exist within the normal court structure. This will secure fair, impartial and proper analysis of the facts at an early stage.

Jury trials

In a recent high-profile English case involving damages for stress from work the judge was struggling with the complex issue, relevant in many personal injury cases, of what is reasonably practicable. He cited from an Australian authority on the point. 'In practical terms this means that the plaintiff must show that the defendant unreasonably failed to take such steps as would reduce the risk to what was reasonable, that is socially acceptable, level. It may be that this takes the court into an area of value judgment for which the inscrutability of a jury verdict may provide a more appropriate means of expression.' Why should such an issue not be resolved by a jury, for what is reasonably practicable should be what society in the form of the reasonable observer considers appropriate?

It is extraordinary that whilst the rules of the court do provide for jury trials in personal injury cases there is practically no imaginable situation where the required judicial discretion will be exercised. Yet there are clearly aspects of liability let alone damages which could be best determined by those who most understand the common good. It will not take many jury trials to secure a significant shift to the preventative cause. If the judiciary will not act, pending strict liability statutory guidance must be issued.

Damages for personal injury

When considering the assessment of damages, the victim's interest should be paramount, consistent with the general principle when awarding compensation of an intention to put the plantiff in the position he/she would otherwise have been in, but for the accident, so far as money is able to do. There are many areas of the law relating to personal injury damages which favour defendants and their insurers at the expense of accident victims, but we believe that amongst the most serious abuses are the following.

General damages

General damages for pain, suffering and loss of amenity have not kept pace with inflation. Problems have arisen in the assessment of general damages through the unofficial 'cap' imposed by the judiciary on the most serious cases. Other awards are then scaled down, with the result that compensation for less serious injuries is extremely low, the 'cap' also providing too little for catastrophic injury. An award of £130,000 or so for paralysis below the neck, or brain damage leading to total dysfunction is just not adequate.

Although inflation should be taken into account in assessing compensation for pain and suffering, the judges have consistently failed to do so. Since the right to jury trial for personal injury cases was all but abolished in England and Wales in the 1960s, society's expectations have ceased to be reflected in court awards.

190

This is especially so in relation to the types of injury which occur rarely, or which have only recently come to light, and where there is little or no guidance to judges in case law: for example psychiatric injury, or certain types of illness or disease such as repetitive strain injury.

A fresh approach to the assessment of general damages is required, involving the wider community in restoring levels of compensation.

This could be done either by allocating a sample of cases to jury trials to set 'bench marks', or alternatively requiring the Judicial Studies Board, who produce from time to time guidelines on the appropriate level of damages, to adopt a more radical approach by completely revising their recommendations upwards to take account of past inflation, working in conjunction with an advisory panel, representative of victims and victims' organisations, and of the public outside the legal profession.

Fatal accidents

Nowhere is the law of damages more at odds with public expectations than in its failure properly to compensate for fatal accidents.

The family of a fatal accident victim may claim for funeral expenses, financial dependency upon the victim, and, for very limited classes of relatives, a statutory payment for bereavement.

This leads to serious anomalies, making it cheaper to kill than maim.

If the victim is a young man in his early 20s, unmarried and with no dependants, his family can claim only for funeral expenses, a few hundred pounds at the most.

The statutory bereavement figure is far too low, and there can be no justification for awarding only half the statutory figure to each parent of a killed child, as if to suggest that if there are two surviving parents, they each only suffer half as much as if there was one. If the child was brought up by other relatives acting in the capacity of parent, they too should be entitled to bereavement damages. The children of a parent victim should also be entitled to bereavement damages if the parent and children lived in the same household. Claims should be permitted on behalf of cohabitees including also those in homosexual relationships.

By substantially increasing the bereavement figure (which should be payable to the deceased's estate if there is no claimant in the statutory categories), some public disquiet over low compensation where a death occurs with no dependency could be avoided.

However, a better approach would be to award, in addition to bereavement damages and dependency, a statutory death payment equivalent to the level of award given for general damages for pain and suffering in cases of maximum severity, as it cannot be right that death is compensated at a lower figure than serious injury.

Dependency claims are calculated on an unscientific basis, treating the assessment of dependency as future loss from the date of death. This flies in the face of reality, as the case may take up to several years to finalise, thus dramatically reducing the potential value of the award. A better approach to calculation of such loss is required (see below).

The permitted extent of a claim for funeral expenses is extremely limited, and does not take into account the diverse expectations of the various ethnic communities in our multicultural society. A wider definition to include the cultural expectations of the deceased's family is needed.

Punitive damages

The criminal law does not provide adequate remedies for accident victims, as has been evidenced by unsuccessful attempts to bring private prosecutions by victims of major disasters. The Health and Safety Executive and other prosecuting authorities rarely mount criminal prosecutions. The penalties imposed by the criminal courts are considered by many victims and their families to be woefully inadequate.

The civil law should provide an alternative remedy through punitive damages. It is not suggested that such damages should become widely available, but it should be open to a court to make a punitive award in cases involving the most serious torts committed in the most reckless circumstances. Such a remedy would go a long way to satisfying public concern over the failure of the law to penalise those responsible for serious and blatant acts resulting in death and injury.

Financial loss: a more scientific method

Despite overwhelming evidence of injustice, most judges refuse to accept a more scientific method of calculation of pecuniary loss. The 'rough and ready' approach adopted over the years in the calculation of such losses, which in the largest of cases, and indeed in many small ones, form the lion's share of the damages, is not acceptable.

Anomalies abound, in that inconsistent figures are often applied to different heads of damage within the same case.

Section 10 of the Civil Evidence Act 1995, allowing the courts to use actuarial tables in calculating damages, is a step in the right direction. The courts must be required to take fully into account prevailing rates of return and interest rates on investments when considering the amount which should be awarded for future losses.

The position of State injury benefits

There are many anomalies in clawing back statutory benefits from accident victims out of their compensation. The victim, who carries the financial risks of the litigation, can often lose the bulk of a compensation award to the DSS, which carries no part of the risk at all.

The system of 'taxing' accident victims by reclaiming benefits for which they paid through their national insurance contributions, is iniquitous and should be scrapped.

If the scheme is not abolished, then benefits should only be offset against the equivalent financial loss for which the benefit was to compensate, and should not be offset against any award for pain, suffering and loss of amenity. The recovery of benefits should be scaled down to reflect any finding of contributory negligence. The benefit position of the plaintiff prior to the accident should be taken into account when considering recovery of benefits paid after the accident. Interim payments should be payable free of DSS recoupment.

Personal injury awards, especially interim payments, should be disregarded for the purposes of means-tested benefits.

NHS expenditure

At present, emergency treatment expenses are directly recoverable by the NHS from the insurer of a person responsible for a road accident. Such a system should extend to the recovery of NHS costs against insurers irrespective of the circumstances of the accident, and especially where the law requires compulsory insurance, for example employers' liability. Private medical insurers such as BUPA are entitled to recover their outlays, and the NHS should not be put in a more disadvantageous position than a medical insurer. If the NHS were able to recover such costs direct from the insurer, more money would be available for the NHS.

It is not right to expect society as a whole to pay for the medical treatment required by a victim as a result of another's fault, when the person at fault is insured.

Proposed reform

We have highlighted the need for reform in a few areas of personal injuries damages. There are many other areas which require attention and the Law Commission is conducting a systematic review. As socialists, we should expect a more radical approach to redress the imbalances and unfairness that riddle the present method of assessing compensation.

Funding of personal injury claims

There has been a great deal of concern about this issue in recent years with the perception that any system of justice in which the costs of pursuing rights to compensation can exceed compensation awarded to the victim, or come close to that figure, must be flawed. We believe that those who seek to find a solution have overlooked the fundamental reasons behind this and as a result, proposed reforms such as Lord Woolf's will ultimately fail to provide a solution except at the expense of the rights of the injured party.

The first and clearest point is that one of the reasons for the adverse relationship of compensation to costs is the inadequacy of personal injury compensation compared with compensation in other areas. If compensation for personal physical injury were to be awarded at the same rate as for libel or trespass to property, the position would be very different.

Generally speaking, the victims of accidents are successful in pursuing their claims for compensation, and, on the 'loser pays' principle, rarely (if ever) have to meet the cost of the litigation. The cost is met by the insurers. The insurers make a great issue out of the amount of legal costs they pay but the reality is that no one has more control over the amount of costs than the insurance industry itself. Inevitably the insurer seeks to dictate the pace and cost of litigation as part of the defence of its commercial interest, in the hope that plaintiffs will be either persuaded to settle early or dissuaded from carrying on litigation at all. Contrary to the arguments adopted by Lord Woolf and others, the issue of costs remains one of the most influential factors in the encouragement of early settlement and the avoidance of litigation.

Attempts to reduce the amount of costs payable in personal injury litigation will therefore (a) encourage insurers to litigate more than now in the defence of their commercial interests and (b) result in the damages available to plaintiffs being eroded by the requirement that they make a contribution towards their own legal costs, as less will be recoverable from the insurers. It is a fundamental principle that the wrongdoer pays. The wrongdoer should not be given the opportunity to reduce the right to compensation through erosion of the 'loser pays' principle.

The reforms that we have suggested above in relation to the issue of liability would in our view go a long way to reducing the cost of litigation without putting at risk the plaintiff's right of recovery or eating into the damages then recovered. But to interfere in any way with the costs arrangement, under which, in 95 per cent of the cases, costs are met by the insurers, will seriously undermine the prospect of achieving prevention through legal process. It will remain cheaper to injure and pay than to prevent. Whilst an expensive costs regime might represent short-term benefit to those who service the compensation system, in the longer term prevention will prevail because it will make economic sense, and the volume and cost of litigation will significantly reduce.

17

Employment Law: Justice at Work

Colin Ettinger

The law provides a series of rights to protect workers in their employment. These range from protection against sex or race discrimination to rights to time off for pursuing public duties, and include the right not to be unfairly dismissed. But much of the protection afforded to workers is inadequate. In order to buttress existing rights there are three particular areas that need specific attention. These are:

  (a) remedies;
  (b) workers' representation;
  (c) dispute resolution.

Remedies

There is little point in providing individuals with rights if the remedies available are inadequate or indeed non-existent. The European Court of Justice has ruled that compensation for breach of directives should be effective, proportionate and have a deterrent effect (see *Von Colson* v *Land Nordrhein-Westfalen* (case 14/83) [1984] ECR 1891 and *Commission of the European Communities* v *United Kingdom* (cases C–382 & 383/92) [1994] ICR 664). This principle overrides the limits placed by domestic legislation on compensation in unfair dismissal cases arising out of sex discrimination (*Marshall* v *Southampton and South West Hampshire Health Authority (Teaching) (No. 2)* (case C–271/91) [1994] QB 126). That case demonstrates that in order to satisfy the European

Court's requirements on compensation, an individual must be compensated for the whole of his or her loss.

It is also clear that the European Court's approach to compensation is that employers breaching employment law underwritten by Directives should be penalised for so doing. In the *European Commission* v *United Kingdom* case (referred to above) it was held that the level of awards given for failure to consult with workers' representatives was inadequate. This was regardless of whether or not individual workers had actually suffered loss as a result of the breach.

For workers subjected to unlawful actions by their employers to receive compensation over and above their losses is not unknown under UK law. For example, special awards are given to individuals who have been dismissed on the grounds of trade union membership or activities, or (more rarely in practice), refusal to join a trade union.

With these two approaches in mind, the current law that deals with compensation for infringement of employment protection rights should now be revamped. The various limits that are imposed on levels of compensation should be removed. This would mean:

(a)   removing the maximum unfair dismissal compensatory award (currently £11,300);

(b)   removing the limit on a 'week's pay' for the purposes of calculating statutory redundancy payments, basic and additional awards for unfair dismissal and certain insolvency payments (currently £210);

(c)   the particular awards applicable in relation to protection against dismissal on certain health and safety grounds and unfair dismissal on trade union grounds.

The Law Society has recently asked for the removal of the limit in unfair dismissal cases. They also highlight the point that had the figure kept pace with inflation when first set in 1971 it would now be £46,000.

There are certain instances where breaches of employment protection legislation have taken place but workers have not suffered losses. In respect of some of these employment protection rights the law actually lays down amounts to be awarded (see, for example, the penalty for failing to inform and consult as required by the Transfer of Undertakings (Protection of Employment) Regulations 1981). In such circumstances the amount of compensation should be assessed in accordance with principles laid down by the European Court, namely, that compensation should be effective, proportionate and provide a deterrent effect.

Consideration must also be given to providing employees with other types of remedies. Injunctive relief in certain circumstances should not be ruled out. If the level of the financial penalty upon the employer is significant then this should act as a sufficient deterrent for employers and ensure that they comply with the law. Consideration should be given to awarding an employee punitive damages on the basis of, for example, an amount of the employer's profits depending on the seriousness of the breach. This is an approach adopted in some States in USA.

It is clear that employers would not like such changes in these rules and compensation. They already complain that enforcement of employment protection rights is costing them too much and they are being subjected to too many industrial tribunal applications. One reason for this may be that they are not complying with obligations imposed upon them and therefore become legally vulnerable to such actions. However, the more expensive litigation becomes the more likely employers will comply with legal obligations imposed upon them. In the area of health and safety it is well established that safety conditions have improved at the workplace as a result of extensive claims for damages having been brought by injured workers.

Workers' representation

The government will have to revise the law to comply with the European Court's ruling in *European Commission* v *United Kingdom*. The Court held that the United Kingdom's current law on information and consultation on collective redundancies and transfer of undertakings was inadequate. The consultation process should be with workers and their representatives and not limited to recognised trade unions. It is at the very least arguable that the legislation that will have to be introduced to implement this will have to ensure that those workers' representatives are independent, have adequate resources and will be able to provide continuity of representation.

Simply to have representatives just for the purpose of dealing with a collective redundancy or transfer of undertaking is likely to prove to be a sham and not to comply with the ECJ's ruling. Unfortunately, regulations introduced by the Conservatives in 1995 allow employers to consult with an *ad hoc* body of employee representatives. This is being challenged in the courts. Taking into account the requirements under the health and safety framework Directive that there be consultation on all health and safety issues with workers and/or their representatives, any proposed legislation should provide a basic statutory underpinning of permanent workplace representatives.

In any event, the current domestic legislation giving workers rights to representation is extremely limited. Section 146 of the Trade Union and Labour Relations (Consolidation) Act 1992 gives protection where action is taken by an employer against an individual for the purpose of preventing or deterring the individual from becoming a union member, or being a member or taking part in the activities of the union, or where an individual is penalised for so doing. A number of amendments to this particular piece of legislation have been suggested in order to provide greater protection, such as:

(a)   The rights should not only cover action taken by employers but also failures on their part to take action resulting in union discrimination. As a result of the House of Lords decision in *Associated Newspapers Ltd* v *Wilson* [1995] 2 WLR 354, s. 146 does not extend to omissions.

(b)   The requirement that the action or failure to act must be taken against the aggrieved employee 'as an individual' should be repealed. In *Carrington* v *Therm-a-Stor Ltd* [1983] 1 WLR 138 the employee was dismissed as a result of an 'indefensible reaction to a simple request for union recognition', but it was a 'reaction to a trade union's activities', i.e., the request for recognition, not to the individual's activities and so, the Court of Appeal held, was not in breach of the section. This is a serious gap in the law.

(c)   The requirement to show that the action was for the purpose of preventing or deterring trade union membership or activities should also be changed. It should be sufficient for it to be established that this was one of the reasons, not necessarily the principal reason, for the action being taken.

(d)   Protection should also extend to preventing the individual from making use of the services of the trade union as well as being a member of it or taking part in the activities of it. The House of Lords in *Associated Newspapers Ltd* v *Wilson* casts some doubt on whether the section covered this aspect.

(e)   Currently compensation is awarded on the basis of what is just and equitable in the circumstances. When a claim is successful but no loss has been suffered the level of compensation is extremely limited. Where there is a breach of this section a special award should be made. This should be the equivalent of the special award given for trade union dismissals where there is no order for reinstatement, that is, two years' pay. There should also be no capping on such compensation. Where the employer fails to comply with an order for reinstatement or re-engagement in such cases, an award of three years' pay should be made in addition.

Section 13 of the Trade Union Reform and Employment Rights Act 1993 was passed to restrict the operation of s. 146. It applies where an employer wishes to change aspects of the relationship with all or any class of employees where there is evidence that there is a contravention of s. 146. In such circumstances there will be no liability on the basis that, as a matter of law, the only purpose is to effect the change in the relationship. The purpose of this section is to allow attempts by employers to offer sweeteners to workers to accept personal contracts rather than allow their unions to bargain on their behalf. The House of Lords decision in *Associated Newspapers Ltd* v *Wilson*, which post-dated this, held such actions are not in breach of s. 146 in any event. Section 13 should be repealed. It is also worth noting that it is likely to be in breach of the UK's obligations under the Conventions of the International Labour Organisation (ILO), particularly ILO Convention 98 (on the right to organise), as well as being contrary to the Council of Europe Social Charter 1961, arts 5 and 6, and the European Convention on Human Rights, art. 11.

Alongside the amended s. 146 there should be a new right for workers to be represented on individual issues. This right to representation should cover all issues touching upon the terms and conditions of employment of an employee that result in dispute with the employer. This would include hearings concerning allegations of misconduct, poor performance and ill health. The right would also extend to grievances brought by the employee.

If workers are members of a trade union they should be entitled to be represented by a union official and this should not depend on the level of membership at the workplace. In addition, such a right should not depend on whether the employee is full or part time, homeworker or casual.

Failure to afford the worker this right should result in the following sanctions:

(a)   The employer's decision would be null and void.

(b)   If the employer still proceeded to act upon such a decision, an employee should have the option of seeking injunctive relief in the High Court.

(c)   The employee would have an automatic right to compensation assessed on the same lines as proposed where a breach of s. 146 has taken place.

Amendment of the law is required to restore formal rights of representation. In 1984 it was announced that staff at the Government Communications Headquarters (GCHQ) would no longer be permitted to belong to any national trade unions. They also lost their statutory protection against unfair dismissal and action short of dismissal for being members of independent trade unions or for taking part in the activities of such trade unions. These restrictions should be removed and the rights restored to those employed by GCHQ.

Another area worthy of reform relates to provisions concerning time off for trade union duties. This right is available only to an employee who is an official of an independent trade union which is recognised by the employer. The reasons for which a union official may claim time off are either to carry out certain official duties or to undergo certain training. The present provisions are much narrower than those set out in the original legislation introduced in 1975. Under the old definition the union official might seek time off for any duties concerned with industrial relations generally. The current provisions setting out the extent to which time off is allowed should be repealed and replaced by the earlier legislation. This will allow union representatives during their working hours to carry out those duties which are concerned with industrial relations between employer and employees. This would include:

(a)   collective bargaining,

(b)   informing members about negotiations and consultations with management,

(c)   meeting with other union officials on matters of concern about the employer,

(d)   interviews with members involving, for example, grievances and disciplinary issues concerning them,

(e)   representing members in disputes with the employer as well as at industrial tribunals,

(f)   explaining to new employees whom the union representative will represent and the role of the union in the workplace.

This is not an exhaustive list but represents the type of issues that ACAS considered relevant and appropriate to be covered by this legislation in their code of practice.

Additional protection should also be afforded to trade unions, their members and activists when they apply for jobs. Some protection is currently available under the Trade Union and Labour Relations (Consolidation) Act 1992, ss. 137 to 143. An individual who is turned down for a job because of union membership has a right to bring a claim before an industrial tribunal. This right should be extended to include rejection of a job on the grounds of the individual concerned being a trade union activist. This approach has received support in the recent case of *Harrison* v *Kent County Council* [1995] ICR 434 in which the EAT held that 'membership' includes activities. Further, the award of compensation to be made in these circumstances should be increased and should represent the equivalent of that proposed where there is a breach of s. 146.

Dispute resolution

In virtually every case, an industrial tribunal is the place where employees go to try to enforce their rights. There has not been any suggestion that this should change. However, the tribunals' jurisdiction should not be extended so as to give them the power to grant injunctions. In respect of the one instance where it has been suggested that injunctions should be available (enforcing the right to representation) the worker should have access to the High Court.

The current time limit of three months in nearly every case is too short. Limitation periods for enforcing individual rights are normally far longer: for example, three years for personal injury cases and six years for contractual claims. I do not suggest that time limits in respect of employment protection rights should be increased to this extent but change is desirable. Six months, the present time limit in respect of claims for redundancy payments, would be more appropriate.

A primary concern in relation to tribunal proceedings is the delay in dealing with cases at certain tribunal centres. There are various strategies that could be put in place to deal with this problem:

(a)   A system of arbitration could be introduced which would be a voluntary, less formal and quicker procedure for resolving disputes.

(b)   The applicant should have the option of having the case decided by written submissions. There should be a right to apply for an oral hearing if the decision is not favourable but with the added possibility of a costs penalty if the tribunal still does not find in the applicant's favour.

(c)   The applicant should have the option of putting forward written offers of settlement to the employer. If these are rejected then the employer may face a financial penalty if a higher award is made. The penalty should be an increase in the amount of compensation.

The role of the Commissioner for the Rights of Trade Union Members should also be changed. The circumstances in which the Commissioner can fund legal proceedings for trade union members should be changed completely. They should no longer be used to finance actions against trade unions but instead against employers who contravene the rights of trade unionists. Similarly, funds should also be made available where there is discrimination on trade union grounds. However, a cautious approach is needed. One of the problems with industrial tribunals is that they have become over-legalistic as a result of the use of legal representation, particularly by employers. Accordingly, access to these funds may be limited to cases where:

(a)   There is an important point of law and complicated factual issues.

(b)   The individual maintains his or her trade union support.

(c)   The case is in the Employment Appeal Tribunal, High Court or county court.

(d)   The employer has legal representation.

It is common ground that workers require legal protection at their workplace. Such protection will only be effective if they have access to adequate and proper representation. Such access must be supported by the full rigour of the law in the event of employers denying or attempting to deny such representation. Similar protection must be afforded to those who are prepared to represent individuals at their place of work.

19

Environmental Rights

Martyn Day

Britain's role as the initiator of the Industrial Revolution, towards the end of the eighteenth century, led to 200 years of British companies taking the environment for granted, at a time when society's main interest was to strive for an ever-increasing standard of living, almost at any cost. It has primarily been in the last 10 to 15 years that the individual has, at long last, stood up and said 'No more!' following the dawning realisation that this headlong drive for increased wealth at home must be balanced against deteriorating environmental standards, whenever we leave our front door.

The Conservative government has, latterly, through legislation such as the Environmental Protection Act 1990, the Water Resources Act 1991 and the Environment Act 1995, started the process of regulating the polluting activities of corporate Britain in a comprehensive and cohesive manner. There are two key problems with the direction in which Conservative policy has moved. The first is that, in balancing the interests of industry as against those of the environment, the Conservatives have leaned far too heavily toward the former. The second is that they have singularly failed to provide individuals with the power and ability to take on the might of industry when their own local environments are under threat.

If a proper balance is to be struck between corporate Britain and the environment, power must be put into the hands of individuals to enable them to play a full part in protecting their local and, as a result, our national environment. It cannot be expected that this will be a role, entirely or even significantly, played by the regulatory authorities.

To provide the citizen with the power to take on the might of British industry, there is little point in talking about giving individuals additional access to the courts if there are no resources to enable the individual to take the action without fear of bankruptcy. There is little point giving the individual access to environmental information that is not put into lay person's language and is not put into its proper context. A part, therefore, of empowering the individual is about giving relevant bodies the ability and perhaps duty to take coordinated action effectively on behalf of the individual.

Considered below are proposals on how the balance can be tipped more in favour of the environment to ensure that future generations are able to live in an improving, rather than a deteriorating, environment.

Individual rights and responsibilities

Every citizen who lives within our shores should be entitled to legally enforceable rights to clean air and water, the ability to live free from the risk of environmental harm (as well as living within a community that is spiritually and mentally pleasing), and to have access to the open countryside. Further, individuals should have ready access to justice, including the right to claim compensation for environmental damage, and the right to obtain environmental information freely.

Information

The most crucial weapon for the individual is information. It should be open to individuals to be able to gain as much information as possible regarding the pollutants potentially impacting on their lives. There are already some requirements for certain products to contain a warning such as cigarettes, drugs and kitchen products. There are, however, no warnings when a dental X-ray is taken, no warnings in relation to the potential impact of electromagnetic fields from the use of electrical equipment, or the dangers from exhaust fumes.

The government currently acts on the basis of only warning people of dangers when the risk arising is very clear. The Maastricht Treaty suggests that European member States should take a 'precautionary approach' to the risk arising from environmental harm, and this is a crucial development that should be adopted in Britain. This would ensure that people were provided with full warnings so that they can make rational decisions about the environmental risks arising from various potential dangers. It is suggested that to warn people when the risk is not certain is to scaremonger unnecessarily. I do not accept this premise. Citizens are well able to take account of risks to health in their everyday lives, provided they are given the information in a dispassionate and non-patronising manner.

To strengthen the powers of the individual in this field I would suggest the following:

(a) The existing regulations requiring companies to produce information are defective for a number of reasons:

(i) The authorities are allowed to charge too much for carrying out the work.

(ii) Too many areas are exempt from the polluter having to provide the relevant information.

(iii) There is no appeal system against a decision by the relevant authority not to release information.

(b) Manufacturers should be under a much greater duty to warn, not only of known risks but of possible risks.

(c) There should be improved access to environmental information which forces central and local government to make available, on request, information for the citizen on their local and national environment and the damage being done to it at a local venue, such as the town hall.

(d) Local authorities should be obliged to provide an annual report to local people on the state of the air, rivers etc. This should also include statements regarding local industry, stating what substances are being emitted, and any concerns regarding health problems. The information behind these statements should be made readily available.

(e) The government should give a far more detailed annual state-of-the-nation environmental statement, setting out the position, nationally and regionally.

Prevention

As well as protecting the individual from harm it is also important to give the individual greater power to influence the development of the environment within that person's life and, where necessary, to prevent it happening in the first place. The most important process in relation to the changing local environment is the planning system (see chapter 20). There should be extended rights for objectors to become involved in this process. There should therefore be a right to appear before planning committees (currently this is only given at the committees' discretion), provided the individual can show that s/he is affected in some way by the particular application. There should be a right given to objectors to appeal against the granting of planning permission. Currently the only right of appeal is that of the developers to appeal against refusal.

When it comes to planning applications for any major development, whether in agriculture or industry, where there will be significant emissions, it should be up to the plant operator to show that no harmful pollution will arise rather than the burden being on the local people to show that the reverse is the case.

Prosecution

Where the relevant pollution control agencies are not prepared to prosecute a polluter, it should be made easier for any of the affected individuals to seek a judicial review of the decision not to prosecute, or to bring a prosecution themselves, with legal aid being available to go down that route where the Board are satisfied that there is a real chance of the prosecution succeeding.

Compensation

Despite the enormous advancement of science it is still extremely difficult for the geneticist and biologist to pinpoint the particular cause of any specific illness, except for illnesses where there is only one known cause, examples being the link between mesothelioma and asbestos, and the link between Buerger's disease and smoking. For other illnesses it is very difficult to determine what has been the cause. Despite this, it is quite clear that pollution does injure and maim people all the time. For example, the emissions of radioactivity from Sellafield are accepted by the scientific community to cause many hundreds, if not thousands, of deaths. However, it has never been possible to prove in any particular case that an individual, who lives outside the plant, has been harmed by the radioactivity. This is primarily because of the continuing lack of sophistication of our scientific knowledge. Further, the burden placed upon the plaintiff in these actions remains too high. It is important that the power is given back to the individual in these circumstances to redress this balance.

There should be strict liability imposed on all environmental polluters, i.e., a victim would not have to prove that the polluter was at fault, which will play a major role in alleviating the plaintiff's burden. This is already the case in relation to those who claim they have been injured as a result of their exposure to radiation, and is a concept already in place in various other European jurisdictions (not least being Germany). Further, where the affected individual can show a prima facie case that the injury resulted from the emissions from the plant, the burden should then fall on the company to show that this is not the case rather than being the other way round. The burden of proof should not therefore lie with the individual but with the polluter.

Responsibilities

In addition to the expansion of individual rights, it is important that individuals also take some responsibility for the role that each of us play in contaminating the environment. Separating our own household waste into reusable piles, curtailing unnecessary journeys by private car, not littering the streets, are all actions that each of us can undertake to reduce the level of environmental pollution.

Environmental Court

There should be one court that deals with all primary issues of environmental damage, i.e., an Environmental Court. This is described as a court but it may well be more appropriate that it operates in the manner of a tribunal, in that it would be far less formal than a court.

The Environmental Court would deal with all environmental issues, including judicial reviews of decisions affecting environmental matters, prosecutions for environmental pollution and civil claims for compensation. Legal aid would be available for the individual going to this court.

At the time of the court being initiated, there would be simply one court, but the intention should be that if the court is successful, the principle would be developed on a regional and then a local basis. Until then the individual should have recourse to the local county court or magistrates' court. The procedure should be one which does not involve a great deal of expense.

This is a concept that has already been seen to work in New South Wales in Australia, where the court sees the protection of the environment as a fundamental part of its role.

Rights of environmental groups

Whilst the rights of individuals are very important, there are times when damage is being caused to the environment that does not specifically impact on individuals. That may be damage to the fauna and flora, to wildlife or whatever. Pumping radioactive waste into the Irish Sea may be a good example of this. It should be open to environmental groups to take on the role of being a detached advocate, rather like an *amicus curiae*, i.e., the sole role of this person would be to protect the environment in legal proceedings. The role of the advocate would therefore not be to take a part in the normal adversarial proceedings, but would be to assist the court or tribunal in coming to a decision that fully took into account the interests of the environment.

The point may be made that in giving environmental groups extra power, they may run amok in the legal system causing all sorts of difficulties for the parties to an action and to the legal system as a whole. The response to this is that every environmental group has a wide responsibility to its membership or to its subscribers. Any organisation seen to be misusing its subscribers' money is likely to be brought to book, and the general expense of going to court is likely to mean that organisations would take this step with reluctance. Further, the court would have the power to regulate the procedures to prevent any such abuses, much as the High Court does already.

Regulation

The Environment Agency, incorporating Her Majesty's Inspectors of Pollution, the National Rivers Authority and the Waste Regulatory Authorities will be established in 1996. The concept of a single, powerful agency, whose role is to protect the environment, must be the right way forward, but only if it can be more effective than the sum of the three constituent parts. The fear is that this will not be the case.

There is no question that since its formation, the National Rivers Authority, with its statutory requirement to protect the rivers and seas of Britain, has gone a long way toward showing what a regulatory authority can do if it is given the power and authority to take appropriate action to protect the environment. In the first five years of its life it successfully prosecuted 2,200 polluters, collecting some £5 million in fines, which may have contributed to the steady decrease in the number of polluting incidents. That is not to say there are not some criticisms of the Authority (not least being its conservative view of the strength of evidence needed before a decision to prosecute and its failure to act against individual directors). However, they are minor in comparison to the successes it has achieved in this relatively short period.

In setting up the Environment Agency, as a result of pressure from industry, the Conservatives have, unfortunately, shied away from giving it the power provided to the NRA. This is seen by the failure to give it a duty to protect the environment, and further by the insistence that it must always take a cost-benefit analysis fully into account.

Whilst the new agency is in general terms a development that is laudable, the watering down of its protective role, when compared with the National Rivers Authority, is to be deplored, and legislation should be introduced to strengthen the protective role of the agency. In addition to strengthening the powers of the Environment Agency, it should be ensured that the agency has the staff and budget that will enable it to operate in a necessarily aggressive manner. The cosy relationships developed by the HMIP with their counterparts in industry, can be contrasted with the more hands-off, aggressive manner of the NRA officers. For the environment to be given the protection it needs to protect it from the rigours of corporate Britain, there must be dedicated officers in an Environment Protection Agency, who retain a strong determination to protect the environment, as against being lured into compromise by the immediate needs and problems of the companies they regulate.

One other feature of the Environment Agency that is important, is to ensure that for the citizen it is a one-stop agency. Individuals want ready access to the information needed to be able to comprehend the environmental position in their locality, and this is only likely to be achieved by there being one office in each area where all matters under the agency's remit can be dealt with. This may well mean the use by the agency of increased levels of technology so that the information is available, but this is clearly a development that is worth having.

Environmental assessment

The country's resources continue to be eroded as the Conservative government allows great leeway to its developer friends to do what they like in their pursuit of profit.

As a result of initiatives at a European level, developers are now required to carry out environmental impact assessments, but only for the most significant schemes. This requirement should be greatly extended to include all medium-scale developments and the assessment should be made more widely available to the affected population. Where there is any question of possible pollution and damage arising from the proposed development, the developers should be ordered to pay for the independent assessment of the damage by experts determined by the local authority, in consultation with the local population.

Enforcement

Private companies

One of the great environmental problems is the failure of local authorities to carry out enforcement action, usually due to a lack of resources, but also because this is not seen as a priority. Enforcement should, however, be seen as an integral part of a good environmental policy. Individuals should have the power to force an authority to take enforcement action where it has not done so. There need to be rights over and above the ability to take a judicial review action, which is a complex process and one that most people would never dream of taking.

Local authorities

It is often the case that the actions that have the greatest impact on a person's life in this area are the failures of a local authority to carry out some of its basic functions efficiently and effectively. The failure to sweep roads regularly, to collect refuse on time, to control fly tipping, to properly control traffic, to prevent significant noise problems, are all matters that can cause significant loss of well-being to the people living in an area.

20

The Future of the Planning System

John Hobson, Stephen Hockman QC and
Paul Stinchcombe

We believe that the role of the town and country planning system as one of the enduring legacies of the post-war Labour government should be affirmed.

The function of the planning system is to regulate the use and development of land in the public interest; to ensure the protection of the environment and observance of the principles of sustainability enunciated at the Rio Conference; whilst also enabling and encouraging acceptable development — especially of underutilised land — which will assist economic advancement and help towards meeting other important land-use needs such as housing.

The arbiters of the public interest are, in the first instance, local authorities. Their role as democratically elected representatives of local communities should be emphasised and, where appropriate, reinforced.

In particular, local authorities are responsible for:

(a) forward planning, through the system of development plans;

(b) controlling development, by deciding whether to grant or refuse planning permission and by defining the conditions and obligations under which acceptable development may proceed.

It is now widely recognised that the best and most democratic planning system is a 'plan-led' system. Such a system enables local authorities to define the policy criteria by which development proposals are to be judged, and more generally to determine the appropriate policy regime for their particular area.

Such a system of development control is inherently incompatible, however, with any broad 'presumption in favour of planning permission'. This presumption has at times gravely hampered the ability of local authorities to set effective parameters within which their development control responsibilities can be exercised.

The introduction (by the Planning and Compensation Act 1991) of s. 54A into the Town and Country Planning Act 1990 was certainly a step towards the kind of plan-led system which is to be desired, effectively providing for a presumption in favour of development only where it accords with the development plan. It was to be hoped that the courts would construe this so as to embrace also its converse: a clear statutory presumption against development which does not accord with the plan. However, the courts have construed s. 54A rather more restrictively (for example, in *St Albans District Council* v *Secretary of State for the Environment* (1992) 66 P & CR 432). Furthermore, the presumption in favour of planning permission has not disappeared from government guidance (see Planning Policy Guidance Note No. 1, para. 5).

Legislation is now needed to make clear provision for a presumption against non-conforming development. This presumption should be rebuttable only where it is demonstrated that no harm will result from that development proceeding; or where there are compelling reasons — for example, a case of overriding need — sufficient to justify the grant of planning permission notwithstanding the harm that would be occasioned.

In addition, a new range of powers should be provided which enable local authorities to ensure that development is more socially responsible. This will include emphasising the materiality of saving energy (together with other principles of sustainable development) and focusing upon town centres rather than greenfield sites as locations for new development. The availability of an alternative site should be a proper reason for refusal of planning permission.

There should also be a review of the General Development Order and the Use Classes Order in order to curtail the categories of permitted development. One aspect to consider is whether there should be a subdivision of the housing use class, to provide for affordable housing; and a restriction to require the express grant of planning permission for any change from housing of that class to another. Another aspect in urgent need of review concerns the various types of business use. Over recent years there has been a crippling loss of light industrial land to offices, causing — on occasions — a fundamental mismatch between local employment needs and the land available to meet those needs; and — in some parts of the country — a wasteful overprovision of empty office blocks. The ability to change from light industrial use to offices without any need for express planning permission has contributed to this and a revision of the law is required to ensure proper planning control over such changes of use.

The problems which can be caused by the failure or refusal of a developer to complete the development for which planning permission has been granted also need to be addressed.

As the law stands, planning permission can be implemented by very minor specified operations. Once development is permitted and the permission implemented, developers can be tempted to leave the land substantially undeveloped for speculative investment purposes. The consequence of this can be very damaging. First, land which should be developed in the public interest can be sterilised. Secondly, as time moves on, land which previously was thought to be appropriate for a certain kind of development might subsequently be seen to be inappropriate for such development and possibly appropriate for development of a different type. Local authorities are, however, discouraged from modifying or revoking the planning permission through fear of payment of compensation to developers for loss of 'hope value'

Legislation is necessary, possibly to strengthen the local authority's powers to require the completion of development once commenced, at any rate where that is in the public interest; and in any event to empower local authorities — in appropriate cases — to modify or revoke an unimplemented planning permission or a permission which has led only to incomplete development without fear of having to compensate the developer for speculative investment loss.

The problems discussed immediately above are often exacerbated by the uncertainty which can arise as to whether, in law, a development has been commenced in the first place. A developer may undertake the most minor of specified operations, such as digging a trench, with no intention whatsoever of completing the development, leaving the local planning authority uncertain as to whether the development has been commenced or not. This uncertainty is compounded where it transpires that the specified operations were in breach of condition. The law relating to the commencement of development is, in each of the above circumstances, complicated and in some ways uncertain: see, for example, *Thayer* v *Secretary of State for the Environment* [1991] 3 PLR 104; and *Whitley and Sons* v *Secretary of State for Wales* (1992) 64 P & CR 296.

Furthermore, the legal complexity which surrounds the commencement of development may lead officers of local planning authorities to express a view to a developer, upon which the developer may rely, to the effect that the development has commenced, when it subsequently transpires, upon legal advice being obtained, that this is not the case in law. This, in turn, leads to further legal complexities since it is far from clear whether the doctrine of estoppel applies in such circumstances so as to prevent the local planning authority from denying the effect of the earlier and erroneous statement: see *Western Fish Products Ltd* v *Penwith District Council* [1981] 2 All ER 204.

Legislation is required to remove the above uncertainties. One option would be to make provision for a developer to apply for a binding certificate of commencement of development, which certificate would be granted only upon the local planning authority being satisfied that substantial works of a specified nature had been undertaken in full compliance with the planning permission and all conditions attached thereto. In the absence of such a certificate, the developer would be disentitled from arguing that the development had been commenced; and the corollary would be that a local planning authority would be disentitled from later denying the effect of any certificate which they had granted. Greater certainty would thereby prevail.

Another of the major planning issues to be addressed is one which has bedevilled the Labour Party for many years — the concept of betterment and the attempts made to recover, for society, the enhanced value that results from the grant of planning permission. There were provisions to this effect in the Town and Country Planning Act 1947, in the Land Compensation Act 1967, which introduced the betterment levy, and in the Community Land Act 1975, which introduced the development land tax. These were highly controversial, time consuming to introduce, complicated and difficult to administer. Unsurprisingly, they were quickly repealed when Labour went out of office.

The focus should now be on the means by which developers can be required to contribute to the needs of the community.

Local authorities are already able to require developers to make contributions, which could be by way of financial payments, for local infrastructure made necessary or appropriate by their development. This can cover not only those infrastructure improvements necessary to overcome the otherwise derogatory effects of a proposed development (for example, sewers and drains), but also additional facilities which might have some linkage with that development (for example, new schools or public open space). In *Tesco Stores Ltd* v *Secretary of State for the Environment* [1995] 1 WLR 759, the House of Lords has made it clear that it is not unlawful to seek such benefits.

At present, however, by government policy, local authorities cannot require such contributions unless they are satisfied that the development ought otherwise not to be permitted: see Department of the Environment Circular 16/91, annex B, para. 8(3). This requirement is too rigid and should be relaxed. Circumstances may arise when, taking into account the proposed infrastructure improvements, the balance of planning advantage lies clearly with permission being granted; and a local authority should be able so to decide when that is the case.

On the other hand, government guidance must continue to make it clear that, whilst local authorities should be conferred with the power to seek benefits which they regard as appropriate, they should not be required to give weight to those benefits which may be offered by a developer but which have no linkage to the proposed development and cannot therefore be considered necessary or appropriate. Otherwise, developers would be enabled to 'buy' planning permissions; and weak local authorities might be improperly influenced.

The risk of such improper influence would be further minimised by the increased weight to be given to the development plan (discussed above); and also by the establishment of a new process of review of planning decisions made by local authorities, part of a thorough overhaul of the current planning appeal process.

Currently, there is a gross inequality between local authorities (with limited resources) and substantial developers, like the major superstore operators (whose resources are immense). This disparity of resources, combined with the right of a developer to force a local authority into a full-blown public local inquiry in the case of every refusal of planning permission, can put excessive demands on the resources of local authorities and their budgets. Furthermore, given that the battle can be so unequal, there is little guarantee that the decision made on appeal will be one which fairly reflects the proper balance of the planning arguments.

Another source of inequality in the system is that, whilst there is an absolute right of appeal for an applicant for planning permission whose application is refused, there is, if permission is granted, normally no such right — nor a legal remedy of any sort — for third parties (such as neighbours) who may have been concerned to try to prevent the grant of permission. There is a need to re-examine the procedure to see if this problem can be addressed.

One option would be simply to graft on to the present system a right of third-party appeal, but this would be difficult and cumbersome, as has been cogently argued by the former Chief Planning Inspector, Mr Stephen Crow, in an article in [1995] JPL at p. 376.

It may be that a more radical approach is required. The essentials of such an approach would be (a) to ensure that there is an absolute right to a formal and independent reconsideration of any planning decision made by a local planning authority and (b) to provide a filter (rather like the requirement for leave to seek judicial review) so as to discourage appeals in cases where the original decision is plainly consistent with the development plan and otherwise an appropriate exercise of a local authority's powers.

We would invite consideration of a system which would enable planning decisions to be reviewed — perhaps by a regional or strategic authority with knowledge of the local circumstances — without the necessity of an inquiry in every case. We envisage that such a review might be initiated by interested parties — such as neighbours aggrieved by the grant of planning permission — as well as by applicants disappointed by a refusal. In many instances the authority would take the view that only by a full inquiry could the relevant circumstances be established and a proper decision taken. In other cases the authority undertaking the review might decide that a more abbreviated or informal procedure could be adopted or that the matter could be dealt with on paper alone.

In certain cases a full inquiry will clearly be justified, especially when issues of national importance are involved — for example, when nuclear power stations, airports or motorways are proposed. The conduct of such inquiries has, however, long been the cause of concern. In particular, the contrast between the resources available to bodies like the CEGB or the BAA and third parties is so stark that there are frequent calls for legal aid to be made available to interested third parties. However, this would be inordinately expensive and difficult to administer, with impossible decisions to be made about which group of objectors should be legally aided, if any.

In so far as there is a continuing role for inquiries of this kind, a more effective and economical approach would be for counsel to the inquiry to be appointed. Counsel would be able to obtain additional evidence as necessary, including commissioning of independent reports from appropriate experts, and would be empowered to cross-examine witnesses upon matters which interested third parties would wish to have tested. This procedure was adopted by Sir Frank Layfield QC at the Sizewell inquiry, but this was exceptional and is not being followed at the current inquiry in respect of Terminal 5 at Heathrow. It should be the norm rather than the exception in cases of such importance.

Summary of Principal Recommendations

1. The Legal System and Law Reform under Labour: Lord Irvine of Lairg QC, Shadow Lord Chancellor

- No capping of legal aid; instead, implement much of the Woolf Report and attempt to cut cost and delay.

- Block franchising is acceptable, but compulsory competitive tendering is not.

- Monitor carefully the operation of conditional fee agreements.

- Introduce a Community Legal Service within the existing legal aid budget; deploy much greater proportion of publicly funded services through law centres, CABx and advice agencies.

- Incorporate European Convention on Human Rights into English law: no derogation from it except by express clause in future Acts; only rights of individuals, not of companies, to be protected; Human Rights Commission to be set up.

- Non-lawyers to be added to final appeal court in human rights cases.

- Introduce public interest defence to official secrets charges.

- Freedom of Information Act to be introduced.

- Strengthen discrimination law; introduce statutory ethnic monitoring for employers; racial motivation in crime to be treated as aggravating feature in sentencing.

221

- A major review of the Asylum and Immigration Act 1993.

- Reverse the encroachment of quangos in favour of decisions being taken by democratic bodies.

- Replace House of Lords by elected Second Chamber; as first step abolish voting rights of hereditary peers.

2. The Penal System in Crisis: Jack Straw MP, Shadow Home Secretary

- A strategy to combat crime must tackle the social and economic inequalities in which crime breeds.

- Action is required on unemployment; homelessness; drug and alcohol abuse; and the policy of care in the community for the mentally ill.

- Community-based management strategies should be used to reduce disorder and anti-social behaviour.

- New orders should be available to deal with persistent criminal behaviour by neighbours.

- Local authorities should be given a statutory responsibility for crime prevention in conjunction with the police.

- Delay in the criminal courts should be reduced by greater use of time limits; more rigorous scrutiny of adjournment applications; and more use of courtrooms.

- Each police force should have a separate prosecution service within the CPS.

- Reparation orders and action plan orders should be available in the sentencing of young offenders.

- The Woolf Report on the prison system should be implemented. Privatised prisons should be returned to the public sector.

3. Legal Aid and Justice: Roger Smith, Director, Legal Action Group

- Oppose capping the legal aid budget.

- Support franchising in principle, but oppose restricting legal aid to franchised firms or introducing CCT.

- Introduce procedural reforms to facilitate class actions.

- Abolish the development risks defence in product liability cases.

- Consider alterations to costs rules in public interest cases.

- More public education about law and legal rights.

4. Delivering Civil Justice: Alternatives to Legal Aid: Professor Ross Cranston, London School of Economics

- There should be national support centres to conduct research and disseminate information for law centres.

- Advice agencies staff should have more law-related training.

- There should be a Public Advocate's Office with the right to bring civil proceedings in the public interest.

5. Judges: Lord Williams of Mostyn QC

- Establish a Judicial College to deal with selection, training, monitoring and promotion.

- Judicial training to include management skills.

- One-month training course for all judges on appointment.

- Move away from reliance on part-time judiciary.

- Retirement at 65 at first instance, 70 at appeal level.

- Proper research and law clerking facilities for appeal courts.

6. Tribunals: Lord Archer of Sandwell QC, Chairman, Council on Tribunals

- Council on Tribunals, when critical of a draft statutory instrument, to have the right to notify Parliament.

- Powers of tribunals to be determined in primary legislation, not by ministerial orders.

- Tribunal members should not be removable by a department or local authority with an interest in the outcome of appeals.

- Tribunal chairmen should have security of tenure subject to competence and good conduct.

- Tribunal clerks should be independent of the department whose decision is under review.

- A small policy unit should provide effective overall coordination of the Tribunal Service.

7. Magistrates: Jenny Jeger JP

- Advisory committees on appointing magistrates should have an annual advertising budget and should actively encourage applications from under-represented groups.

- Employers should be encouraged to allow release from work to sit as a magistrate or lay member of a tribunal by the introduction of a Queen's Award for Public Service.

8. The Legal Profession: Two Views
Henry Hodge OBE

- Publish service standards for solicitors and barristers and ensure their effective enforcement.

- Separate regulatory complaints and disciplinary systems from trade union functions of Law Society and Bar Council.

- Allow multi-disciplinary partnerships between solicitors, barristers, accountants and others.

- Allow direct access to barristers.

- Allow solicitors to incorporate with limited liability.

- Improve specialist accreditation, training and management skills.

Benet Hytner QC

- The scandal of a profession and Bench not representative of society can only be tackled by education policy, and by schoolchildren and students from 'working class' or ethnic minority backgrounds being actively encouraged to study law.

● Touting and advertising of alleged skills should not be permitted.

● Multi-disciplinary partnerships, by cloaking conflicts of interests, can provide a vehicle for fraud: the proposal should be abandoned.

9. Legal Education and Training: Professor Peter Jones, Nottingham Trent University

● The Law Society and Bar Council should allow universities to develop legal education with only a light regulatory touch.

● The Lord Chancellor's Advisory Committee on Legal Education and Conduct should be abolished; its replacement should set standards rather than imposing control.

10. A British Bill of Rights: John Wadham, Director Liberty

● The European Convention on Human Rights should be incorporated into English law, although it is not an adequate Bill of Rights: a domestic model should be framed.

● Breach of the Bill of Rights should of itself be actionable.

● Subordinate legislation in conflict with the Bill of Rights should be declared *ultra vires*.

● The 'notwithstanding clause' model should be used to entrench the Bill of Rights, so that Parliament could expressly overrule it; but a few basic rights should be placed beyond even such overruling (as in the Convention): the right to life from the moment of birth; freedom from torture, slavery, discrimination; the rule against retrospective criminal offences.

● Where legislation is struck down by the courts, a special Select Committee, with no overall majority for the governing party, should have the right to refer the matter to Parliament which could then re-enact it.

11. Judicial Review: James Goudie QC

- A new Administrative Justice Act should specify the bodies subject to judicial review and require them to give reasons for their decisions. It should specify the grounds for judicial review and the remedies available.

- Local authorities should have a power of general competence subject only to justified exceptions.

12. Freedom of Expression: Geoffrey Bindman

- Defamation law should be scrapped and a fresh start made.

- A new tort of infringement of privacy is on balance not required.

- Any greater legal protection of privacy should be balanced by freedom of information legislation.

- A comprehensive code should be introduced implementing the European Convention rights to freedom of expression and freedom of information.

13. Discrimination Law: Towards a Principle of Equality: Rabinder Singh

- Extend powers of EOC and CRE to bring actions themselves.

- Shift burden of proof to respondents where prima facie less favourable treatment.

- Improve training of tribunal members and judges in discrimination matters.

- Permit awards of exemplary damages in suitable cases.

- In the longer term, create a constitutional right to equal equality; prohibit discrimination on the grounds of religion, disability and sexual orientation as well as race and sex, and take initiative on these issues within the EU.

- Establish human rights tribunal to hear cases and human rights commission to implement rights.

226

14. Immigration: Keith Vaz MP and Maria Fernandes

- Rights of appeal should be restored for visitors seeking entry into the UK; families' rights to visit should be recognised.

- The primary purpose rule should be abolished.

- Once a marriage is accepted as genuine there should be no probationary period.

- The right to family life should extend to couples in same-sex relationships.

- Immigration detention should be a last resort; written reasons should be given; there should be independent and regular review.

15. Official Secrecy: Michael Supperstone QC

- A Freedom of Information Act should be passed.

- Access to official information should only be denied in certain limited categories causing identifiable harm.

- There should be a public interest defence to Official Secrets Act prosecutions.

- Interception of communications should require judicial approval.

16. Family Law: Wendy Mantle and Maggie Rae

- There should be a network of publicly funded centres providing information about mediators, counsellors, solicitors specialising in family work, etc.; and assistance to lay people in compiling documents for ancillary relief cases.

- There should be a more flexible route of appeal to the courts from decision of the Child Support Agency.

- Guardians *ad litem* under the Children Act 1989 should be in a nationally organised service.

- Adoption law should be reformed on the lines of the proposals in the 1992 Consultative document.

17. Personal Injury: Andrew Dismore and Fraser Whitehead

- There should be strict liability for injuries on the roads and at work, thus saving costs of litigation; as an interim measure the burden of proof in such cases should be reversed.

- Inquests and inquiries should have the power to make binding determinations of culpability.

- New, higher benchmarks should be set for levels of general damages, either by sample cases being tried by juries or by the Judicial Studies Board working with an advisory panel including lay people.

- Bereavement damages should be increased and eligibility for them widened.

- Punitive damages should be permissible in the most serious cases of reckless acts causing death or injury.

- Recoupment of benefits should be either ended or confined to being offset against financial loss, as opposed to being deducted from general damages for pain and suffering.

18. Employment Law: Justice at Work: Colin Ettinger

- Artificial limits on compensation in unfair dismissal and redundancy cases should be abolished.

- Defects in the law on dismissing or penalising employees for trade union membership or activities should be removed to provide greater protection.

- Members of trade unions should have the right to be represented by the union in disciplinary proceedings, grievance procedures, hearings concerning sickness, and disputes as to terms and conditions; this right should be enforceable by injunction.

- Trade union rights at GCHQ should be restored.

- The time limit for unfair dismissal claims should be extended from three to six months.

19. Environmental Law: Martyn Day

- The requirements to provide information on environmental hazards should be strengthened.

- There should be a duty to warn of possible risks, not only of known risks.

- Local authorities should be required to produce an annual environmental report.

- There should be strict liability for environmental pollution.

- A specialist environmental court should deal with all cases including prosecutions and judicial review applications; where appropriate environmental groups should be allowed to appear in an *amicus curiae* role.

- Legislation should strengthen the protective role of the Environment Agency.

20. The Future of the Planning System: John Hobson, Stephen Hockman QC and Paul Stinchcombe

- Any presumption in favour of planning permission should be ended and replaced by a presumption against development not conforming with local development plans.

- Local authority powers to ensure more socially responsible development should be increased.

- The categories of permitted development should be reviewed.

- Where planning permission has not been implemented or completed the local authority should be able in certain circumstances to revoke the permission without having to compensate the developer.

- The power to make developers contribute to infrastructure costs as a condition of planning permission should be widened.

- Neighbours and others aggrieved by the grant of planning permission should be able to require a review by a regional or strategic authority.

Index